OCR HISTORY A

A2

Russia and its Rulers
1855–1964

Mike Wells with Nick Fellows

www.heinemann.co.uk

✓ Free online support
✓ Useful weblinks
✓ 24 hour online ordering

01865 888080

Heinemann is an imprint of Pearson Education Limited, a company incorporated in England and Wales, having its registered office at Edinburgh Gate, Harlow, Essex, CM20 2JE. Registered company number: 872828

www.heinemann.co.uk

Heinemann is a registered trademark of Pearson Education Limited

First published 2008

12

10 9 8 7 6

British Library Cataloguing in Publication Data

A catalogue record for this book is available from the British Library

ISBN 978 0435 312 42 8

Edited by Anna Woodford

Designed by Pearson Education

Typeset by Saxon Graphics Ltd, Derby

Original illustrations © Saxon Graphics Ltd, Derby

Cover design by Pearson Education

Picture research by Zooid

Cover photo: Stalin and Lenin © Illustrated London News Agency

Printed in Malaysia (CTP-VVP)

Acknowledgements
The author and publisher would like to thank the following individuals and organisations for permission to reproduce photographs:

Every effort has been made to contact copyright holders of material reproduced in this book. Any omissions will be rectified in subsequent printings if notice is given to the publishers.

Photos and Images
Fig 1.1 a: akg-images; Fig 1.1 b: AFP PHOTO/SCANPIX/Getty Images; Fig 1.1 c: W. & D. Downey/Hulton Archive/ Getty Images; Fig 1.2: (Lenin) Mary Evans Picture Library/Alamy, (Stalin) Bettmann/Corbis UK Ltd, Khruschev: Hulton-Deutsch Collection/Corbis UK Ltd; Fig. 1.3: (Kerensky) George Grantham Bain Collection/Library of Congress; page 16: Illustrated London News/Mary Evans Picture Library; Fig. 1.4: © David King Collection; Fig. 1.5: Bettmann/Corbis UK Ltd.; Fig. 1.6: National Art Museum of the Republic of Belarus; Fig. 1.7: State V.I Surikov Art Museum, Krasnoyarsk/© ADAGP, Paris and DACS London 2008/Bridgeman Art Library; Fig. 2.1: akg-images; page 58: © SCRSS; page 51, Fig. 2.3, Fig. 2.4: © David King Collection; Fig. 3.1a, b: TopFoto; Fig. 3.2: Visual Arts Library (London)/Alamy; page 81: 1 & 3 ITAR-TASS Photo Agency, 2, akg-images; Fig. 3.3: RIA Nowosti/akg-images; Fig. 4.2: The Print Collector /Alamy; Fig. 4.3: Collection International Institute of Social History, Amsterdam; Fig. 4.4: Collection International Institute of Social History, Amsterdam; Fig. 4.5: RDA/Lebrecht Music and Arts; Fig. 5.1: Fotomas/TopFoto; Fig. 5.3: RIA Nowosti/akg-images; page 135 : Wikipedia Commons; page 141: RIA Nowosti/akg-images.

Written sources
p. 34: Richard Pipes, The Unknown Lenin, used by permission of Yale University; p. 34: Dmitri Volkogonov, Lenin: A new Biography, Simon and Schuster; p. 36: Dmitri Volkogonov, The Rise and Fall of the Soviet Empire, Harper Collins; p. 36: Rethinking the Russian Revolution by Edward Acton © 1990, reproduced by permission of Edward Arnold (Publishers) Ltd; p. 39: Moshe Lewin, The Soviet Century, Verso; p. 94: Merle Fainsod, Smolensk under Soviet Rule, reprinted by permission of the publishers, Harvard University Press, Cambridge, Mass, copyright © 1958 by the President and Fellows of Harvard; p. 108: Allen Monkhouse, Moscow 1911 to 1933, Gollancz 1933; p. 116: Quoted in Munting, The Economic Development of the USSR -Pg. 86 from Stalin CW 1947, St. Martins Press; p. 131, Rulers & Subjects: Government & People in Russia, 1801-1991 by John Gooding © 1996, reproduced by permission of Edward Arnold (Publishers) Ltd; p. 146, "Companion to Russia Since 1914" by Martin McCanley © 1997, used by permission of Pearson Longman.

Websites
There are links to relevant websites in this book. In order to ensure that the links are up to date, that the links work, and that the sites are not inadventently linked to sites that could be considered offensive, we have made the links available on the Heinemann website at www.heinemann.co.uk/hotlinks. When you access the site, the express code is 2428P.

Contents

How to use this book

Notes for teachers

The Historical Themes unit (A2 Unit F966) is a **synoptic** part of the specification that seeks to develop an understanding of connections between different elements of the subject and for candidates to draw together knowledge, understanding and skills of diverse issues centred upon a common theme. Although there are no restrictions within the specification about the selection of themes, candidates are encouraged to study one or more themes linked to options that they have studied in other modules (see for example the routes through the specification tabulated in section 2.4). Six topics cover the period from 1066 to 1715 and six cover the period from 1789 to 1997.

The topics are based on Themes covering an extended period of approximately one hundred years with an emphasis on continuity, development and change appropriate to the topic. The emphasis is on developing and interpreting a **broad overview** of the period studied. The modules are historical perspectives, so concern is focused on making links and comparisons between different aspects of the topics studied, and on testing hypotheses before reaching a judgement.

Theme 4: *Russia and its Rulers 1855–1964*

This book focuses on Theme 4 (F966 Option B): the nature of Russian government and its impact on the Russian people and society.

It is important to understand the nature of the Themes paper. This will be the only unit taken under examination condition at A2 and will be a very important part of the A level as a whole. The skills involved may have been encountered previously, but not to such an extent as the skills of explanation, evaluation and source analysis. In the themes paper the skills required are to be able to look at the period **synoptically, i.e. to discuss it as a whole,** to take a sort of aerial view and to be able to write about elements which run through the whole period. Previously students will have done essays on individual people or events in a relatively narrow frame. For example, 'How successful were Stalin's economic policies 1929–41?'; or 'Does Tsar Alexander II deserve to be known as the Liberator?' Now the focus is on a much longer period in which these policies have to be seen in the light of what went before or what came after.

Key skills

This book will help students to develop the key skills for this specification of:

- making **connections** between different elements of the subject
- **drawing together** knowledge, understanding and skills of diverse issues
- understanding **continuity, development and change**
- developing a **broad overview.**

The starting point may well be to encourage students' ability to formulate a *thesis* (i.e. a possible explanation or view) and to test this thesis by analysing different elements. To get

---

Synoptic

means looking at the same time. Synoptic analysis considers a theme over a period of time, looking at patterns of continuity and change, making comparisons and contrasts. This involves taking an overview of a period, not necessarily considering events in chronological order.

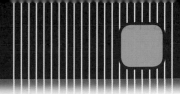

students started, the topic of parties in people's lives could be used as an everyday example. The question might be '*How useful are parties in making new friends?*'

A thesis may be as follows; that the less formal and organised a party is, the more the chance of making new friends. So teenage parties where people just dance and chat or adult parties where people just come together to meet each other are more likely to result in new relationships than formal dinners.

Now take the title '*Assess the impact of war on Russian history 1855–1964*'. The thesis may be that wars which have involved very severe losses and consistent defeats have had more impact than wars which have either been relatively less costly or have been victorious.

You could develop this example further by considering which war has been the greatest agent of change and why? Or which type of party is most likely to lead to new friendships and why? It would not be sensible in either case to describe the elements of each party or each war in turn and then try to offer some conclusion.

Therefore, the approach of this book is not to offer a comprehensive history of Russia between 1855 and 1964, but to cover the specification content exactly and provide activities and information on how to approach the ideas of the unit synoptically.

A simply chronological approach would not be successful, especially in view of the exam time given: one hour per essay. Students will need to sift information and consider it in the light of their broad ideas and theses. The question in their minds should always be 'will this fact support my thesis'?

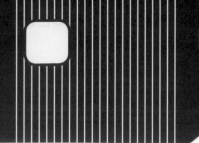
How to use this book

Notes for students

This book has been specifically written to support you through the OCR A GCE History course. *Russia and its Rulers 1855–1964* will help you to understand the facts and concepts that underlie the topics you are studying. It can be used as a reference throughout your course.

You should also refer back to this book during your revision. The **Exam Café** section at the end of Chapter 5 and on the CD-ROM will be particularly helpful as you prepare for your exam.

Each chapter includes the following features:

Key questions

Each chapter will start by asking some Key Questions. The content of the chapter will help you to find answers to these Key Questions.

Key Question:

In what ways were these rulers similar and in what ways were they different?

■ They might be compared in terms of personality and background.
■ They might be compared in how they reacted to the situations they found when taking up power.

In this chapter you will be invited to think about differences and similarities, but you will not be given a comprehensive history of Russian rulers between 1855 and 1964. Issues of continuity and change will be addressed by an analysis of Lenin as 'Red Tsar'. (The success of their major economic policies will be considered in Chapter 4.) You will also be encouraged through exercises to practise the skills of comparing rulers and situations and framing overall explanations and analyses. You will be asked to develop supported judgements and to weigh arguments about continuity and change.

Analysis

These analyse the situations described in each chapter and stimulate ideas on how to approach each line of enquiry, such as repression.

ANALYSIS

Consider this analysis

The scale and range of discontent – social and political as well as geographical – showed the Tsar that massive change was necessary. It could have reappeared, but in fact the success of opposition in 1917 did not depend on a repeat of 1905. There were important elements of similarity in the mass demonstrations of 1905 and the situation in February 1917 (and indeed in the fall of the Russian empire in 1918) but the October revolution – the most significant and lasting success by an opposition group depended on different factors.

Stretch and Challenge

These activities pull together all the work done in each chapter giving you chance to practice the skills needed in your final exam.

Stretch and challenge

What follows is a general survey of the period 1855–1964.

1   After reading the overview, make a list of the major attempts at opposition and change and form a *thesis* about why opposition was difficult both before and after 1917. Are there common factors?

2   Then consider under what circumstances opposition was successful and why these problems were overcome, particularly in 1917.

There follows a more detailed look at the different periods and you can check to see if your thesis holds good.

Information

These highlight content and provide extra detail to the main questions in the chapter.

The Russo-Japanese war, 1904–5

In 1904 Nicholas II (1894–1917) fought a war against Japan. His government hoped for a quick victory. Instead the war went badly, with heavy losses and a major naval defeat. The war led to unrest and in 1905 Russia was in a revolutionary situation with a great deal of discontent of various sorts. The Tsar had to make concessions and offer a national parliament.

Case studies

Case studies are used to further illustrate the chapter content. Most of the examples can be applied in some way to the topic you are studying for your A2 exam.

Case study: changing attitudes to the Russian Orthodox church

The Church of Christ Saviour, Moscow

Under Khrushchev (1956–64) there was a renewed persecution which was by and large maintained by his successors. Not nearly as severe as the period 1917–41 it nevertheless reduced the number of churches. to less than 7000 An interesting case study is the Church of Christ Saviour in Moscow. This huge cathedral was built to celebrate the victory over Napoleon in the reign of Alexander I. It was destroyed in 1931 and Stalin's plan was to build a new Soviet Palace. The war prevented progress and the site became an open-air swimming pool. Then after 1997 it was totally rebuilt and reconstructed and is now one of Moscow's major tourist sights.

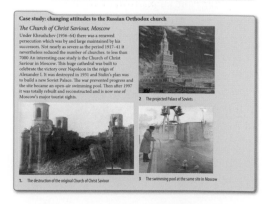

1.   The destruction of the original Church of Christ Saviour

2   The projected Palace of Soviets

3   The swimming pool at the same site in Moscow

Activities

These have been designed to help you understand the specification content and develop your historical skills.

ACTIVITY

Taking these as at least some of the possible criteria, does Lenin emerge as a new Tsar or is the discontinuity with the Tsarist era more significant than any similarities?

Biographies

These provide more detail on key people such as 'Stolypin'.

BIOGRAPHY

Otto von Bismarck 1815–98 went on to be Minister-President of Prussia in 1862 and was the Chancellor of a united Germany from 1871 to 1890. Here he is referring to the failure to create free peasant holdings, such as existed in France and Germany, but to keep peasants on communal holdings.

Definitions

Definitions of new words can be found in the margin close to where the word appears in the text to help put the word in context.

Thesis

Usually an extended essay, as in a university PhD thesis. Here, forming a 'thesis' is proposing an explanation on a particular subject that relates to the whole period.

Exam Café – print and electronic

In our unique Exam Café you'll find lots of ideas to help you prepare for your exams. You'll see the Exam Café at the end of each unit. You can **Relax** because there's handy revision advice from fellow students, **Refresh your memory** with summaries and checklists of the key ideas you need to revise and **Get that result!** through practising exam-style questions, accompanied by hints and tips on getting the very best grades.

Free CD-ROM

You'll also find a free CD-ROM in the back of the book. On the CD you will find an electronic version of the Student Book, powered by LiveText. As well as the student book and LiveText tools, you will also find an interactive Exam Café. This contains a wealth of interactive exam preparation material: interactive multiple-choice questions, revision flashcards, exam-style questions with student answers and examiner feedback and much more!

Note from the author to the students

Judgement is a very important element of A2 History generally in both Themes and Investigations. It is a requirement that a judgement is made. The assessment objective uses the term **substantiated judgement** (i.e. a judgement which is supported from evidence and understanding). Examiners are not looking for a right answer and you are not expected to write a definitive history of Russia. It is your views that the examiners are looking for – the examiners *know* what happened, and they *know* what the explanations are: what they *don't know* is what you think and how you have interpreted the broad developments. Analysis of this sort is a very high level skill, but one which offers considerable rewards: in the world of work the ability to process and use information is much more important now than the ability to acquire and transfer information. A2 history is demanding, but it is also immensely rewarding and interesting, so good luck!

All three married foreign princesses: Alexander II married, a German princess, Marie of Hesse. An American visitor in 1871 wrote of the Empress of Russia, that she was:

> 'a tall stately lady, with a sad face and the appearance of an aristocratic invalid, is rarely seen in public. She appears only at the State balls and other festivities where etiquette demands her presence, and it is evident that she would prefer to be shut off altogether from the stare of curious eyes. Maria Feederovna, formerly Princess Dagmar of Denmark was more vivacious – a keen dancer and horsewoman.'

Alexander III married Princess Dagmar of Denmark on 9 November 1866. Nicholas II's marriage was the only true love match of these Tsars and Alix of Hesse-Darmstadt in Germany was his choice, despite the opposition of his father. She took the place of the beautiful mistress, the ballerina Kschessinska.

Lenin too married a soul mate, and rejected a glamorous mistress whereas Stalin's first marriage ended in tragedy with his wife's death from cholera. His second wife committed suicide. Unlike the Tsars neither he nor Khrushchev enjoyed an easy married life. Khrushchev had three wives: his first Yefrasina died in the famine of 1921; he left his second, a peasant girl called Marusa and he lived with Nina Petrovna for over 40 years before finally marrying her in the 1960s. The only wife to exert political influence was the Empress Alix, whose favourite Rasputin was allowed power and influence. Lenin's wife shared his interest in politics but because Lenin was a stronger personality, lacked decisive influence. Alix was the only one of these wives to suffer execution, though not the only one to have a tragic death.

Two of these leaders came to power with a view to reforming an existing system. Alexander II was convinced that a more liberal rule than his father Nicholas I had established was necessary; Khrushchev though he had risen to prominence under Stalin thought that a more liberal communism was necessary. Neither man was prepared for the implications of change and both showed weaknesses in dealing with it. Both had unhappy endings in their different ways – Alexander II by assassination in 1881, Khrushchev by a humiliating removal from power in 1964.

In physical appearance, Khrushchev's burly physique most resembled Alexander III, who displayed his strength in rescuing his family from a railway accident by holding up the roof of a carriage. Neither he nor Nicholas II had the reforming impulses of Alexander II or Khrushchev. They were determined to uphold autocracy and restrict change to agricultural reform and industrial growth. Alexander III, shocked by his father's murder, was determined on a broadly conservative policy, whereas change had to be forced on Nicholas II by external events. Of all of Russia's rulers, the weakest personality was probably Nicholas II. The finest featured and most sensitive, he nevertheless, for all his sense of duty, failed to come to terms with Russia's problems, and his conservatism was more rigid and unthinking than any of the other rulers.

The two rulers who forced through change and overcame the most opposition were Lenin and Stalin. They have been compared with Tsars; if they were indeed like the Tsars, they were more like the Tsars of Russia's more distant past in personality than the rulers of the later 19th century. Lenin was by the far the most academic and intellectual of Russia's non-Tsarist rulers of the period; trained as a lawyer from an intellectual background, he relished the obscure debates about Marxist theory and concocted elaborate intellectual defences for policies which were based on practical considerations. Here there is little parallel with the Tsars. However, like Alexander II and Nicholas II, Lenin did make reforms which nevertheless kept the basic power structure intact. Like the Tsars he could be pragmatic and also he did not shift from a basic belief in a political system – not autocracy but Communism. Stalin was the least Russian of all the rulers. Lenin described him as 'Asiat' – someone from Asiatic Russia with a different outlook and traditions. For all the German influences and foreign culture, the Tsars were Russian in outlook; whereas Stalin the Georgian, like Napoleon the Corsican and perhaps Hitler the Austrian, may have seen the people he ruled as essentially alien and dispensable. He had had a harder early life than any of the other rulers; his personal power in terms of his ability to change Russia was greater than any other ruler in practical if not theoretical terms. Certainly, no other ruler in the period had such an enormous impact on the everyday life of Russians, or on the historical development of the country.

Figure 1.3 Aleksandr Fedorovich Kerensky (1881–1970).

And of the leaders of the Provisional Government? Bizarrely Aleksandr Fedorovich Kerensky (Fig. 1.3) who became Prime Minister in July 1917 came from the same town – Simbirsk – as Lenin; his father, like Lenin's was a teacher. He even taught Lenin briefly. Like Lenin, Kerensky studied law and History at St. Petersburg University. Like Lenin he was drawn to radical politics and joined the **SRs**. He was elected to the **Duma** in 1912 as a moderate socialist (a member of the **Trudovik party**). His oratory made him noticed and he came into his own after February 1917, serving as Minister of Justice and then Minister of War. Unlike any of the other leaders he had to grapple with parliamentary politics and not exert dictatorial powers or assert autocratic principles. His rule was the shortest; like Nicholas II he was the victim of a revolution; like the Tsars before him he found that reforming measures were too little and too late. Intellectually more able than the Tsars, he lacked the ruthlessness of Lenin and Stalin and did not inherit, like Khrushchev, a powerful state with little opposition. Like the Tsars he failed to cope successfully with war. He bungled an attempt to use the army to increase the authority of the government. Unlike the Communists, he could or would not put power before every other consideration in order to maintain Russia's brief interlude of genuinely constitutional government.

SR: Social revolutionaries

They were the heirs of the 19th century radical intellectuals who put their trust in peasant democracy, advocating redistribution of land to the peasants. They formed a party in 1901 under Victor Chernov which was the largest revolutionary group before 1917. They split in1917 and were suppressed by Lenin.

Duma

The Russian word for State (i.e. National) Assembly to Parliament. The first Duma met in 1906 after Nicholas II agreed to a constitution with an elected assembly in October 1905. It met in the Tauride Palace in St. Petersburg. In practice it had little power until its members formed the Provisional Government in 1917. It was suppressed by Lenin. Duma is still the word used to describe the Russian parliament.

The Trudoviks

A group of peasant deputies and intellectuals who numbered 130–140 members in the first and second Dumas and who were more moderate than the SRs and sometimes aligned themselves with the Liberal Cadets. The word comes from the Russian Trudovaya Gruppa (Toilers' or Labouring people's group). Kerensky is their most famous member but Zarduny, a Trudovik, was a minister in 1917 and played a leading part in trying to suppress the Bolsheviks. Lenin suppressed the Trudoviks in 1917–18.

BIOGRAPHY

Otto von Bismarck 1815–98 went on to be Minister-President of Prussia in 1862 and was the Chancellor of a united Germany from 1871 to 1890. Here he is referring to the failure to create free peasant holdings, such as existed in France and Germany, but to keep peasants on communal holdings.

Zemstvos

There was a Zemstvo (plural Zemstvos) for each province and district. They were elected in separate meetings by peasants townsmen and nobles. They could not levy taxes but oversaw local matters: roads, poor relief, prisons, public health and some industrial development. There were urban councils created in a similar way in 1870.

control of the peasantry who continued to be in communal agriculture and to pay communal taxes and heavy redemption payments to the state, which had compensated the nobles, was more important than 'modernisation'. The liberal ministers were dismissed when the peasants protested about loss of land and the imposition of obligations to the state in a wave of peasant unrest. The Tsar Liberator had no intention of introducing a modern system of money relationship into the countryside, or a class of capitalist peasant farmers, or even peasant citizens – there was no equality before the law or real economic freedom to develop individual lands. The nobles, who had been the privileged order, remained so throughout the Tsarist period. Their share of wealth increased from 1861–1914 rather than decreasing. Alexander II was a long way from the reforms of the French revolution – the Emancipation was a very Russian, very traditional and very communal act, and its consequences were not really foreseen. It was supported as much by pan Slav Russian nationalists as pro-western modernisers.

In 1864 came another major reform – the creation of the first elected local governments (**Zemstvos**). There were three categories of voters for these councils who were chosen for three years. As well as assemblies at local level there were provincial assemblies. There were also urban councils. In these assemblies there were assemblies and executive councils. The guiding principles here were respect for property and wealth. Regional and provincial nobles of the highest rank chaired the rural assemblies; the wealthy and titled had more voting power; those who paid the highest taxes had a greater representation. The councils were there to make improvements not to discuss matters pertaining to politics in a wider sense.

The consequences were not foreseen; because they were an outlet for political hopes and a chance for the educated elites to meet, there was some political development. Even a restricted electoral process encouraged hopes and demand for greater change. At no time was there an intention that there should be any greater political development. The Tsar was rooted in autocracy and the Zemstvos were a means to support it by making local administration more efficient.

The reforming impulse was also seen in law reforms. There was no equality before the law because the freed serfs were under a separate jurisdiction. There was a reorganisation of local and regional courts to hear relatively minor civil and criminal cases by local justices of the peace. The Judiciary was to be more independent of the state. Bribery of judges was to be reduced by paying them better and making their appointments permanent. The office of examining magistrate was created to take away the role of the police in establishing a legal case for the prosecution. These magistrates would decide whether there was justification for prosecution. The Higher courts too were reorganised with the huge reform of criminal trial by jury. In theory, the reforms were linked – a modern Russia without a mediaeval class system needed modern laws. More local consultation logically led to an independent judiciary and trial by jury. But the implications proved to be too much – what if traditional authority were eroded by new ideas? To deal with possible unrest, censorship was taken out of the jurisdiction of the new courts in 1866; crimes or possible crimes against the state also did not come within this system. Important political cases were tried by special courts from 1872. Flogging was retained as a punishment in prisons and in colonies of exiles; police powers to investigate political offences and prepare cases were restored in 1871.

The greater freedom in society as a whole and economic progress seemed to call for educational changes. If there was a move from serf to citizen and if Russia were to develop economically, then a literate workforce with greater technical skills would be needed. The liberal education minister Golovnin introduced a number of reforms in the Universities and a Charter for Secondary education; but he, like Miliukin and Samarin was dismissed in a wave of fear about student radicalism following an assassination attempt on the Tsar in 1866. A more restricted curriculum based on classical studies was imposed, and moves towards more science – associated with liberalism and irreligion were discouraged. Inspectors were appointed to keep a close eye on primary schools to ensure that teachers were not encouraging disrespect for authority. The impact of reform was not really foreseen – such as the growth of radical ideas and the development of the Narodnik revolutionary movement. Alexander II lacked the intelligence to see what change might lead to and the confidence to deal with it. Instead there was a stop/go policy. At the end of the reign, there were considerations of extending the representative assemblies and increasing liberalism once more which were ended by the Tsar's assassination and Alexander III's dismissal of the liberal Loris-Melikov.

Army reforms and financial reforms pointed the way to the future. Universal conscription in 1874 pointed the way to a very large-scale armed force – with six years service and a long period in the reserve. This replaced the old-fashioned 25-year service, which was really the equivalent of a serf army. It also put the Russian state on the path to developing a modern army on the Prussian model. Economic reforms attempted to stabilise the currency and encourage foreign loans and investment. The Russo-Turkish war of 1877–78 revealed the limitations of the new armies and caused a financial crisis which saw the devaluation of the rouble and a loss of foreign confidence.

The situation facing Alexander III in 1881

The Russia of 1881 was a very different country in some ways to that of 1855. Personal serfdom had gone; local assemblies offered a taste of consultation and some political experience. Up to 1878 there had been financial reforms, a public budget and major reforms in finance; new notions of judicial independence and trial by jury had been introduced and there had been military changes. However, for all this there were strong elements of continuity. Autocracy dominated: Alexander III was educated in strictly orthodox ways; the power of traditional institutions like nobility and church was as strong as ever; the countryside was dominated by communal peasant agriculture and profitable market-based estates able to take advantage of new rail links – therefore the rich were getting richer and the poor remained poor. Tradition was still very strong. Pan Slav beliefs hailing tradition and the old Russia were stronger in official circles than Liberalism. The Opposition (like the remnants of the Narodiks, the People's Will and small groups of revolutionary anarchists) was still dependent on the influx of ideas and materials from a handful of exiles, and felt enough frustration to resort to violence and terrorism. The Crimean War was one measure of Russia's limitations at the start of the reign; by the end of the reign it was clear from the Russo–Turkish war of 1877–78 that Russia could not stand still. However Alexander IIIs situation in 1881 was different.

ANALYSIS

How did Alexander III's position compare with that of Alexander II in 1855?

Alexander II faced growing rural discontent and opposition from liberal elements in the upper class with the rigidity of the regime established by Nicholas I, but he did not face organised opposition with distinct ideologies and a commitment to terrorism. Total numbers of opponents may have been small, but as with the case of terrorist groups in the 21st century, small groups of dedicated and fanatical opponents can have a huge impact. The assassination of the Tsar generated a massive amount of insecurity and a determination to crush opposition and maintain tradition. Unlike his father, Alexander III did not approach his reign with optimism,

but a grim sense of duty – he wanted no celebrations for his coronation and his military background led him to consider himself a soldier at war with internal enemies.

The external situation, too, was threatening. For all Russia's good relations with Germany and her support of German unification, the results had been disappointing. When Russia needed support over the **Eastern Question** in 1878, she had not found it and had been forced to make unpopular concessions. She had expanded considerably in the east and the empire had grown, but relations with Britain, Austria and Germany had worsened; the alliance of Italy, Austria and Germany left her isolated and though there were treaties of friendship with Germany, there was a growing rift. Russia would need to have strong armed forces and this depended on economic growth.

So the basic dilemma was that the Tsar wanted a traditional Russia; he wanted no opposition; he wanted strict control over peasant communities; he wanted no growth in either local or national democracy. However, Russia could not retreat to a pre-industrial past, as it needed to be a great power and compete with other great powers. This meant that towns and industries and transport had to develop, but with that development came dangers. Workers gathered together would pick up new ideas. Communications would help the radical groups to spread ideas. A growing middle class would mean more intelligentsia, increasingly attracted to socialism. Modernisation would make the rigid autocracy seem old fashioned. The Tsar's train crash of 1888 is a perfect example of the problems he faced. The new trains gave Russia advantages – they developed the market opportunities of the peasants; they brought raw materials to factories; they carried the Tsar's troops; they unified the empire. But they also crashed.

The train crash of 1888. Tsar Alexander III sustained internal injuries in helping his family during this crash which contributed to his death in 1894.

On the face of it the reigns of Alexander II and Alexander III offer total contrasts, but there are similarities as well. Neither Tsar veered from a belief in autocracy, but had different strategies to preserve it – Alexander II by moderate reform, Alexander III by repression. Neither was consistent: the reforms were restricted by retreats from liberalism and an increase in state censorship and control; Alexander III did not entirely abandon concession and reform. Both were keen imperialists and expanded an essentially Russian empire; Alexander III was more determined to Russify his Empire, but the Polish revolt of 1863 showed the limits of Alexander II's liberal policies as severe repression was employed. Both encouraged economic and military development and neither really came to terms with the possible consequences.

The Eastern Question

This was the question of what would become of the decaying Ottoman (Turkish) Empire which still ruled large numbers of Balkan Christians? Russia was deeply concerned because the Turks mistreated the Balkan Christians who were Slavs and believed in the same Orthodox religion as the Russians.

Many in Russia wanted to protect the Balkan Christians and end Turkish rule, establishing Russian domination instead. This was deeply opposed by Austria-Hungary, also a Balkan power, and by Britain who did not want to see Russian forces in the Eastern Mediterranean threaten the Suez Canal and the route to British India. So Europe was deeply concerned about the future of Turkey and the Balkans.

The ways in which Alexander III reacted to the situation

There *were* changes after 1881. Peasant redemption payments, set up after 1861 to pay the state for compensating landlords for the loss of serfs were reduced; a peasant land bank was established in 1882 to allow farmers access to capital for improvements; the poll tax was abolished in 1886. Interestingly, the regime took up an idea from Bismarck's Germany and regulated working conditions in factories in 1882 imposing official limits on hours worked by women and children. The Tsar was also a patron of the arts and encouraged the first collection of Russian art which now forms the Tretchyakov Museum. So the idea of Alexander III as an angry bigoted and reactionary figure needs some modification. But not much. The tone of the reign was set by its tragic beginning and by relentless repression and a desire for political and social control.

There was some pressure from below, not just from the Tsar's ministers but also from nationalist groups and the growing popularity of anti-Semitism which linked attacks on Jews with attacks on revolutionaries and traitors. The Tsar embraced both Russification and anti-Semitism. A famous comment on a law restricting Jewish entry to university reveals his attitude 'Let us never forget that it was the Jews who crucified Jesus'. A strong bond between the Orthodox Church and the Tsarist regime led to measures against Jews and a big rise in emigration. The same nationalism also put pressure on the nationalities to accept Russian language and control. Press censorship was increased in 1882; control over the peasants was increased by the appointment of land captains and a law making violation of contracts between landlords and tenants a criminal act. There was an increase in closed (secret) trials for political offences and the position of the Zemstvos was changed. The executive boards of all local and regional councils became government officials, becoming part of the state. The electorate was reduced: in elections to the Moscow city council for instance, voting rights were removed from 13,000 people, leaving only 7,000 of the richer electors. Peasants voted but peasant representatives to the Council had to be appointed. Thus the Tsar did not end the reforms of Alexander II but he ended any chance of them evolving into broader or more liberal changes. Serfdom was not restored, but peasant independence was reduced; assemblies still met but clearly as part of government, not as a means of control or criticism; university education was restricted and religious tolerance was eroded. The secret police – the **Okhrana** – became a much more important element in Russian life than it had done before. By modern standards the power of repression was not overwhelming, but the restrictions of the state were very widespread – writers, teachers, local councilors, peasants, Jews, Catholics, Protestants, Finns, Poles, Lithuanians, Ukrainians, Estonians, reformers, editors and students were caught up in growing state control. The bureaucracy, police and army were dedicated to enforcing religious, racial and national orthodoxy.

The Okhrana

The Okhrana dates back to 1881. Following the assassination of Alexander II a new Division for the Protection of Order and Social Security was set up. In Russian this was shortened to Okhrannoe Otdelenie (security division) and thence to Okhrana or Okhranka. Okhranka is more informal – an ironic reference – rather like the British use of 'old bill' for police by criminals. Its aims were spying, data collection on political offenders and infiltration of terrorist organisations. Plain clothes detectives collected information. There were specialist officers and undercover agent provocateurs who led terrorists into actions for which they were arrested. There were branches in the Russian provinces and also abroad from 1883 to watch foreign exiles.

The Okhrana was abolished after the February revolution in 1917. Instead Lenin quickly set up his own secret political police, the Cheka – again having as its aim state security.

The Okhrana's HQ was at 16 Fontanka in St. Petersburg – the house still stands.

ACTIVITY

Was Alexander II more successful than Alexander III in coping with the problems he inherited?

1   Write down the successful points of Alexander II's policy on cards. These should be linked to the problems that he faced in 1855. If, for instance, one problem was that the Russian empire faced a mass of peasant discontent, how successful was Alexander II in solving it?

2   On the back write ways in which the Tsar had not been successful in dealing with the problem. For example, one side of the card might be 'The Tsar was successful in persuading the nobility to accept a more modern Russia by emancipating the Serfs'. On the other hand, you might say that the serfs were not equal citizens and were not given freedom to cultivate land independently.

3   Do the same with Alexander III.

On the basis of the balance between the two sides of the cards, who was more successful? Share and debate your views with others in the class.

What was the situation facing Nicholas II?

With the death of Alexander III and the accession of Nicholas II the pressures of a dual policy of repression and quite rapid economic growth had changed the situation once more. Unlike Alexander II, Nicholas brought no humanitarian impulse or broad concern for change to his role. But neither was there a furious revulsion about terrorism to motivate a change of policy, as there was with Alexander III. Nicholas's high-level tutors had made relatively little impact; his foreign travels had not brought a breath of vision; the Tsar's outlook was more domestic and limited than either of his predecessors. An intelligent analysis of the situation in 1894 might have revealed a dangerous development of urban growth and a suffering and resentful working class gathered in large units in urban centres. Statistics revealed a growing population with huge pressure on land. Surveys did reveal low levels of literacy, productivity and Russian technical progress. Foreign expertise still dominated. Communications in Russia were worse than in any other of the great powers.

Nationalism was growing and resentment of Russification increasing in a way not true in 1855 or 1881. Russia's anti-Semitic reputation was a moral blot, and religious and political exiles took with them a resentment which blackened the reputation of the Tsar's regime abroad. In the literature and political commentary of the time Russia was seen as an isolated and backward police state. The nobility's political and economic power had increased with the result that a number of modern developments – in agriculture and military expertise, for instance – were made more difficult than in other countries. Even if the Tsar's regime were to be maintained then changes would have to be made. Russia's towns, industries and communications were developing in the 1890s at an unprecedented level and doing nothing was no more an option for Nicholas II than it had been for different reasons for Alexander II in 1855 or Alexander III in 1881.

These Tsars had 'hit the ground running' but it took war and revolution to shift Nicholas into change and this is a major difference between him and nearly all the other Russian rulers of the period. The other rulers, for good or ill, had quite distinct visions of change; this vision was lacking in Nicholas II.

How did Nicholas II react?

The changes that were made in Nicholas II's reign were in some ways greater than those of his predecessors, but there is one overwhelming similarity. They were brought in after a period of crisis to conserve autocracy and the key features of traditional Russia as it was in 1894. They were much less motivated by a vague liberalism than the reforms of Alexander II. Their leading proponents in Nicholas II's government were both strong supporters of autocracy and less liberal than some of the ministers of Alexander II thirty years before. Domestic policy did not really engage with the scope of economic and social change in this reign any more than it had under his predecessors, but the degree of change seemed greater.

Nicholas II continued the policy of state-supported industrial expansion (*see* Chapter 4), Russification and control of the nationalities in the Empire and suppression of political discontent. There was no sense of Russia moving in a different direction until a catastrophic war with Japan from 1904–5 led to a revolution. This revolution was seen as the most serious challenge to the regime since 1855 and was unique in its extent and scope (*see* pages 134–40).

Unlike his predecessors, Nicholas was forced to proclaim political concessions in the 1905 **October Manifesto** which promised a national parliament. The Tsar promised freedom of speech, press, association and conscience. There was to be an end to arbitrary arrest and a wide franchise was promised for the election of a new state Duma. No **UKASE** or Imperial edict would become law without the Dumas's consent and the Duma would have a role in controlling officials. What had been too great a reform for Alexander II and unthinkable for Alexander III introduced a hope for a liberal Russia and was the biggest potential development of the period. Had it been successful, then Russia's industrial modernisation would have been mirrored in its political development.

On one level the Manifesto, urged on a reluctant Tsar by an almost equally reluctant but realistic Count Witte, who had been most responsible for economic growth, was a success. It split the revolutionaries and swung moderate opinion back to the Tsar. On the other hand, the subsequent betrayal of the manifesto promises and the creation of only a token and restricted parliament eroded respect for the Tsar and failed to give him the cooperation of the nation in the war effort after 1914. Like the Emancipation of the Serfs of 1861 it promised more than it delivered.

The October Manifesto

This was issued in October 1905 on the advice of Witte to give concessions to the liberals who wanted constitutional change. It offered freedom of person, conscience, speech assembly and union' and a legislative assembly or Duma elected by a broad franchise. The Duma would be consulted by the Tsar and given the right to pass laws. By 1906 the Tsar had regained power and made the position clearer in the Fundamental Law of 23 April 1906 which reasserted his autocratic powers, veto of any laws, appointment of all ministers and to hold all government power.

UKASE

An arbitrary decree. In 1906 the Tsar reserved the rule to rule by UKASE when the Duma was not meeting – something he could decide on by dismissing it.

The creation of a national assembly – the **Duma** (see below) – as a result of the promises of 1905, was the first outlet that political opposition had that was legal; it was a major step forward from the Zemstvos, but was treated in much the same way. That is to say the initially liberal and forward-looking reforms were eroded when the regime felt more confident that restrictions would not lead to revolution. The powers of the Duma were very limited and the voting qualifications amended in such a way as to favour the rich. At a time when the rich were actually getting richer, they were also given more political influence. When the crisis of war came and there was a need to involve the nation in Russia's greatest national effort, the Duma was not developed or used as a channel of communication with the nation. The war revealed the regime's attitude to democratic parliamentary government – that it was a foreign idea irrelevant to Russia. The Tsar's response to failure in war was rather similar to his father's response to the rail crash – he would take the weight. The effects on both men were similar – it hastened their deaths. The Tsar's perception in 1915, that in a modern state a situation might be saved by a leader with little or no military experience taking on the role of Commander in Chief leaving his unpopular German-born wife in charge at home, shows the limited ability of this regime to move with the times and the Tsar's bad judgement.

The Dumas

The First Duma was elected in the spring of 1906 on a wide franchise, from 19 May to the 21 July. There was little agreement on the power of the Duma. It was dissolved by the Tsar. The second Duma, 5 March to the 16 June 1907, was more radical and had even less agreement. After its dissolution restrictions on the electoral power of the lower classes as the electorate is reduced. The third Duma, 1907–1912, was more conservative in nature. Modest reforms were agreed. No development of responsible government, i.e. control by the parliament over ministers, Ministers not responsible to the Duma but directly to the Tsar. No financial control by the Duma. The fourth Duma, 1912–1916, had little role in wartime administration. There was little attempt by government to use it in generating national enthusiasm for war. Strong criticisms were made of government and tension increased.

Tsarist Russia moved forward however after 1906 in many different ways. It adopted radical agrarian policies (*see* page 76). Its economic development continued rapidly. Railway development grew and military expenditure jumped dramatically as huge efforts were made to rebuild the ships sunk by the Japanese navy at the battle of Tsushima. Efforts were made to bring the army up to the level of its European counterparts, and foreign experts were used to modernise production. There was some attempt to come to terms with industrial working conditions and to offer measures of health insurance.

The key element of the previous reign, however, remained. As the celebrations for the 300th anniversary of the dynasty in 1913 showed, Russia remained essentially rooted in its autocratic past. The attempt to share power failed. Liberalism was increasingly discredited and political change was focused on the more extreme groups.

Tenure

How land is officially owned. For example if land is Freehold Tenure it means it is owned outright. If it is Leasehold, then the occupier pays for it. Tenure literally means 'holding'.

The story of the lack of development of parliamentary government has a parallel with most of the Tsarist reforms since 1855. They encouraged hopes of change which were not fulfilled. The agricultural reforms of Stolypin (*see* Chapter 3, pages 86–87) may have gone further in changing Russia from a communal to an individual agrarian society, but essentially were concerned with the arrangement of the peasants' own lands into new forms of **tenure**. They did not tackle the land hunger that population growth had brought to the countryside nor did they deal with the greater concentration of landed wealth into fewer hands. During this period the bulk of **agrarian** produce being sold on the market came from private estates. The growth in urban markets and communications benefited this sector rather than the peasantry as a whole. Though there was more economic freedom, this was not matched by political freedom. Peasant discontent found more outlet in the revolutionary SRs than in Duma representation so when the regime tottered, there was little loyalty from a mass of peasants eager only to seize lands.

Economic growth both before and after the 1905 Revolution was promoted by the state just as it had been earlier. Neither Alexander III nor Nicholas II could see the implications of huge urban growth; neither provided adequate infrastructure for growing cities. Neither could even provide real law and order and prevent the hideous crime rise that accompanied urban growth. By 1914, slum districts became a noticeable feature of major cities and were unpoliceable with a modicum of personal safety only being preserved by lynch mob 'hue and cries'. Faced with potentially huge urban discontent, even Nicholas II's secret police, the Okhrana, were more in support of social and political reforms than the Tsar.

Agrarian

To do with the countryside and farming. Agrarian disturbances are riots or violence by peasants.

ACTIVITY

Which reign saw the most significant domestic reforms, Alexander II's or Nicholas II's?

Construct two arguments based on clearly supported points involving the strengths and weaknesses of their respective domestic policies.

In one Alexander II's reforms 'win', for example, the creation of the Zemstvos. In the other, Nicholas's reforms 'win' and, had not the war intervened, they might have given the monarchy the chance to survive. For example the October Manifesto.

Which argument seems the more convincing?

The problems facing the Provisional Government (March–October 1917)

The Provisional Government

They were a group of Duma deputies who took over the Government of Russia when the Tsar abdicated. They filled a gap until a new constitution could be established. They chose a chairman, Prince George Lvov who became Prime Minister, though reluctantly. No-one had expected the Tsarist regime to collapse so quickly, so both Lvov's leadership and the new government were temporary measures. The Provisional Government faced another body claiming the right to rule in the Soviet. This was the Petrograd Soviet. Thus there were two bodies claiming authority. The Provisional Government never made their rule legitimate because by the time an assembly met to draw up a new constitution, Lenin was already in power and he sent it away in January 1918.

Few of Russia's long-term problems had really been solved before the First World War and the war had created many new ones, but the problems facing the **Provisional Government** in March 1917 were perhaps the most serious facing any of Russia's Tsars. Unlike the three Tsars the government did not come to power with any real legitimacy. So why should they rule at all? Not because of custom and inheritance or divine will. Not because of popular sovereignty, since Duma elections took place on such a restricted franchise. Not because they were people of outstanding ability: the new premier Prince Lvov was such a nonentity

Soviets

These were councils of workers that emerged in the Revolution of 1905. Hastily elected councils of workers and soldiers were formed again in February 1917. They sent representatives to a larger body – the St. Petersburg Soviet – which claimed power over the armed forces. All over Russia these councils were formed and there was an all Russian Congress of Soviets due to meet in October 1917. After the Bolsheviks seized power the Soviet became the unit of local government, though controlled by the Communist party.

KEY IDEA

Was democracy possible in the Russia of 1917?

Democracy can work in agrarian societies with limited traditions of parliament – as was shown in India after 1947. However, India had the British model; some talk of parliaments had been going on since 1909; the Indian middle class was educated on English lines with English traditions. Most important, anti-democratic groups were not strong and India did not try and establish a new democracy while engaged in a massive war and during wholesale peasant land seizures.

that few knew whom their new rulers were. Not because of a theory of history – later the Bolsheviks could claim that the laws of historical development had put them in power. Not because they represented a dominant class – the peasant parties might have claimed that; the Marxists could claim they represented a key class in the industrial workers, who would grow. Not because they were the only established body, because in the cities an alternative form of government – the **Soviets** – had been formed. This offered the problem of working with another body which claimed to control the armed forces. The Soviets claimed to represent the people. But whom did the Provisional Government represent – the liberal upper class; the small Russian middle class? Neither was a strong base from which to continue to rule.

Unlike the Tsars, they came with a clear liberal agenda in which they believed that the changes they made were not to preserve an outdated autocracy, but to introduce the benefits of 19th century liberalism. However, the context for establishing this was much more unfavourable than the context which the three Tsars had faced in preserving their ideal type of regime. The world in 1917 was a distinctly illiberal place, with freedom everywhere subordinated to the needs of war. It was extremely unlikely that without a liberal market economy, a strong educated middle class, a democratic tradition and a period of peace to ease a transition that Russia could suddenly become a liberal democracy. The great majority of the opposition did not believe in this and the supporters of the old regime had not valued it.

How did the Provisional Government react to their situation?

The liberal reforms after March 1917 were more whole-hearted than those of the Tsars but freedom of press, movement, association, political activity and the end of political police and control added to the problem. The enemies of democracy got free rein. The ability to change enough to meet a crisis situation was a common feature of the Provisional Government and the Tsars. The **peasant land seizures** were neither prevented nor recognised, leaving a state of uncertainty in the countryside. If the government had issued a Land Decree accepting the new ownership, then perhaps the history of Russia might have been different. But that would have been asking the liberal middle class politicians to betray their entire ethos of respect for property and law and order. Lenin, who had no interest in either could easily promise the peasants land; as could the peasants' own party the SRs. Lenin could also promise peace – international obligations to capitalist powers meant nothing and in any case he believed that a world revolution was on the way. But the Provisional Government needed foreign recognition, believed in honouring obligations and respecting the sacrifice millions had made. By 1917 they also ignored the fact that German militarism had been more successful than any democratic alternative in the war so far. In a way they were as controlled by ideology as the Tsars had been and the Commissars were to be. Had a constitution been established and elections held quickly then the Provisional Government might have achieved legitimacy. However, they allowed themselves to be distracted by the practical problems of organising all this in a time of war.

The problem for the Provisional Government was that that the Tsar had been overthrown by events in the capital rather than in the country as a whole. The revolution had spread to the cities, but the bulk of Russia had not been involved. Therefore the new political leaders were not known on a national level and the authority of the government had not been imposed nationally. Whole areas had drifted out of any control when the Tsarist regime collapsed – as was shown by the **peasant land seizures**. Troops were drifting home by late Summer; local police forces were disintegrating. The Provisional Government was having a limited effect outside the capital by the time it was overthrown by the Bolsheviks – another group about which the majority in provincial Russia had a limited knowledge. The sheer size of Russia, its poor communications and education reduced the effectiveness of the Provisional Government. Russian traditions of disintegration at time of crisis made it hard for it to assert control.

Into this political vacuum came a number of competitors – the Soviets, the extremist groups and some discontented military units. However, none of these groups succeeded at this time. The Soviets did not succeed in controlling the government and a stronger leader, Kerensky, emerged; the Bolsheviks were suppressed in July and General **Kornilov's** attempt at a coup was defeated. However the cost of this was just too much; the Provisional government had survived but had not generated much support; its reforms had little impact on the wider population and clever and ruthless opponents made the most of the crises. Popular support for greater change was building; Lenin made good use of it and offered a range of promises which he neither could not meet nor really believed in. However, by a well-organised coup at just the right time (October), he gained control of the two major cities (St. Petersburg and Moscow) and proclaimed a new government.

Peasant land seizures

In the Summer of 1917 there had been widespread takeovers of landed estates by the peasants. The government refused to authorise a widespread redistribution of land, so the peasants simply took it. This was accepted by Lenin in his Land Decree in November 1917.

BIOGRAPHY

Lavr Kornilov (1870–1918) was a career officer in the Russian army and fought against Austria in the First World War. Made Supreme Commander of the army of the Provisional Government in 1917 he bitterly disliked Lenin and any idea of peace. He thought that Kerensky wished him to occupy Petrograd and suppress the Bolsheviks. Kersensky dismissed him on 9 September but he ordered an advance on the capital. The Bolsheviks organised a defence against what seemed like a military take over. Kornilov's troops were unable get to Petrograd and there was no take over. Kornilov was arrested, but escaped and was killed by a shell during the Civil War.

ACTIVITY

Why did the Provisional Government last such a short time, while Tsarist Russia survived the major crisis of 1905 and lasted for over three years in a terrible war?

This piece of analysis will help as a building block for the consideration of the whole period. Was it because Nicholas II and his ministers were more skilful than Kerensky and his colleagues or was it because the problems they faced were so much greater than those facing Nicholas II? You will be able to expand your ideas by considering why Lenin and the Bolsheviks, facing far more numerous enemies, did survive when the Provisional Government did not.

Think in terms of reading through the text, looking at some additional material on 1905 and its aftermath and on 1917. Then propose a *thesis* on the main reason that might explain this. See if your thesis is similar to others in the class.

Note: Whilst it is important to write your ideas down, do not go beyond a page and a half at most.

The situation facing Lenin

Lenin had a little more legitimacy than the Provisional Government. He could claim that by the Marxist view of history (suitably adapted to suit his position) and by popular support he ruled in the name of the people. In March 1917 there had been few alternatives to some sort of provisional rule by the only elected body in Russian, the Duma. Lenin claimed that there was now a real alternative – rule by the industrial proletariat through the Bolsheviks, the party destined to rule in the name of these workers. Many did not agree. None of the Tsars had faced a succession crisis on the level of the Civil War which followed Lenin's accession to power; and none of his successors faced such acute challenges to their power (*see* pages 144–48, Chapter 5). For historical parallels one would have to go to the early 17th century and the '**Time of Troubles**'. More dominated by ideology than any of their predecessors, the Bolsheviks issued decree after decree revolutionising Russia. Most were meaningless because they were unenforceable. The peasants were sitting on the lands they had seized from the nobles and landowners in the summer of 1917. The workers still faced the hardships they had faced throughout the war. Opposition – among nationalities, former Tsarists, and liberals – solidified around hatred of the very harsh Brest-Litvosk peace treaty (*see* page 68, Chapter 2) that Lenin agreed with the Germans in March 1918. Foreign powers joined in such as Britain, France, Japan and the USA and Russia spiralled into chaos. It was not the first time that a regime had faced widespread violence and opposition but even compared with 1905 or the peasant riots of the 1850s, or the Polish Revolt, this was unprecedented.

How did Lenin respond to the challenges that faced the Bolsheviks after the October Revolution?

What was unprecedented, too, was the level of determination and energy shown by Lenin and the Bolsheviks. Lenin was convinced that world-wide revolution would follow, and in this exalted mood was prepared to sign away to the Germans large areas of western Russia in a separate peace, the Treaty of Brest-Litovsk. This decision tipped the scales as opposition gathered against what seemed to be a tragic waste of 5 million Russian casualties. Lenin was faced with not only establishing a completely new type of state, but also defending it against a variety of enemies, the so-called Whites, and also peasant resistance, the Greens.

Not intellectually limited, or weak in any way, Lenin showed himself to be more Tsarist than the Tsars. Power was rapidly centralised and decisions taken with a complete ruthlessness. Any suggestion that power was to be shared was ended by the dispersal of the Constituent Assembly after one day in January 1918. The elections had not given the Bolsheviks a majority, so as the assembly was clearly flying in the face of History, it had to go into the dustbin of History. There was a short-lived alliance with the left wing of the SRs, from whom Lenin had virtually stolen his peasant policy, but other parties like the Mensheviks were seen as enemies and persecuted. To fight the war for control of Russia and implement a series of hasty communist decrees, the strictest control was needed: grain was confiscated, hostages taken and killed; the war was fought without any restraint. The secret police were quickly reinstated as the Cheka. Any controls necessary were imposed, whatever the cost and resistance met by extreme force: White officers had their epaulettes nailed to their shoulders in some areas and some naked Polish officers were impaled on branches of trees. Even more so than for the Tsars, defeat was unthinkable. The period of War Communism turned Russia, at least that part controlled by the Bolsheviks, into an armed camp. The element of discussion in the party was subordinated to a disciplined unity. Opposition to left and right was repressed. Lenin became the target of assassination by leftist terrorists just as the Tsars had been. Meanwhile hopes of a world-wide revolution faded. The revival of the Workers' International organisations of the previous century took place with the founding of **the Comintern** in 1919, but Russian domination was vital. This was also true of the old Empire: the nationalities were brought under soviet control and hopes of independence were dashed. Communism became a means of binding together the nationalities to Russia as much as loyalty to the Tsar had been. Bolsheviks from outside great Russia, such as the Georgian Stalin were also eager to repress their fellow nationalities and force them into Soviet control. The term Union of Soviet Socialist Republics disguised the maintenance of political control.

By 1921 against all odds, the Bolsehviks had crushed internal and external resistance, foreign powers had left and the Poles had been driven back. But the costs were huge. Both sides, Reds and Whites, had waged war violently and against civilians as well as troops. Agriculture was disrupted by a programme of huge requisitioning and there were major revolts on the level of post-1861 or 1905. Industry had declined. There had been major droughts, famine and a humiliating dependence on American humanitarian aid. There was an opposition movement among the very class that the Bolsehviks represented, and even the sailors of Kronstadt – previously the heart of the revolutionary movement – had mutinied and had to be bloodily suppressed. In 1921 Lenin was forced to give way massively on the party's major policies – he allowed private trade in the countryside and small-scale industrial enterprise. In contrast, the party was rigidly controlled by a ban on factions. Already the death toll of political trials was mounting and the **Cheka** enforced a high level of supervision and political repression. But the heart of Bolshevik policy had gone, as had Lenin's health. The preservation of the Bolschvik state had been an amazing achievement, but how much was left of the original idealism of the Bolsheviks and how far had Lenin been forced to become more and more like the Tsars he so hated?

> ### Stretch and challenge
>
> #### To what extent do you consider Lenin to be a Red Tsar and why?
>
> At this point, a more extended synoptic view can be attempted.
>
> 1. Read the following arguments carefully and make a judgement on whether Lenin was a Red Tsar.
>
> 2. Look at how much continuity there was between Russia before February 1917 and between October 1917 and January 1924.
>
> What follows is included to be evaluated, not accepted as true. You may disagree with the criteria for establishing how Tsarist Lenin was. This is fine and you can use your own ways of judging the issue, if they can be defended. You may find some of the arguments which follow much more plausible than others. Think about why. You may wish to bring in material of your own. The object of the exercise is to offer a power point presentation to the class showing to what extent you consider Lenin to be a Red Tsar and offering clear evidence for your view.

The 'Red Tsar' argument

In order to discuss this then certain aspects of Tsarism have to be identified and it has to be kept in mind that, even since 1855, not all the Tsars had behaved in the same way.

The Comintern

The third Workers International Socialist Organisation (March 1919 to May 1943). The first International Socialist Organisation lasted from 1864–76; the second from 1889 to the First World War. The third was the first dominated by an actual Socialist workers' state. Its aim was to spread revolution and it coordinated socialist movements in other countries. The Comintern became a tool of the Russian leaders rather than a genuine international workers organisation. It was revived after the second world war as Cominform.

The Cheka

This was the Russian Extraordinary Commission for the Struggle against Counter Revolution and Sabotage – founded late in 1917 by Felix Dzerzhinsky. It was the heir to the Okhrana which had ended when the Tsar fell in March 1917. Russia was without a secret police for only a few months in the entire period 1855–1964.

ACTIVITY

Taking these as at least some of the possible criteria, does Lenin emerge as a new Tsar or is the discontinuity with the Tsarist era more significant than any similarities?

Some of the characteristics of the post-1855 Tsarist regimes were as follows.

1 A continuing belief in autocracy – the rule of a divinely chosen individual to whom the Russian people owe obedience. The monarch represents something higher and something deeply rooted in the Russian past.

2 Tsarism depended on control by the state bureaucracy of key elements in Russian life. In theory the land was the Tsar's, there was a huge input into economic development and the Tsar was closely linked to the spiritual and religious life of the country through the Orthodox Church. The Tsar had control over opinion, censored publications and political life.

3 Russia's destiny and that of its Rulers were seen as linked. The Tsars did not retreat behind ministers but played a leading part in decision making, accepting this as a matter of responsibility.

4 Despite all this, the aristocracy since 1855 had accepted a degree of change and was prepared to try and adapt to circumstances. They looked back to Tsars who had taken their Empire forward in the past and attempted modernisation.

5 The Tsars were major cultural patrons and promoted new architecture and the arts, though without allowing complete freedom of expression.

The argument for continuity

Ideology and power

Lenin did not claim to be divinely chosen but there was more behind his claims to power than simply himself. He did not base his right to be obeyed on having been elected, like a democratic politician. Nor did he base his claim to power on his own political abilities or administrative skills. He did look to a higher source of legitimacy, like the Tsars. This was not religion, but the laws of History. In Marxist theory, revolution takes place when the historical process has reached a certain point. The French Revolution took place when bourgeois capitalist elements in the economy had reached such a point that the time was ripe for the old feudal regime based on land ownership to be overthrown. By 1918 Capitalism had entered its final phase – Imperialism. That had brought about war which had been a disaster for the old regimes. Now it was the time for the proletariat to take over, just as the middle classes had taken over before them. History not God was the higher power and Marx not Jesus was its prophet, but Lenin was guided by something beyond himself, just as the Tsar was guided by his obligations to God as a divinely appointed ruler.

A lot followed from this that made Lenin like a Tsar. He had a higher purpose. All three Tsars since 1855 had grappled with fears of change because they felt that had to maintain autocracy as a duty to God. Autocracy went beyond a conviction that rule by a single person was the best way to get results, or to help their country. It was a binding duty and a real ideology. Lenin, too, felt a huge responsibility to be guided by an ideology and to meet his historical destiny, whatever the costs.

The state and the people

The Tsars had inherited a monarchy with an aristocracy owing service to the Tsar and all lands belonging to the Tsars. By 1855 this had been modified in practice, but there was no contractual idea of a mutual obligation by rulers and ruled. The state was very dominant in theory if not in practice. The elements of the state – the bureaucracy, the army and the official church – were much stronger than was the case, say in America or Britain. In strict

Marxist theory the state would wither away after the Revolution and the state was simply a means of class oppression. But in the short term, the state would be used by those who had taken power for the workers to impose a dictatorship of the proletariat. The state would be used against the class enemies of the workers until the time that the golden age would emerge of true socialism. So Lenin, like the Tsars needed a strong state.

The bureaucracy

The official bureaucracy remained. The so-called Lenin Recruitment drafted thousands into the party and the measures taken to control Russian economic life demanded a considerable administrative machine which was to be a major feature of Soviet life. The police apparatus was important for both Tsarist and Leninist Russia: for instance, the Okhrana was replicated by the new Cheka early in the Soviet regime.

The army

The army was a major element in Lenin's Russia because of the Civil War. The Red Army fought dissidents just as the Imperial army had; it was at war with foreign powers just as the Imperial army was. The Red Army struggled with Polish forces just as the Imperial army had. The functions of both Imperial forces and Red forces in suppressing internal dissent remained the same. Indeed this reached its highest point under Stalin when police and army uniforms were made the same. This political deployment of regular military forces had not been a feature generally of America or Western Europe in the period 1855–1917. Nor was it general practice after the First World War. Lenin inherited and developed a particular feature of Tsarist Russia.

Industry

In economic terms, the state in Russia had been a major contributor. Businesses were not nationalised, but were heavily dependent on the state to commission and purchase products, to provide investment and infrastructure. The massive industrial expansion after 1891 would not have been possible without the state. Lenin took over industry for the state, so in a sense went further, but he did not move far from Tsarist industrial policy, especially with the greater influence of the state on production that had occurred during the war.

Rural life

In agriculture, the state – or the Tsar – was a major landowner; the state dictated much about the organisation of landowning and in theory the land was the states. Lenin permitted greater freedom initially to the peasants, but he made it clear that all land belonged to the people – not individually but collectively. As the people's will was interpreted by the party and the party was the state, then really the land was owned by the state on behalf of the people. Like the Tsars, Lenin reserved the right to control the land. When he needed to, he took the products of the land by wartime requisitioning.

The church

The Orthodox Church which had supported the Tsarist regime was not obviously a pillar of Lenin's rule. However, both regimes rested firmly on doctrines – Orthodox Christianity and Marxism; both had an interest in spreading these doctrines; both liked ceremonies; both taught ideologies in schools. There is greater contrast between, say, Britain and France which were largely secular societies whose politics was not based on theories and ideology

and in which religion was essentially a private matter, than there is between Lenin's Russia and the Russia of the Tsars where ideologies played a much larger role.

The role of the leader

The Russian Empire

The Tsars believed strongly in personal responsibilities. The Emancipation was driven at key points by Alexander II himself and the nature of the state changed because of the ideas and personality of the ruler. Alexander III too ruled personally. The liberal direction in which Russia was heading was reversed because of the personal influence of the Tsar. Nicholas II, a less thoughtful or forceful personality nevertheless saw his duty in terms of personal leadership and went further than his two predecessors in taking personal charge of the armed forces in a major war. A cabinet system did not exist; advice was given by ministers personally. There was even after 1905 and the creation of a Duma, little mechanism for controlling the Tsars or formal limitations on their power. The main limitations were practical; the repressive forces at their command were, by modern standards, relatively limited; communications in their vast empire were poor; there was the threat of urban riots, national resistance, peasant violence which offered considerable dangers. There was too the need to consider international opinion.

The USSR

Lenin as a Bolshevik leader before 1917 had been part of a loosely-knit revolutionary movement. There were considerable differences of opinion within the Social Democrats which meant that Lenin's ideas were scrutinised and criticised in a way that none of the Tsar's views had been. Lenin was a fierce debater and found plenty of opposition to his views about the nature of the party and the interpretation of Marxist theory. As Bolsheviks were spread all over Europe and Russia, the establishment of any firm central control was difficult and Lenin was not a Tsar of his party before 1917. In 1917 his ideas were greeted with some horror by his party comrades. His insistence on taking power was thought unrealistic and inconsistent with the views of Marx. How could true Communism come before the necessary bourgeois phase in a country's history had been developed? Only by applying all his powers of persuasion and his natural leadership qualities did Lenin persuade the Bolsheviks to support a take over in October 1917. After that, Lenin ruled not as undisputed 'Tsar' but with a cabinet of Commissars. So on the face of it, a head of a party which openly discussed both theory and tactics, could not really be a Tsar. Lenin's colleagues offered opposition and sometimes advice that no Tsar would have received. Lenin was advised to curtail his affair with Inessa Armand after his wife had complained to the Central Committee! Lenin had on occasion to plead, to offer his resignation; and he had to persuade and cajole the Party Congresses in a way that the Tsar did not. Yet, for all this key decisions were Lenin's. The most important of these were the timing of the Revolution. Lenin personally encouraged the harshest repression in the Civil War; he pushed through the acceptance of the peace Treaty with the Germans, the Treaty of Brest-Litovsk; his energies were behind the economic measures which rapidly nationalised finance and industry. Above all the Land policy, which seemed to give lands to the peasants in November 1917 against all Marxist theory, was his policy.

Lenin saw most of all that power must come first and that the opportunity for taking power must be seized. He saw that keeping power by any means must be the priority; his interpretation of Marxism was the theoretical basis of the new regime. When he deviated from ideology or even what the bulk of the party believed, as with the introduction of the New Economic Policy in 1921, then his personal authority and persuasion were the key to the change.

In appearance and manner, Lenin was far from appearing a Tsar – but the worker's cap and the three-piece suit (Fig. 1.4) were as much symbols as all the robes and uniforms of the Tsars (Fig. 1.5).

Figure 1.4   This propaganda poster shows the iconic depiction of Lenin.

Figure 1.5   Nicholas II reviewing troops in 1915. The photo shows a short man – the splendid horse, the sword, the military uniform seem very different from Lenin.

Modernisation and adaptability

None of the Tsars after 1855 was totally opposed to change. Whether it arrived as economic development, or offering concessions to the peasants, or attempting some sort of institutional development, they did not stand still. They were also forced to adapt to changing circumstances by wars or the emergence of discontent. But they did not change the fundamental political philosophy of their regime. Autocracy and tradition remained. In this respect, Lenin can be seen to be in line with the Tsarist tradition. Once Communism had been established as the dominant ideology, this never changed. Lenin's Ban on Factions restricted discussion. Opposition was not allowed to function; there was little chance for any alternative political philosophy to be debated. However, there were adjustments to circumstances. Lenin made concessions to the peasantry first in November 1917 with the Land Decree and then in March 1921 with the New Economic Policy. In no way did Lenin give up the theory that land belonged to the people as a whole; in no way did he give up his belief that collective agriculture was beneficial. In practice, to keep power, he made concessions. This is very similar to Nicholas II after 1905. Autocracy was central, but to keep power there had to be elections, a new national Duma and the concept of 'loyal opposition'. Alexander II offered a series of modernising reforms which were curtailed if they seemed to be a threat to the underlying autocracy. Even Alexander III made some concessions to the peasantry. Conservatives opposed even the limited Tsarist reforms, just as those in the Communist party who looked back to the strict orthodoxy of Marx were concerned about the concessions made in 1921. The Tsars found reforming ministers who were nevertheless deeply committed to the underlying principles of the regime. Lenin found in the party those who accepted and defended change – like Nikolai Bukharin who defended the NEP concessions. The difference is that Alexander II and Nicholas II were more prepared to compromise their underlying principle of concentrated power than was Lenin. The local councils in town and countryside offered opportunities for debate and participation. Nicholas II's Duma marked a big departure from total absolute monarchy even if its powers were limited. Lenin offered no such political concession or opportunity. Aware that economic change is linked to political change, there was a determination to maintain the political monopoly of the Bolsheviks at all costs and not to even offer the possibility of a 'loyal opposition'. In that respect he was closer to the rigidity of Alexander III and possibly 'more Tsarist than the Tsars'.

The arts

The Tsars and Lenin shared artistic interests. Culture was an important political weapon for both; for the Tsars Russian cultural achievements were linked to Russian national pride and cultural superiority over the subject peoples. The grandeur of the palaces and the royal architecture was a visual expression of autocracy. The state offered patronage – even Alexander III had a keen interest in Russian art and established a major gallery. Russian art thrived after 1855. The Imperial opera and ballet saw a golden age of masterpieces by Tchaikovsky, Rimsky-Korsakov, and the young Stravinsky. Elite patronage was an important element. Innovation was not discouraged and the roots of the post-war avant-garde developments in painting (Fig. 1.6), architecture and music can be seen in pre-war culture.

The Revolution provided a different sort of stimulation. With a sense of political re-birth, many artists were moved to develop new ideas that they had been considering before 1917 and to take them forward (Fig. 1.7). In many ways artistic developments happened regardless of revolution, but in some cases were inspired by Lenin's new Russia

Figure 1.6 Ilya Repin, *Ukranian Girl by a Fence*, 1876. Oil on canvas. The Art Museum of Belarus, Minsk, Belarus.

Figure 1.7 *Improvisation 209*, Vasilii Vasilliyevich Kandinsky, 1917. Collection of the Surikov Museum of Art, Krasnoyarsk.

The distance between Repin's portrait and Kandinsky's abstraction (Figs 1.6 and 1.7) is huge, but both the Tsarist and Leninist regimes saw flourishing artistic life, which did not seem to depend on political liberty.

A major difference is the politicisation of art under Lenin. Initially this did not compromise artistic standards as the best artists of the day, like Dimitri Moor, made Soviet posters works of art. Also, nascent cinema was used to take propaganda to the countryside in a way unknown under the Tsars

More avant-garde posters show the influence of artists like Malevich and Kandinsky. Later Soviet art was far more conservative. The same is true of music. Shostakovich's 2nd and 3rd symphonies combine intense modernism with praise of the revolution. The composer Alexander Mosolov tried to put the sounds of an iron foundry into music.

The argument for discontinuity

The dominant theme of rule under the Tsars was essentially conservatism. The ceremonial, the vocabulary – the recitation of the Tsar's long list of titles – the lifestyle were essentially backward looking. The reforms which were made were the result of external pressure – mainly war or threat of revolution. Tsarism compared even with similar regimes in Europe was old fashioned from 1855–1917, and there was little sense of vision or progress. The three Tsars from 1855 were essentially holding back more fundamental change. The closest

Sources

Ⓐ To Tsaritsyn Province Labour Committee

You are directed as a battle order to take decisive measures to mobilise 3,000 men and 8,000 women for the Astrakhan Fishing Industry without fail. Implementation is your personal responsibility.

Ⓑ Lenin, Chairman of the Defence Council, 25 March 1921

At a stroke, 11,000 people would be drafted into forced labour.

Treat the Jews and urban inhabitants of the Ukraine with an iron rod; transfer them to the front; do not let them into any government agencies.

Ⓒ Draft resolution of Policy in the Ukraine, 21 November 1919

11 August 1918.

Letter to V. A. Kuraev and other Bolshevik leaders in Penza province

Hang (hang without fail, so that people see) no fewer than one hundred known Kulaks, rich men, and bloodsuckers.

Publish their names

Take from them all their grain

Designate hostages

Strangle to death the bloodsucking Kulaks

Telegraph receipt and implementation

Yours

Lenin

Ⓓ To Comrade Berzin, 14 August 1918

Do not spare money on publications in three or four languages (propaganda). The Berliners will send some more money; if the scum delay, complain to me formally

Yours

Lenin

Letters all quoted in: Richard Pipes, *The Unknown Lenin*, 1996

that they came to a dynamic mission was Pan Slavism, and even that was mostly reduced to its more negative aspects of Russification. This cannot be compared to the strong sense of vision and forward movement which motivated Lenin. His philosophy was based on progress towards a golden age of socialism, not back to golden age of Tsarist grandeur. His famous saying 'One step forward, two steps back' was a realisation of the huge difficulties that he faced in pursuing a vision, but to see him as trying to preserve power for its own sake on the model of the Tsars is wrong. It is a superficial comparison to say that both rulers were motivated by something higher when their political outlooks and philosophies were so very different. There is no equivalent in any Tsar's outlook to the influence of Marxist theory on Lenin.

It is true that the state did not wither away under Lenin and that it was violent and oppressive. But the nature of state control was very different. The state bureaucracy of the Tsars was often inefficient, as the wars of 1904–5 and 1914–17 showed; it was slow and inadequate. It could be cruel, but often this was a result of poor communications and inefficient control from the centre. Its procedures were cumbersome, but it owed its ethos to service to a Tsar seen as the father of his people. The Soviet state was highly politicised and its ethos dominated by class war. The domination of local areas from the centre was a strong feature of Lenin's rule and he engaged in a sort of micro management that the Tsars did not.

Lenin: a personal rule

The revelation of Lenin's correspondence show him personally ordering slave labour, executions, hostages, waging class war, directing propaganda and acknowledging funds received from Germany.

There are similarities – the Tsars repressed, they punished; there was terror and encouragement for the populace to obey. However, there is a new element in Lenin's personalised control over the minutiae of the process and the sheer scale of politically directed violence that is alien to the world of the Tsars. The use of the party to carry out repression has no real parallel in Tsarist times. The world of Lenin seems much closer to that of twentieth centuries dictators like Hitler, Mao ZeDong and the inheritor of the system, Stalin, than to Alexander II and his successors. Comparisons can be made superficially, but the evidence from letters and telegrams sent by Lenin seems to place him in a different world from that of the Russian rulers.

In terms of the economic development, there are more differences than similarities. The motivation for the collective farms, which Lenin tried with limited success to promote, was different from the motivation of Alexander II and III to sustain traditional peasant farming. Lenin was looking forward to a Soviet agriculture in which the peasant would be a sort of rural proletarian. The Tsars, on the other hand, were seeking to preserve traditional authority. Imposing requisitioning on the peasants went beyond anything attempted by the Tsars, who would never have interfered with property to that extent. The direct control of industry and finance imposed by a rapid series of decrees went beyond the indirect impact of the Tsarist state on industry, even in the First World War. The lack of care about money supply and the roaring inflation of the Lenin period were in marked contrast to the Tsars preference for secure money and foreign confidence. The Tsars lived in a world where they needed to interact with other countries; Lenin lived in a fantasy world where other countries were enemies or territories ripe for control.

As has been clear both Lenin and the Tsars were deeply personal rulers. What is without parallel is the period where Lenin was too ill after having a stroke in 1923 to rule effectively and power passed to the triumvirate of Trotsky, Kamenev and Zinoviev (*see* Fig. 2.3, page 69).

Source

23 July 1919, Lenin to Stalin

The revolution in Italy should be spurred on. Hungary should be sovietised and perhaps also Czechoslovakia and Romania. Lithuania should be sovietised first and then handed over to the Lithuanian people.

In ignoring pleas from Jewish communities in Poland to stop attacks on Jews by the Red army; in having no sympathy for nationalist feelings and revealing a clear intention to bring all parts of the Tsarist empire under control, Lenin reveals similarities with certain aspects of the Tsars, but it is the notion of sovietizing that marks the real discontinuity. The emphasis is not on Russian or Imperial control of internal nationalities and other countries, but the use of class war and political propaganda. Lenin's imperialism was more effective, systematic and politicised that that of Tsars and that makes him more than just a Red Tsar.

Letters all quoted in: Richard Pipes, *The Unknown Lenin*, 1996

The personal responsibility of Lenin for key decisions can be illustrated by sources on the execution of the Tsar and his family July 1918.

Sources

A Memoirs of Yurovsky

A leading Bolshevik in Ekaterinburg wrote in his memoirs of 1922 that as the newly appointed commandant of the House of Special Purpose (where the Tsar and his family were imprisoned) he established a harsher regime 'until a definite decision came from the centre' about the fate of the Tsar

Lenin Dmitri Volkogonov, p. 214, 1995

B Nikunin, a participant in the executions:

There was a volley of shots: one, two, three! Some of the royal family weren't quite dead and had to be finished off later. In my opinion we did the job humanely. I doubt if the Urals Soviet would have taken the responsibility themselves, you know, for the shooting, without an order from Lenin, or one of the other leaders without their unspoken agreement.

C Ioffe, the ambassador in Berlin wrote in his memoirs that he was simply told that the Tsar had been executed:

I knew nothing of his wife and family. I thought they were alive. When Dzerzhinsky visited Berlin, incognito, I made him tell me the whole truth. He told me that Lenin had expressly forbidden that I should be told anything. He had said 'Better if Ioffe knows nothing, It'll be easier for him to lie'.

D Trotsky writing in his diary, recalled in 1935

I asked Sverdlov in passing, 'Oh yes, and where is the Tsar?' 'It's all over; he has been shot'….. 'And who made the decision?' I asked. 'We decided it here; Lenin believed we shouldn't leave the Whites a live banner to rally around, especially in the present circumstances'.

(All these quoted in Volkogonov, *Lenin*)

This indicates a personal level of decision making with a strong element of cynicism and deliberate deception beyond what might be described as Tsarist behaviours but comparable perhaps to that of a Hitler, Stalin or Napoleon.

The way that Lenin's incapacity was covered up – he was a sick man since the assassination attempt made by the SR Fanya Kaplan in August 1918, who did think Lenin was a sort of Tsar as she had been an active terrorist against Tsarist officials before the revolution – may indicate that the Bolsheviks believed that Lenin had the mystique of a Tsar. However the cult of Lenin, which began in his lifetime and grew to epic proportions after his death, continuing until the fall of Communism, went beyond *any* posthumous cult image of any of the Tsars. The evidence can be seen today by visitors to his embalmed body in the tomb outside the Kremlin. The leader as a sort of god was a unique phenomenon rather than a continuation of Tsarist practice.

Reform and change

Lenin, like Alexander II and Nicholas II, like Khrushchev but less like Stalin or Alexander III, bent in the face of widespread opposition and the realities of the political situation. Faced with a huge peasant revolt in Tambov province, evidence of a workers' opposition, a considerable revolt by the sailors of the Kronstadt naval base (not incidentally the same ones who had been loyal supporters of the revolution, as the rebels of 1921 were recently drafted into the naval base) Lenin, gave way to survive.

However, it is doubtful if this makes him in any similar to the Tsars. There is little suggestion that the Tsars were hostile to the Russian peasants or saw them as a means to create a new industrial society (and when this caused massive resentment gave concessions which they knew were temporary). There is no suggestion that the Tsars were so dominated by class hatred that they were willing to destroy sections of their subjects in a way that Lenin envisaged for the richer peasants. There is no suggestion that the Tsars were so hostile to representative democracy that they controlled all outlets for expression and all democratic institutions. Nicholas II may not have liked his Duma and may have restricted its powers and controlled its electorate, but he did not, as did Lenin, go to the Duma and lounge contemptuously in the chamber before dispersing it with troops after one day. Nor did any Tsar justify concessions by reference to a theory which claimed that they had been planned all along: Lenin justified an obvious retreat in 1921 by claiming that NEP was necessary in ideological terms and had been pre-planned from the start. This type of outrageous political lie was not a common feature of Tsarism.

One of Lenin's closest pre-Revolutionary comrades summed him up in a memoir published in Paris in 1937,

> 'No one else possessed the secret of Lenin's hypnotic power over people, or rather his dominance over them. They unswervingly followed only Lenin as the sole undisputed leader. Lenin represented that rare phenomenon in Russia, a man with iron will, indomitable energy, who poured fanatical faith into the movement and the cause, and had no less faith in himself. . .. Behind these good qualities lurked great deficiencies, negative qualities, more appropriate perhaps in a mediaeval or Asiatic conqueror.'
>
> (Volkogonov, p. 81.)

If Lenin were like a Tsar, it was not a Tsar of the previous century, as none of them had these qualities or aspired to that sort of leadership.

The arts

Here the comparison is at its most superficial. Russian art did flourish in the late Tsarist period and it did flourish in the Lenin period. However, the atmospheres of the period were different and the priorities of art were different. Thoughtful artists like Tchaikovsky and

Chekhov were representative of a depressed feeling. Tchaikovsky's best work has a sense of dissolution and despair made more poignant by the obvious beauties. It is also quite conservative – his first symphony differs very little in terms of harmony or orchestration from his last. This is true of much of the art, music and architecture of the post-1855 period, and foreign influences are very strong.

Folk songs are often orchestrated in the French or German style in Russian music. The influence of French art is very pronounced: just as foreign investment dominated Russian industry, so French and German techniques and aesthetics dominated much of Russian cultural life. This was less true of literature, but there is a distinctly pessimistic air in much of the writing. Chekhov's plays do not celebrate a new world; they reflect on the passing of the old. What most pleased foreign observers was the celebration of a Russia that never was in Diaghilev's clever commercialisation of Russian folk art in dance and Bakst's colourful reworking of traditional elements in Russian art. The artistic developments under Lenin inhabit a different world, because Lenin's regime, for all its brutality and dictatorship, looked forward and required positive attitudes from the art that it patronised. Those who rejected this, like Rakhmaninov, went abroad.

Traditionalists like Glazunov and Miaskovsky who remained had to put a positive spin on their essentially late-Tsarist music. In Lenin's Russia, prominence was given to the adaptation by the avant-garde to social and political needs. New buildings were for the people. Cubist or abstract art was turned into posters to exhort support for the Bolsheviks. In the end, this 'formalism' was condemned and political art became much more old-fashioned; but the temporary alliance of a radical state with radical art produced a very different artistic atmosphere and very different products form those of the pre-1914 period, and comparisons break down.

Sources

A Marcel Liebman, Leninism under Lenin, 1975

Let there be no misconception, however, the authority that Lenin enjoyed had nothing dictatorial about it, and if he sometimes sought to impose his on his followers an attitude of unconditional acceptance, he aimed to do this not so much to ensure allegiance to himself personally, but to obtain unity round a theory that he believed to be correct

B Edward Acton, *Rethinking the Russian Revolution*, 1990

In a few short years Lenin was able to do so much that it is hard to believe one man capable of it. The party had become a state within a state, its dictatorship a fact. Religion had been replaced by the harsh Bolshevik ideology of Leninism. Party absolutism had replaced Tsarist autocracy…The fact that Lenin's system survived for seventy years depended on its harsh authoritarianism and the manipulation of the public mind than any inherent virtues.

Sources A and B: Dmitri Volkogonov, *The Rise and Fall of the Soviet Empire*, 1998

The fact that Lenin's policies were adopted owed as much to the fact that they were in accordance with rank and file radicalism as to Lenin's persuasiveness. Lenin was perhaps not an all-powerful dictator, and if he is to be criticised it should be on the grounds of ill-founded optimism, rather than insincerity

The situation facing Stalin

Lenin's death in 1924 led to a period of collective leadership. There were some very influential figures in the ruling council, the **Politburo**. It was the bureaucrat, the General secretary, whom Lenin had seen as 'too rude' to be trusted, that emerged as the leader. Stalin emerged as the dominant influence on policy gradually, but was seen as the heir to Lenin by the end of 1926 when the so-called 'left' opposition to him in the Politburo was removed and his greatest possible rival **Trotsky** forced into exile. But his ascendancy might be dated from the defeat of the supporters of **NEP**– the so-called 'right opposition' in 1928. Bukharin said to his former rival Kamenev,

> *'Stalin is a Genghis Khan, an unscrupulous intriguer who sacrifices everything to the preservation of his power.'* (Quoted Radzinsky, *Stalin*.)

In January 1929 Stalin confirmed his ascendancy and Trotsky was sent out of Russia. The former influential Bolsheviks were powerless and the central committee was dominated by Stalin supporters.

BIOGRAPHY

Trotsky (Lev Davidovich Bronstein) 1879–1940 was a Ukrainian Jew. He was a revolutionary activist who met Lenin in London in 1902. He tried to unite the Bolshevik and Menshevik wings of the Social Democrats and was associated with the more moderate Mensheviks for a time. In 1905 he organised the first Soviet during the Revolution. Arrested after the Revolution he escaped and was a revolutionary in exile. He came back to Russia from the USA in 1917 and organised the Military Revolutionary Committee, masterminding the actual Bolshevik take over in October. As Commissar for war he took a leading part in the victory of the Civil War and was the creator of the Red Army. He failed to take the initiative and gain power after Lenin died and was pushed out of office and out of Russia by Stalin. He opposed Stalin's foreign and industrial policy in the 1920s and condemned Stalin's purges in the 1930s. He was eventually murdered in Mexico by a Stalinist agent.

Unlike Lenin, Stalin had risen to power through a long process of using the Soviet system and in the face of talented rivals. Lenin had always been seen as a potential leader. Stalin had been portrayed by his enemies as a provincial boor and dull bureaucrat. In reality Stalin was a well-read and relatively cultivated person, more highly regarded by Lenin than has been thought. However, unlike the Tsars he had not necessarily been expected to rule. Unlike the Tsars and Lenin he had had to intrigue, use the party, use the cult of Lenin and exploit divisions among his possible rivals and Trotsky's reluctance to use his military connections to establish his power. So Stalin's rise was untypical of the period.

However, the problems he faced were by no means untypical for the period 1855–1964. Unlike Alexander II in 1855, Stalin did not face the results of an unsuccessful war, but in a sense the effects of both the First World War and the Civil War were still being felt.

Unlike Nicholas II, in 1905 there were no revolutionary outbreaks to cope with, but like Nicholas he had to consider the ongoing survival of the regime.

Unlike Lenin, he did not have to establish a completely new form of Communist state – that had been done and was even gaining some international recognition. However, like Lenin, he did face the problem of establishing something new – a communist state that was

Politburo

The ruling executive body of Communist Russia – the equivalent to the British cabinet

NEP

The New Economic Policy was introduced by Lenin in March 1921. It replaced requisitioning (seizure) of crops by a tax in kind and allowed private trade by the peasants. It also allowed smaller industrial businesses to be owned and to trade privately. It was seen as a betrayal by hard line Communists; but in reality it was the only way for the regime to survive.

not based on peasant landowning but on communal agriculture which would support a massive industrial drive. Stalin was faced with the need to undertake a second revolution almost as momentous as the first in order that Communism could become a reality and that the regime could be secure. A continuing peasant society with a slow-growing mostly private industry would, in the Communist view, which linked economic and political factors, lead to counter-revolution. Also, the USSR was not strong enough to withstand a foreign invasion. A repeat of the defeats by the smaller foreign powers of 1904–5 (or indeed 1853–56 or 1877–78) might well result in the fall of Communism. Disputes with Britain and anti-Communist sentiment in the USA, the strengthening of bonds between France and Germany, and the French diplomatic links with anti-Communist countries such as Poland, made this more of a reality for Stalin than it seems to be in retrospect. The countries of Eastern Europe were predominantly right wing, as was Italy. The USSR was isolated; for example, Communists were persecuted in China. The strengthening of defences was as much a priority for Stalin as it had been for the Tsars and was to be for Khrushchev facing an ongoing arms race with the West. In terms of infrastructure, Russia needed to advance as much as it did under the Tsars; there were *still* backward communications. However, like his predecessors, Stalin did not approach these problems in a disinterested way. Development was associated with the need to secure his own power and to destroy his real and imagined enemies. Stalin was deeply influenced by Marxist theory in a way that the Tsars, of course, were not. Lenin had had to adapt theory to reality, but Stalin was in a stronger position to apply it. What the balance was in Stalin's internal policies between, on the one hand, the rational consideration of Russia's economic, social, defence and political problems and, on the other hand the desire to dominate and to exercise power on a ruthless scale, is still debated. Also still under debate was whether Stalin's ideas were *reflecting* strong elements within the party or were *manipulating* the party into policies of massive social and economic change for his own advantage.

How did Stalin respond to the situation?

What characterised Stalin's domestic policies was their sheer lack of compromise , in contrast with the policies of all the other rulers in this period, and the enormous scale of change that he effected. Though it is possible to see similarities in aspects of the economic policy with what had gone before, the massive scale of industrialisation makes Stalin's policies unique. The collectivisation of agriculture might have gone back to Russian traditions and some might think it recreated aspects of serfdom and communal farming. However, the scale of violence applied in the countryside and the disruption this caused have no real parallel. The social changes involved have something in common with the impact of population growth and urbanisation under the Tsars, but again the transformation in society was so great that comparison is not really justified. Finally, the massive impact of state power on the population which, though not uniform throughout Stalin's rule, marked out another unique feature: that of unprecedented terror.

Stalin was not the only ruler to repress the Russian people. For most of the period there was a heavy reliance on state power to prevent opposition and to enforce policies about which there was little possibility of public discussion. Exile, penal colonies in remote and bleak parts of the Empire, harsh prisons, spies and fear were aspects of Russian life which were common to Tsarist and Communist rule. However Stalin's rule differs in two significant respects: firstly in scale and secondly in the phenomenon of the Purges. These have no real parallel before or after his rule in the widespread effects they had on the life of the people and the development of the country.

ACTIVITY

Can Stalin be seen as a Red Tsar?

■ Look at the criteria of the Stretch and challenge activity on page 25.

■ Make up five arguments for this proposition and five against. Put your ideas clearly on post-its and on a board, marked *Stalin as Tsar,* stick up your arguments with some supporting evidence. On a board marked *Stalin not a Tsar* put your post-its for this view.

■ When the class has finished, look at the arguments and come to a conclusion.

Write down that conclusion on no more than two sides of A4.

Year	Death sentences	Those sent to camps or prisons	Those exiled	Other measures
1921	9,701	21,724	1817	2587
1922	1,962	2,656	166	1,219
1923	414	2,336	2,044	
1924	2,550	4,151	5,724	
1925	2,433	6,851	6,274	437
1926	990	7,547	8,571	696
1927	2,303	12,267	11,235	171
1928	869	16,211	15,640	1,037
1929	2,019	25,853	24,517	3,741
1930	20,201	114,443	58,816	14,609
1931	10,651	105,683	63,269	1,093
1932	22,738	73,946	36,017	29,228
1933	2,154	138,903	54,262	44,435
1934	2,056	59,451	5,994	11,498
1935	1,229	185,846	33,601	46,400
1936	1,118	219,418	23,719	30,415
1937	353,074	429,311	1,355	6,914
1938	328,618	205,509	16,342	3,289
1939	2,552	54,666	3,783	2,888
1940	1,649	65,727	2,142	2,288
1941	8,011	65,000	1,200	1,210
1942	23,278	88,809	7,072	5,249
1943	3,029	70,610	649	821
1944	3,029	70,610	666	458
1945	2,896	116,681	1,647	668
1946	2,896	117,943	1,498	957
1948	–	72,509	419	298
1949	–	64,509	10,316	300
1950	475	54,466	5,225	475
1951	1,609	49,142	3,425	599
1952	1,612	25,824	773	591
1953 (first half)	198	7,894	38	273
TOTAL	799,455	2,634,397	425,512	215,942

Figures taken from B. P. Kurashvili (1996), *A History of the Stalin's System,* quoted in Moshe Lewin, The Soviet Century, Verso 2005

Table 1.1   The number of people whom the Security forces of the soviet regime, the 'secret police', brought to trial and their fate between 1921 and 1953, when Stalin died.

Gulag

This was the name given to the prison/labour camps which spread throughout the Communist USSR, particularly under Stalin. Often situated in cold and remote regions, they housed millions of prisoners, especially in the late 1930s. Conditions were inhumane and death rates were high for the ZEKs (prisoners). They were still heavily used after 1945 though fell into disuse after Stalin's death.

KGB

The KGB was the Committee for State Security; the name given to the secret police, spy and security organisation of Russia from 1954–1991.

Kulak

peasants who owned their own farm and as a result were strongly opposed to communist Collectivisation. The term 'kulak' literally meant 'fist' – the idea was to encourage a sturdy Russian peasant middle class to stand between the state and the masses. Under Communism it came to mean 'tightfisted'. (*See also* Chapter 3.)

VOZHD

The title Stalin adopted. It roughly means 'the Boss' or the Chief. Stalin was in theory only the Secretary of the Party; in practice he was the national leader.

The scale

Huge numbers are often spoken of when the '**Gulags**' or prison/labour camps of the Stalin period are discussed. After 1989 more documentation was available and the statistics in Table 1.1 are based less on 'guesstimates' than the record keeping which the Soviet administration valued.

To help to put these extraordinary figures into some sort of perspective: The **KGB** brought 5413 criminal prosecutions to court between 1959 and 1962. They brought 58,298 in for suspicion of anti-Soviet activities between 1967–70.

The figures for those executed between 1921 and 1953 exceed the total British war dead for the First World War.

Political violence had been part of the Soviet regime since the beginning. The Civil War had been a particularly bitter experience with mass executions, tortures and imprisonment. While the level of violence fell after 1921 it never disappeared. In effect another civil war in the countryside increased the political violence, with agrarian resistance being met with force and class warfare waged on the so-called '**kulaks**'. The death toll here was high and the famines, which followed the disruption of the countryside, can be seen as an additional punishment imposed by the state on its people.

Added to this was a political struggle within the party which led to the disgrace of both right and left opposition groups and the strengthening of the centre group of the party leadership under Stalin. In 1933 there was a large-scale 'purging' of the party membership, with perhaps 400,000 expulsions. With the Japanese invasion of Manchuria in 1931 and the rise to power of Hitler in 1933, there is no doubt that Russia did face potential enemies. Hitler had made quite explicit that he linked the threat from the Jews and the Communists to Germany and thought that Judaeo–Bolshevism must be eliminated: that Germans needed 'Lebensraum' in Slav lands. The dangers exceeded anything faced by the Tsars or perhaps even Lenin, as the determination of the allied intervention force during the Civil War 1919–20 was not great and allied action was not popular in their home countries. Given this, there was an unprecedented need for internal discipline and security.

Stalin did face opposition from his own party about the conduct of the Five-Year Plans. A possible rival was Sergei Kirov, the Leningrad Party boss who was assassinated in 1934. Kirov's death was used as justification for the existence of counter-revolutionary plots.

There followed a series of Show Trials of leading party members in 1936. At first elite groups were chosen. Tortured and pressured, they admitted working against the Soviet system and were executed. The accusations spread to the armed forces, to specialists in industry, to managers, to ethnic groups (like the Polish communists) then to 'kulaks' and ordinary soviet citizens. The persecutions reached a peak in 1937 and fell away by 1939, but the atmosphere of suspicion and fear they created were unique in the period and more akin to the random persecutions of Ivan the Terrible or Peter the Great.

While this fantastic terror was going on, Soviet society was becoming more diverse, the economy was growing, the population rising, public works flourishing and the arts offering more conservative products but with a strong flavour. Composers like Shostakovich may have had a bag packed ready for when they were arrested at night and taken to imprisonment and possible death, but they produced distinctive Soviet music, some of it, like the composer's fifth symphony, among the most distinguished works of the century.

Cinema reflected a world far removed from the backward Russia of the early 20th century and presiding over this modernisation was the new Tsar – the **VOZHD** – the 'Leader' now seen as all-knowing and infallible by a dazed nation.

Though it was Stalin who was dazed by **Hitler's invasion** of 1941 – the great Leader distrusted millions of totally innocent people but had a seemingly complete faith in a pathological German dictator who had widely written that his intention was to destroy Communism and enslave the Russian people and who had built a huge army to do just that!

Wartime Russia resisted the Germans with a superhuman effort, but at least a million and a half collaborated and guerrilla warfare was being waged by anti-Soviet partisans well after the defeat of Germany. Stalin saw no reason to change the basic policies which had produced victory and established him as complete dictator. The post-war years saw the application of the basic tenets of Stalinism to Eastern Europe and even more stress on central control at home. There was a likelihood that the purges of the 1930s would begin again in Russia in 1953 (they had already been a feature of the new so-called Eastern European 'satellite states'). However Stalin died before this could be implemented.

ACTIVITY

Can Stalin be considered similar or different to Lenin?

- Make up five arguments that there was considerable continuity between Stalin's dictatorship and that of Lenin and make up five arguments that there was no real continuity.
- Share your arguments with the class, using post-its on two boards.
- Then write on no more than two sides of A4 your view as to how similar Stalin and Lenin were as rulers of Russia.

What problems faced Khrushchev?

Like Stalin, he had to dominate the Politburo and eliminate rivals. In the Stalinist tradition, **Beria** was shot; other rivals lost influence and were demoted. There was something of a repeat of the post-Lenin era but the death toll was not comparable, and when Khrushchev himself was ousted in 1964 he was not tried and executed. The Stalinist terror had left huge scars and Khrushchev had the problem of dismantling the repressive system but not ending the control the party had over its people and its enlarged empire.

Khrushchev faced a similar situation to Alexander II – to maintain the power he needed to make reforms. Unlike Nicholas II he was not being forced into this by unsuccessful war and popular revolution. But as with Alexander II his own inclinations, more liberal elements among the elite, discontents among the subject nations and a need for a more effective and modern economy to match rival nations were pressures for change. He lacked the liberal background of the Provisional Government of 1917; he did not inherit power like the Tsars, but like Stalin he had intrigued and struggled for power. Like all his predecessors he was strongly opinionated, but unlike them he came from a peasant background and had actually worked in industry.

How did Khrushchev respond to the situation?

The fear of popular uprising in 1953 can be seen by Beria bringing in tanks and troops into Moscow after Stalin's death. For all the repression of Stalin's last years and the absence of any indication of organised opposition, the leaders of Russia were still nervous enough to do this. Beria gave the orders, but the tanks could not save him from his enemies in government and he was tried and shot as a supposed British agent. The feeling was that the Soviet people could not endure the high levels of repression of the Stalin era. Amnesties, the gradual dismantling of the Gulags, a reduction in political arrests and execution, and the

Hitler's invasion

Stalin believed that Hitler would be faithful to the pact of friendship signed in August 1939 and ignored warnings from agents that the Germans were preparing for an invasion of Russia. Stalin was so shaken by Hitler breaking his word that he became withdrawn and issued no orders for some time after the invasion.

BIOGRAPHY

Lavrenti Beria was one of Stalin's major henchmen. A fellow Georgian born in 1899 he replaced Yezhov as Commissar for Internal Affairs, the head of Russia's security forces. Made a Marshal of the USSR in 1945 he was the major figure behind Stalin's repression. Corrupt and toadying he alienated the army and other members of the Politburo who had him shot when Stalin died.

public admission, at least to the Party in the 1956 Congress that errors had been made and that Stalin had pursued a 'cult of personality' were indications that high profile leadership on a sort of 'Red Tsar' level – with statues, uniforms, processions, ceremonies, a sort of adulatory court of followers – had given way to a more normal form of European political leadership. The new law code of 1958 limited the power of the police; but rather like Alexander II's introduction of trial by jury, could be overridden if necessary.

However there was a break with many aspects of the Stalin era, just as Alexander II broke with many aspects of the reign of his more repressive predecessor, Nicholas I. The naming of towns after the great VOZHD or leader had seemed to indicate that not only was Stalin aiming to emulate the Tsars but to go beyond them. Old titles were not enough. Stalin had taken entirely new ones like 'Generalissimo' and had been proclaimed an 'all-knowing expert' in every aspect of life – arts, science, and foreign affairs. This had gone beyond what was claimed by the Tsars since 1855 though it may have been true of earlier megalomaniac rulers like Peter the Great. Khrushchev did not appear in uniforms, was not an icon, condemned the cult of personality and did not destroy his rivals like an oriental despot. But he was not a liberal politician like the men of the Provisional Government either.

Khrushchev, unlike Stalin, did not rise by promoting a cult of the former leader, but rather by removing Stalin's supporters from office and suggesting a new way forward based on more concessions to consumers, more freedom of expression and better relations with the West. The most original feature of his rise to power was his accusation in the 1956 Party Congress that Stalin was a despot and had suppressed the people. It was Stalin who had ordered the purges, been behind Kirov's murder and left Russia unprepared for German attack in 1941. In other respects there were similarities. Like Stalin he had controlled the party machine as general secretary, like Lenin he condemned the former regime.

For the first time since the Zemstvos created by Alexander II, there was a move to decentralise and give more authority to the localities. A hundred regional councils, the *sovnarkhozy* were given control over production and not the central production ministries. Like Alexander II, this reform was challenged by revolt. The Tsar's liberalism had been checked by the emergence of terrorism; Khrushchev's changes were threatened by the 1956 Hungarian revolt. However he overcame conservative opposition and gave more power to local party officials.

Like Stalin, he faced some opposition in the party, but interestingly his opponents, Malenkov, Kaganovich and foreign minister Shepilov who tried to oust him in 1957 ended up with demotion to lesser posts, and not in KGB torture chambers. Kaganovich, one of Stalin's associates ended up managing a cement factory. Khrushchev certainly had the best sense of humour of any of Russia's rulers in the period. However, one characteristic that Khrushchev shared with his predecessors was a careful fostering of his own authority. When Marshal Zhukov aimed at more independence for the Red Army from the control of the party, he was ousted (October 1957). Then in 1958 Khrushchev became Premier. The party and the state were well within his control and the expansion of party membership to ten million gave him huge powers of patronage.

However the trappings of power, that Stalin and the Tsars so cultivated, were not emulated – in a person of Khrushchev's appearance, they would have been ludicrous. Nor did he adopt the head teacher persona of Lenin. He behaved in an uncouth way at home and abroad and posed as a simple farmer. To stress the change, Stalin was removed from Lenin's tomb in 1961 and the large number of places named after him and his allies were changed back. Stalino became once again Donetsk; Molotov became Perm again; Stalinsk became Novokutznetsk. To remain true to the Bolshevik past, Leningrad remained. Lenin remained an icon because his simple image – the overcoat – the suit – could be linked to Khrushchev's lack of grandeur and his rumpled suits. But like Lenin, power was focused on him; he took key decisions and initiatives; he had huge control over the party and he played on his personal traits of character, exploiting outrageous behaviour, such as banging his shoe on the table at a UN meeting when the British prime minister Macmillan was speaking (Macmillan wittily asked for a translation). In the end that was his downfall. Personally associated with grand plans to bring more agricultural land into cultivation than the total sown acreage of 1928, pledged to increase the living standards and pledged to take the pressure off the Soviet defence spending by 'peaceful co-existence', failure would rebound directly on him and not the collective leadership of the party. By 1964 the Virgin Lands Scheme was showing weaknesses (*see* pages 95–98) and food shortages were evident; consumer goods had not flourished in line with expectations. Peaceful coexistence had given way to a massive example of confrontation with the USA (the Cuban missile crisis of 1962) in which nuclear war had been a possibility and troops and police had crushed a demonstration by workers (in 1962 at Novocherkarsk) in the spirit, if not of Stalin, then at least that of Nicholas II at *Bloody Sunday*. For all their faults, Russia's leaders since 1855 were imposing figures who kept their dignity and maintained the mystique of government. Khrushchev was not an imposing or dignified figure and he could not offer much in the way of leadership quality in place of that sustained success.

Stretch and challenge

Which of Russia's rulers from 1855 to 1964 served the interests of the Russian people best?

1   This can be approached by first of all deciding how the interests of the Russian people can be interpreted. Discuss this with a partner and draw up a list of categories (for example, who offered the Russian people more freedom; who offered the most opportunities; who offered more security).

2   Then consider what each ruler offered and try to colour-code your notes according to the list of categories.

3   Then establish a thesis.

Does the answer depend on what benefits are considered? Did Kerensky offer greater liberty than other rulers, but Stalin offer greater opportunities? Did Lenin offer more equality, but was the greatest benefit the break from the past offered by Alexander II? Were the interests of the people in a largely agrarian society best served by traditionalists like Alexander III or Nicholas II, who tried to protect the people against violent political change?

Note: The important elements in this exercise are reflection and comparison. You will need to take time to think about this and to discuss it inside and outside the classroom, using the material in this book and your other research to make a frame for your thesis. You will not find a complete answer in a book or by a search on the internet. The thesis will need comparison of the key figures and categories.

Conclusion

You have now completed an overview of the period by looking at the similarities and contrasts of the rulers of Russia from 1855 to 1964. Later chapters will look in more detail at government, the economy and the impact of war. However, before moving on, you need to make an interim judgement by completing the exercise above. This can be reviewed and added to later in the course: reflection and additional knowledge will probably alter your view. But it is important that you do begin to make judgements.

The history of opposition to the different regimes from 1855–1964 is generally a tragic one. The forces of the state and its methods of repression (*see also* Chapter 5) seemed very much stronger than the forces for reform or change. The overwhelming exception is the abdication of the Tsar in the face of mass demonstrations in 1917 and the successful opposition to the Provisional Government offered by the Bolsheviks. This chapter focuses on how the state was challenged between 1855 and 1964; the problems that opposition faced and how governments dealt with opposition.

Key Questions:

In this period the central questions are:

- Why did the revolutions in 1917 succeed when other opposition failed?
- What are the similarities and differences between the different opposition groups in the period?
- What common features in Russian history can be found that made opposition generally in the period so problematic and unsuccessful?

In this chapter you will be invited to think about differences and similarities of the nature of government between Tsarist and Communist rule. You will also be encouraged through activities to practise the skills of thesis development and synoptic thinking.

An overview of the period

Stretch and challenge

What follows is a general survey of the period 1855–1964.

1   After reading the overview, make a list of the major attempts at opposition and change and form a *thesis* about why opposition was difficult both before and after 1917. Are there common factors?

2   Then consider under what circumstances opposition was successful and why these problems were overcome, particularly in 1917.

There follows a more detailed look at the different periods and you can check to see if your thesis holds good.

The concept of 'loyal opposition' did not exist in Tsarist Russia when Alexander II acceded to the throne in 1855. Tradition derived from various sources (*see* Fig. 2.1):

- the Greek Byzantine world with its ritual elevation of emperors to be close to divine beings;
- the oriental despotism of the Mongol hoards;

- the Viking war bands with their dependence on complete obedience to the war chiefs;
- and the tribal organisation of the Slavs.

Figure 2.1 The Byzantine Roman Emperor Justinian succeeded his uncle Justin in 527. Justinian was a very strong ruler who ruled for a long time.

These traditions did not offer any precedents for participation in government. The great Tsars of the past had been **autocrats**, violently suppressing real or imagined opposition. Where there had been some interest in the enlightened ideas of the 18th century, for example by Catherine the Great's interest in improving the life of royal serfs, this had not extended to ideas of social contracts between ruler and ruled, or any ideas of the rights of the subject. Russia was dominated by the concept of a **service state** where rank depended on loyalty to the state and the bulk of the people were unfree. This left no room for debate or discussion about policy, and there was no concept of popular sovereignty. Where these ideas flourished in other parts of Europe there was an educated urban elite and a liberal aristocracy. These were in short supply in Russia. Nevertheless, Tsarist Russia was not nearly as isolated from Western Europe as Communist Russia was to become under Stalin, and new ideas did come in. The wars against Napoleon tended to make French ideas even more alien, but there was still a feeling among a minority of educated Russians that some form of liberalism was desirable. The **Decembrist** revolt by liberal officers and nobles in 1825 lacked organisation and popular support and was little more than a demonstration. The organisers paid heavily in terms of executions and banishments, and Nicholas I (1825–55) clamped down severely on any expression of liberalism – that is support for the rights of the subject, a constitution implying some sort of mutual obligation between ruler and ruled, and policies which were in the interests of the nation.

Autocrat

Autocrat comes from the Greek – self rule. The Tsars saw themselves as selected by God to rule without being responsible to anyone on Earth; they ruled as absolute monarchs.

Service state

Peter the Great (1689–1725) had reduced the power of the traditional Russian aristocrats or boyars, instituting a Table of Ranks which made noble status dependent on the military or administrative service given to the state. The state thus overrode class and tradition.

The Decembrists

A group of young army officers had been influenced by the ideas of the French Revolution and the reforms of Napoleon. They formed a secret society which later split into two, the Northern and Southern Societies. The Northern group led by Nikita Muraviev favoured a constitutional monarchy; the Southern Society led by Paul Pestel favoured a radical republic with some socialist elements. The groups had been infiltrated by spies and the Tsar Alexander I knew about them. The issue was complicated by uncertainty about succession. Alexander had named as heir his younger brother, Nicholas, but his other brother Constantin was theoretically the heir. He however had renounced the throne in order to marry a commoner, having divorced his wife.

Constantin had a false reputation as a liberal. When Alexander I died in December 1825 some regiments declared that Constantin would be Tsar. Nicholas met a mutiny in Congress Square in St. Petersburg by artillery fire; revolts in the South were suppressed by loyal troops. The so-called Decembrists were arrested. Five of the leaders were hanged and over a hundred exiled. Mutinous regiments were dispersed. Like so many later revolutionaries, the Decembrists were divided, spent too long on pointless theorising and lacked in-depth support. They were betrayed by spies, observed by secret police and met with overwhelming military power.

New ideas

These originated from 18th century thinkers, America and the French Revolution. They included the idea that a state should recognise the rights of its citizens to 'life, liberty and the pursuit of happiness'; that a constitutional monarchy should share power; that there should be free trade with an end to restrictions on trade and manufacture to allow private enterprise to create wealth; that social equality was desirable.

In as much as any early 19th century could be, Russia was a police state. The Tsar, the bureaucracy, the church, the army and educational institutions were united in support of an autocratic tradition. Traditional attitudes were repressive enough, but the rulers of Europe saw themselves under threat from forces unleashed by the French Revolution. Nationalism would have undermined the Russian empire which ruled over many different nationalities. Most were too backward to have developed ideas of self-government, but the large Polish population acquired since the late 18th century were certainly strongly nationalistic and had to be suppressed. Liberalism was seen to have led to the execution of Louis XVI of France in 1793 and the rise of a populist dictator Napoleon Bonaparte who had threatened the entire European order and caused huge numbers of Russian deaths by his campaigns of 1805–7 and 1812–14. Democracy meant only the anarchy of serf revolts – like the **Pugachev rising** of the 1770s which remained a frightening and violent episode in the minds of the Russian establishment.

To the religiously devout ruling class the **new ideas** were a threat not only to internal peace but also to eternal salvation. The idea of democracy seemed meaningless in a country where most people were serfs, where there was mass illiteracy and where urban populations were limited. So by process of elimination, the only ideas that were feasible for the government and the ruling class were the traditional ones – autocracy, orthodox religion and an established class system which tied the nobles to the state in return for a guarantee of their power over their serfs.

The Pugachev rising

In 1773 a Don Cossack Emilian Pugachev led a major rising in the South which brought together a mass of discontents – peasants objecting to conscription, serfs, national groups like the Bashkirs, Tartars and Kirghkiz who resented increasing Russian control. In all 30,000 rebels occupied the government for two years before larger-scale royal forces and internal squabbles among the insurgents led to the rising being crushed in 1775 and Pugachev executed. It set up a fear of serf rebellion which lasted until 1861. There are very interesting parallels with the disturbances of 1905 and even the Civil War in which divisions among the opponents of the state proved the decisive factor in the failure of opposition.

Nicholas I was so disturbed by the Decembrist revolt that his reign is characterised by repression. The **Third Section** of 1826 used spies and informers to root out revolutionary activity throughout the empire. Schools and universities were restricted. The principles of 'Autocracy, Orthodoxy and Nationalism' held sway and the Tsar, backed by the Orthodox Church, refused any concessions to other nationalities and the empire remained strictly Russian. Revolt in Poland was brutally suppressed in 1830–31, and Russian troops supported the monarchs of Europe in putting down European revolts in 1848, for example assisting the Austrian emperor to put down a revolt in Hungary.

The small literate Russian middle class found the situation in Russia so unfavourable for reform that they concentrated instead on cultural pursuits or on economic development. This isolation from mainstream Russia did result in the growth of a very special social phenomenon – **the Intelligentsia**. This word is used in a much more limited way in modern speech, but in Russian terms it was more than a vague concept. There developed a distinct section of the population devoted to learning, philosophy, poetry, music and the arts generally. From this class came some of the most significant products of 19th century civilisation – Pushkin, Glinka, Tchaikovsky, Mussorgsky, Dostoyevsky are household names in western culture, yet they emerged from a largely rural society and a repressive and old fashioned autocracy. Out of this impressive but limited class also came opposition. Many revolutionary leaders came from the Intelligentsia. Stalin did his best to wipe them out.

Repression and opposition in the reign of Alexander II

In 1856, 'Opposition' meant underground groups of critics who deplored Russia's political and social backwardness and who sought like-minded idealists; it meant restless peasants; it meant nationalists – mainly Poles, hostile to Russian rule. However, during the reign of Alexander II despite or perhaps because of reform a more organised form of opposition emerged. **The Polish revolt** of 1863 was one of a line of nationalist revolts (*see* page 48) – heroic but doomed.

Narodniks

Narodniks is from the word *Narod*, meaning people or peasants. The Narodniks were supporters of a revolutionary movement. From 1873 they met secretly and were largely intellectuals who believed that Russia could be reborn by giving power to the peasants who they saw as inherently pure but terribly oppressed and corrupted by the state.

They had the idea of 'going to the people' to convert them to socialism in 1876 – this failed and they were persecuted by the state from 1877. The Narodniki or Populists were a phase of the more general Russian Populist movement which developed into the more organised Social Revolutionary party in 1901.

More general opposition came from the Populists or **Narodniks.** As censorship was relaxed and educational, social, legal and governmental reforms were introduced in the wake of the Crimean War (*see also* Chapter 5, pages 127–33), hopes were raised for more fundamental change. Strong currents of opposition emerged among the intelligentsia and from the liberal nobles. The widespread debate about **emancipation** provoked other debates. While not strictly opposing the Tsar, elements of the educated classes discussed ideas which went against traditional autocratic methods. There was no intention to abolish the monarchy but

---

Third Section (1826)

was a precursor of the later Okhrana and Cheka (secret police). It was a department of the Royal Chancery, run by a close friend of the Tsar, General Benckendorff. It investigated political opposition and rooted out corruption among officials. It relied on spies and denunciations and intervened in a wide range of matters – business disputes, immorality among the higher classes. It processed 31 million documents in 1850 alone.

ACTIVITY

Why was political change likely to be difficult for reformers in 1855? List as many points as you can and then attempt to put them into order of importance.

Emancipation

The freeing of the serfs by royal decree in 1861 from being the personal property of their owners. Black slavery in the USA was ended in 1863. There were interesting similarities. Both ex-slaves and ex-serfs found themselves tied by economic necessity to their former lands and both had to wait a long time for full political rights.

Case Study: The Polish revolts and changing boundaries

One of the largest states of 18th century Europe, Poland was weakened by noble in-fighting and weak, elected monarchs. In three partitions from 1772–95 Poland was divided by Austria, Prussia and Russia. France restored it as the Grand Duchy of Warsaw (1795–1810) but it was restored to the rule of the three monarchies of Austria, Russia and Prussia in 1814. Elements of the Polish nobility and middle class resented this, especially after the heroic nationalist rising of Tadeusz Kosciuszko in 1794. This patriotic soldier had fought in the American War of Independence and acquired ideas of freedom. He led an army against Russia, which was defeated at Raclawice in April 1794, setting a precedent for the major armed revolts of 1830–31, 1863 and 1918. It was still uppermost in Russian minds in 1941 when Russia massacred leading Poles in Katyn Forest to ease the Russian occupation of Eastern Poland arranged in yet another partition with Germany in the Nazi–Soviet Pact of 1939. Then in 1944, Stalin allowed the Germans to crush a Polish revolt in Warsaw before moving in to occupy the country). After the Second World War, the borders shifted again so that south of Poland became Czechoslovakia (now the Czech Republic and Slovakia). It is worth looking at a modern-day Atlas to see just how much the political-landscape has affected the physical since the period discussed in this book.

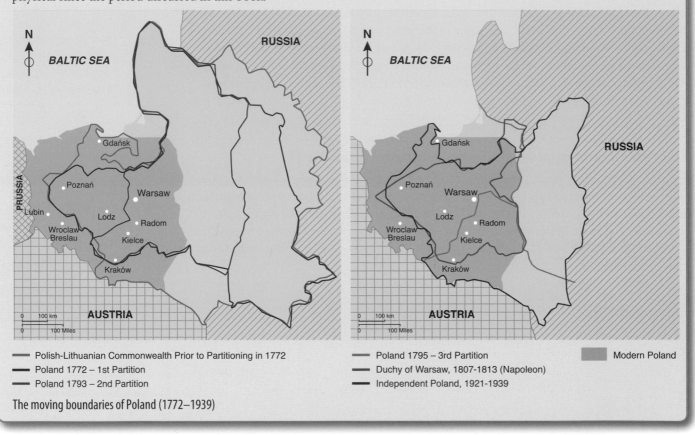

—— Polish-Lithuanian Commonwealth Prior to Partitioning in 1772	—— Poland 1795 – 3rd Partition
—— Poland 1772 – 1st Partition	—— Duchy of Warsaw, 1807-1813 (Napoleon)
—— Poland 1793 – 2nd Partition	—— Independent Poland, 1921-1939

Modern Poland

The moving boundaries of Poland (1772–1939)

there was an intention to press the Tsar to continue to take the lead in change. The first organised group of reformers was founded in 1861 . However, what also emerged as well as these limited moves for greater freedom was terrorism, initially by **Land and Liberty**.

The varieties of opposition

In retrospect what is striking is the mixture of ideas and methods:

- ■ liberalism, which hoped for peaceful parliamentary developments;
- ■ movements which wanted a peasant democracy and believed in the soul and purity of the Russian rural community; and
- ■ extremist terrorism.

Land and Liberty

a revolutionary group formed in 1877. They relied on terrorism and murder. They evolved into the People's Will group which assassinated Alexander II in 1881.

In 1866 there was an assassination attempt on Alexander II; by the 1870s there was a distinct terrorist movement which culminated in the assassination of the Tsar in 1881. If one adds in the first strike in 1870 by industrial workers, the seeds for future opposition movements had been sown at the time of greatest reform and change.

However, it is easy to see why these movements achieved little. They were limited in numbers and relied on secrecy; they never developed mass support and faced a powerful state with a developed spy system. They could not campaign openly and their violent methods alienated many potential supporters. Their socialist ideas were too complicated for the peasants, the industrial working class was too small to offer a base, and they faced heavy repression in the years after 1881 under both Alexander III and Nicholas II.

Opposition, 1881–1905

Different forms of opposition came to Russia in this period. Socialist ideas which had been growing in the West resulted in the first Marxist groups in Russia; peasant-based opposition was reborn in the Socialist Revolutionary Party of 1900. The Zemstvos (Zemstva in Russian, *see also* Chapter 1, page 14) created by Alexander II stimulated a liberal movement aiming at a Western-style parliamentary state. Russification policies and the growth of pan Slav enthusiasm encouraged nationalities within the Empire, particularly in the west, to aim at national independence. Often this opposition took cultural forms: an interest in native literature or nationalistic music. Then the growth of industry meant the development of urban opposition – if not overtly political, then certainly a demand for change in industrial conditions – which was seen as political by the authorities. Then came the failures of the 1904–5 **Russo-Japanese** war. Thus by 1905 resistance had grown considerably. There was a greater development of revolutionary theory and a more diverse opposition.

The Russo-Japanese war, 1904–5

In 1904 Nicholas II (1894–1917) fought a war against Japan. His government hoped for a quick victory. Instead the war went badly, with heavy losses and a major naval defeat. The war led to unrest and in 1905 Russia was in a revolutionary situation with a great deal of discontent of various sorts. The Tsar had to make concessions and offer a national parliament.

Opposition could take the form of regular political activity after the creation of a parliament, but in practice this was ineffective because the Dumas had such restricted powers. Thus most opposition remained outside standard political processes and depended on illegal organisation: agitation; violence and apocalyptic visions of the future rather than limited goals. This fantasy element in opposition was increased by many of the leading opponents having to work outside Russia. The tradition here went back to the first part of the century in which dissident groups and individuals had been forced into exile. The amazing tolerance of other countries in allowing this was a feature of the international disapproval of Russian dictatorship that was widespread before 1914 and perhaps also a result of much freer travel before the age of universal passport control. With little prospect of power after the failures of 1905 and the improvements in the economy after 1906 the exiles then clashed with each other. There were acrimonious conferences and sub-groups – the most famous were the **Bolsheviks and Mensheviks** formed from the Russian Social Democrats (Marxists) in 1903.

KEY IDEA

The division of opposition

This division was probably what preserved the autocracy. Before 1855 there were examples of division being key to the survival of autocracy. The opposition groups could not unite and though there was a massive rebellion in 1905 in the wake of the unsuccessful **Japanese war**, the different groups had only one uniting factor – opposition to the regime. They had very different ideals and looked to support from very different groups, both socially and geographically. Concessions were therefore effective and the Tsar survived.

The Bolsheviks and Mensheviks

The Russian Social Democrats divided in 1903 into two groups: the largest were the Mensheviks but in the London conference of 1903 they happened to be a minority, so they were called 'Minority Men' (the Russian word for minority is *menshinstvo*); the Bolsheviks, actually a minority were wrongly labelled 'Majority Men' (in Russian *bolshinstvo* is majority). So 'bigs' and 'littles'. The Bolsheviks believed in a tightly-knit disciplined revolutionary party; the Mensheviks believed in a wider, mass party which operated as openly as possible. Their leader was Julius Cedarbaum, a Jew from Odessa, better known as Martov. The split was not made formal until 1911.

War as a key element

Once again war brought the prospect of change, with the First World War bringing the problems of Tsarist Russia to a head. Within the Duma greater opposition developed, as the Tsar failed to use parliament as a uniting force and the war revealed the inefficiencies of the regime. Far more effective than the exiled revolutionaries was a feeling within the Tsarist establishment that for sheer national survival there had to be major change. This was closest to the Decembrist movement or the palace revolt which saw the assassination of unpopular and incompetent rulers like Peter III (deposed and killed in 1762) and Paul I assassinated in 1801. However, there was little ideological or political will behind the growing resentment of many at the heart of the regime – more a simple desire to rid themselves of the present ruler.

The massive popular demonstrations in St. Petersburg of 1917, unparalleled in Russian history, gave them the opportunity.

- On February 23rd 1917 there were bread riots in St. Petersburg.
- By February 24th 200,000 people were on the streets.

In the following days, the army and police lost control of the streets and the authority of the Tsar was destroyed.

This was people power opposition the like of which was not seen again until the fall of Communism in Europe in 1989. Unlike the demonstrations of 1905 there was no will among the armed forces and police for mass slaughter to clear the streets. Nicholas, isolated from the capital by his unwise decision to be near the Front, found few supporters among his leading generals and abdicated.

The suddenness of the fall of the monarchy meant that no ready-formed political group could step in. (Unlike, for instance in Germany in 1918 where the SPD or Socialist party was so popular and well organised that it could take over government and take the lead in establishing a new Republic.) The huge divisions in opposition led to a situation in which effective government in large parts of Russia disappeared. In very special and very disturbed circumstances the most unlikely of the contenders for power emerged victorious. In the only successful example of revolutionary opposition in the period, Lenin and the Bolsheviks gained power in October 1917.

Opposition and the state after 1917

Thereafter the pattern was similar to that of the previous century. Opposition to the new rulers was as unsuccessful as opposition to the older ones. The opposition of the Whites in the Civil War against Bolshevik rule failed because, like the opposition in 1905–6, it was disunited and the Reds used a more effective armed force.

From December 1917 opposition to the Bolshevik take over built up and the unpopularity of the Brest-Litvosk treaty signed in March 1918 confirmed many in their campaign against Lenin. Former Tsarists, liberal democrats, nationalist groups eager for freedom, and allied forces eager to defeat the Bolsheviks, and to get Russia back into the war, formed the so-called **White Armies**. Angry peasants also joined the opposition in 1920. But by 1920, campaigns in the Ukraine, Baltic, Northern Russia and Siberia had ended with Red victory. Just as power was more concentrated in the hands of the Tsars after 1881, so after the Civil War power was more concentrated in the hands of the Bolshevik party and its leaders.

Stalin and opposition

Opposition to the rise of Stalin (1928–53) suffered from many of the faults of opposition to the Tsars:

- Trotsky followed the same path of exile taken by so many of the opponents of the Tsar.
- Repression was as constant a feature of Communist rule as of Tsarist rule. By 1930, both Left and Right oppositions had been eliminated.
- Further, any hopes of nationalist independence were eliminated by economic policies which standardised central control (*see* Chapter 4, pages 116–17).
- Opposition within the party was met by violence: the party boss of Leningrad, **Kirov**, met the same fate as another reformer who seemed to go too far – Stolypin. Both were assassinated.

BIOGRAPHY

Sergei Kirov (1886–1934)

Kirov was an active revolutionary and close to Stalin personally. He was the boss of the Leningrad party. From 1932 he had argued that there was the need to reconcile opponents and not to rely so heavily on repression. He was assassinated by Leonid Nickolaev, a party member with contacts in the police, on 1st December 1934. Stalin used his death as an excuse to purge the party. Count Pyotr Stolypin (1862–1911) was killed by Dmitri Bogrov, a police informer, on 18 September 1911. Like Kirov he had been deeply associated with the ruling of the country and had favoured change. Both men died under mysterious circumstances and both had tried to persuade an autocratic ruler to institute reforms. Both were victims of intrigues, and the death of both preceded periods of greater repression.

Sergei Kirov

Where any comparison ends is in the period after 1936. The Tsars did not persecute imagined opponents on any scale, but Stalin eradicated not only real opponents but also anyone who might conceivably be in the smallest way possible a critic or opponent.

Any deviation from the views of the party leadership was impossible within Russia. Exiles, like Trotsky, still opposed the regime but Stalin's reach was longer than that of the Tsars

White armies

formed from disparate opponents of Communism, the White Armies were geographically separated and their supporters were united only in their opposition to the Reds.

and Trotsky was murdered in Mexico in 1940. Only the advent of the Second World War allowed opposition. Anti-Bolshevik elements *did* join forces with the Germans; but potential opposition was rendered pointless by the short-sighted policy of the Germans in treating the occupied Russian areas as slave pens and wreaking an even greater violence on them than Stalin. Had the Germans come as liberators, then opposition to Communism might have been successful, especially in Western Russia where nationalism had been suppressed.

What impact did the Second World War have on the power of the State?

From 1941 to 1945 Russia fought the greatest war in her history to defeat the Nazi invasion and then to impose Soviet rule on most of Eastern Europe. After the war instead of greater liberalisation, as had followed previous wars, even greater control of opposition or potential opposition was launched and purges spread to the new empire in eastern Europe (*see also* Chapter 5, pages 149–50), where anti-Communist parties were suppressed with an even greater thoroughness and violence than that used by the Tsars to impose Russian rule.

Purges were a way of expressing the high level of repression pursued by Stalin and his supporters, both within the Communist Party and then in the country as a whole. The severe years of terror were 1936–1938, but throughout Stalin's rule there were large numbers of arrests. Under Nicolai Yezhov, the head of the NKVD, very large numbers of party leaders, officials, officers in the armed services, technicians, creative artists, minority groups in the empire and ordinary citizens were arrested and sentenced to imprisonment in the gulags, or executed. In 1938 Yezhov himself was purged.

The Tsars lacked the means of modern control – telephones, card indexes, 'scientific' methods of interrogation and torture, and massive structures like prison camps (gulags). Opposition stood even less chance than it had under the most rigorous persecution of Alexander III. As during the Civil War, criticism was linked with foreign interference: any murmur of protest was enough to brand one as a Western spy. The control of communication meant that exiles had less chance of getting access to Russian citizens than had been the case under the Tsars. Then the so-called **Leningrad affair** neutralised any potential opposition within the party.

Reform and resistance after 1953

By 1953 there was indeed a feeling within the highest sections of the party that change was needed, but whether this could really be seen as opposition is doubtful. It was more resentment, as was shown by the rapid coup which had Beria, Stalin's secret police chief, arrested and shot by order of his enemies in the **Politburo** in 1953. There was change in the Khrushchev era (1956–64) but it was limited by the fact that Soviet Russia, like the Germans before them, had to control a potentially hostile population in its European Empire.

The Poles had been major opponents of the Tsars. Now there was unrest again in Poland, in East Berlin and most significantly in Hungary in 1956. Yet this resistance met with a similar lack of success to the nationalist movements of 1863, 1905–06 and 1918–20. There were similar elements – a divided opposition, the power of the state, and the lack of foreign support. Limited concessions were gained, but the aims of liberation were not achieved until the strains of another war – this time the **Cold War** – had weakened Soviet power.

The Leningrad affair

A purge of the party leadership in Leningrad of whom Stalin had become suspicious. Stalin's henchman Malenkov condemned 'anti party' activities in 1949. The leaders of the Leningrad party, Kuznetsov and Voznesensky together with their associates and even family members were tried in 1950 and executed. Those executed were entirely innocent.

Politburo

The ruling executive council of the USSR.

The very limited internal opposition met formidable resistance by a Soviet machine which had developed repression from years of practice. The massive gulag system was wound down, but there were severe controls (for example, the state control of all education). The only successful opposition was at the very top – comparitive to the fall of the Tsar in 1917 – when the politburo overthrew Khrushchev in 1964. This was unique in Soviet history but had little to do with public opinion or mass demonstrations and much more to do with the failures of economic policy and the humiliation of the Cuban Missile crisis. It was these which had robbed Khrushchev of credibility among top communists (just as the policies of Nicholas II had robbed him of credibility with the Tsarist elite in 1917). The parallel is with the palace coups of 1762 and 1801, which eradicated Tsars in the 18th century, not with the success of any form of organised opposition.

> ### ACTIVITY
>
> How would you start to explain the problems faced by those who wanted to change the regimes after 1855?
>
> ■ What are the key reasons for failure.
>
> ■ What elements in Russian history favoured the existing state, apart from the special circumstances of 1917?

This chapter will now consider in more depth the theme of the state and opposition in different eras from 1855 to 1964.

Opposition in the reign of Alexander II

Of the three main elements of opposition, historians have shown most interest in the least significant element in terms of numbers. The major upheavals were first the Polish Revolt of 1863, followed by three years of unrest and secondly the agrarian unrest both before and after emancipation. However, the third, the growth of the Populist movement, has been of more interest because it pointed to the future

The main elements of revolt

Political unrest

The ruling classes of Poland had never accepted Russian rule, even the devolved version set up by making Poland a semi-autonomous state within the Empire. The risings of 1830 were commemorated by demonstrations in 1860 and a revolutionary committee was set up. By 1863 the Polish rebels had some hope that they might succeed because Alexander II's reforms had given them the hope that there might be the possibility of change in Poland, with more self-government. The Poles not only had more hope – they had a potential force since a recruiting campaign launched by the Russians to expand the army had led to an extensive flight from the Polish villages of young men eager to escape Russian military service, but willing to serve as a Polish army. However, the Poles were divided in aims and methods. The so-called 'Reds' supported armed revolt – even in the face of 195,000 Russian troops; the so-called 'Whites' – mainly the nationalist nobles – preferred to rely on negotiations and the possibility of foreign diplomatic assistance which had been effective in the case of Italian unification. The terms Red and White were to remerge after 1917. The 'Red' secret society 'Earth and Will' had similarities with the Russian Narodniks, but there was no question of any joint action.

Cold war

Relations between Russia and the West had been strained during the war; the failure of Russia to abide by the West's understanding of the Yalta and Potsdam agreements led to a higher level of tension by 1946. The so-called Cold War escalated in 1947 and persisted through this period.

The Polish rising of 1830 failed because of the following factors.

- The Polish countryside was not effectively mobilised by the rebels and Russian concessions (commuting service for cash payments to the serfs) undercut support.
- The Poles could not form regular units and they relied on guerilla activity which often lacked the support of the population, especially in the Ukraine.
- The rebels were divided in aims. Conservative nationalists were not committed to land reform. There was distrust of the Warsaw-based committee in Lithuania and the Ukraine.
- Russian military power was too great.
- The most decisive foreign intervention was that of Prussia who closed the frontier to the rebels and handed over rebel leaders who had fled.
- No help came from France or Britain.

The results were brutal – execution of members of the revolutionary committee and 25,000 Polish deaths. The Russification of the former 'Congress Kingdom of Poland' set up in 1815 intensified and extended to the Ukraine, despite the limited support given there to the rebels. Treatment of Polish dissent was far harsher than that of Russian reformist movements and anticipated later events – the cooperation of Hitler and Stalin in crushing Poland in 1939 and the Red Army's occupation in 1944. When Polish rebels in Warsaw were left to their fate at German hands by a Communist regime as eager to control the country as Alexander II had been. Polish nationalism was as distrusted by the Commissars as it was by the Tsars.

Peasant unrest

In terms of violence and disruption, the opposition of the peasantry was almost as great a problem. Since 1856 the countryside had seen an unprecedented level of disturbances, but these increased after 1861, as disappointment was intense about the sharing out of the lands after serfdom had been abolished. The peasant revolts in the Pezna and Kazan provinces

Figure 2.2   Map of 19th century Russia showing Penza, Tambov and Kazan as major areas of peasant unrest.

(Fig. 2.2) were the most extensive since the 18th century (*see* Pugachev's revolt page 46) and a peasant army was formed under Anton Petrov. Military force was deployed in an anticipation of the battles against the Green (peasant) armies in 1919 and later the Communist assault on the peasants during **Collectivisation**. Over 500 deaths resulted.

The peasants wanted more land but they lacked a focus in terms of their ideology and political demands. They were easily crushed by overwhelming forces, but also because the different groups failed to unite. It is easy to see why they failed. The results put pressure on the liberals who were urging reforms – if so much upheaval had been caused by change, some argued, would it not be better to fall back on the traditions of authority and military force?

The final element of revolt

The third element in opposition had its focal point in two developments. The first was the so-called 'Going to the People' in the summer of 1874. Three thousand young members of the intelligentsia, mostly students went to the villages to spread their ideas of 'the truth' to the peasants:

1 that Russia's hope lay in a peasant democracy;
2 that the purity of rural life was in strong contrast to the corruption of the cities;
3 that the peasants had been oppressed and that the land belonged to them; and
4 that men were equal and a rebirth of Russia should be made on the basis of that equality and freedom.

These ideas had been developing in various forms since the 1830s. They were discussed in secret and by exiles living abroad and smuggling publications into Russia. They appealed to certain elements in the liberal nobility and to the young men of humble birth who had managed to get an education – the poor students. These were seen as classless (*raznochinetski*). With Russia's limited urban middle class, these radicals were bound to be much smaller in number than the Polish rebels or rebellious peasants. Mainly composed of small reading and discussion groups, often in universities or in literary circles, they devoured radical publications like Alexander Herzen's *The Bell* or Chernayevsky's *The Contemporary*. Had it not been for later developments, these radicals would be a footnote of history but out of this loose movement came the ideas and men who would rule Russia from 1917.

Their revolutionary aims centred on freedom, but also a belief in the 'wholeness' of Russian society, in the community of the land. In a way, they were similar to the officials who preferred establishing peasant communities rather than individual farms in the reforms of 1861. They had similar roots to the pan Slavists, who thought of all Slav peoples as a huge community and to the Bolsheviks, who thought in terms of collective farms and huge industrial communities. However, they stand in contrast to the individualism of the post-1905 Tsarist regime and also to the Westernised individualism which followed 1989.

The 'coming out' of 1874 was a remarkably open expression of radicalism that met with limited support among an illiterate peasantry, benefiting from the transport expansion, population growth and greater marketing opportunities of the 1870s. The authorities clamped down and over 700 activists were arrested. Unlike the Polish rebels they were not executed. The leaders of the Populist (Narodnik) movement were exiled and the dissent was driven back to secrecy.

Collectivisation

This was the process of collecting farms together for communal use. The main campaign was 1928–1933 but the process continued until 1941 and was resumed after the war.

However, the official foundation of the distinct organisation for radical change called 'Land and Freedom' was launched by a public demonstration in St. Petersburg in 1878. This referred to earlier attempts in the 1860s by different groups to establish some kind of structure. 'Young Russia' founded by a student, Zaichnevsky was a small student group, easily suppressed. The first 'Land and Freedom' was a very secret society founded by Nickolai Serno-Solovyeitch in 1861. Intercepted letters from this group to exiled radicals – Herzen, and the anarchist Bakunin – led to 32 arrests. The techniques for being a secret revolutionary were not developed enough even to outwit the rather basic police organisation of Tsarist Russia. Secret societies by their nature, however, tend to proliferate and one feature of this period is the gap between those who preferred peaceful measures and those who favoured direct action. A turning point, and indeed the signal for the second major development of opposition was the attempt by a member of one of these groups – called 'Hell' – to murder Alexander II in 1866.

Thus the Populist movement of 1878 had two models:

1   the idealistic secret discussion groups devouring the ideas of exiles and dedicated to persuasion, and

2   terrorism.

The 'movement' (if it can really be called that given the limited organisation) split. The more peaceful element had limited impact; the terrorist elements achieved a high profile.

KEY IDEA

Modern revolutionary theory argues that terrorism by driving established states into greater repression and dependence on force not consent weakens the state and paves the way for revolution. This was the case after 1881 and political repression together with rapid industrial growth was to provide a lethal cocktail for revolution in 1905.

ANALYSIS

- The different elements of opposition were very divided, even among themselves.

- Resorts to violence could not succeed against the military power of the Russian state.

- There were no means to organise which were not illegal and dangerous.

- There were influential ideas but little structure to put them into effect.

- After the Polish Revolt and the assassinations, radicalism came to be associated with a lack of patriotism, and all radicals were seen as 'nihilists', i.e. pointless destroyers.

- The middle class base for the development of strong reformist pressure did not exist.

- Though there was industrial growth, the number of workers in cities was too small to make mass working class agitation a possibility; the peasants were not interested in revolutionary ideas and too conservative to enlist as agents for more general change.

- The nobility had shown an interest in change – for example the nobles of Tver province called for a constitution in 1863, but generally, they swung away from change as a result of violent opposition activity.

What had been achieved?

- The provenance of some ideas had been established, such as democracy.

- The revolutionary attempts had established models for later radicals and lessons had been learnt.

- Martyrs and heroes had been created (Vera Zasulich).

- Father figures had been established. It was no coincidence that Lenin's most famous revolutionary work What is to be Done' had the same title as a novel of that name by the radical writer Chernayevsky.

The larger group was peaceful – the so-called Black Partition. The terrorists of the People's Will – possibly with membership as low as 50 – gained huge attention by the shooting of the Governor of St. Petersburg General Trepov by a woman, **Vera Zasulich**, in 1878 and by the assassination of the Tsar himself on 1 March 1881. The immediate result was severe repression, an end to the liberal proposals being considered by the regime and an increase in the power and activity of the police. The populist groups disintegrated; propertied opinion swung to the rigid autocracy supported by the new Tsar Alexander III and hopes for reform of the land or an increase in freedom seemed further away than ever.

Vera Zasulich born 1849 died 1919. From a poor family she became involved in revolutionary groups in St Petersburg and joined land and Liberty. She shot the military governor in 1876 as a protest against police brutality. She was acquitted by the jury and the crowd prevented her re-arrest. She escaped and joined the more peaceful Black Partititon group, rejecting terrorism. She became a Marxist and helped to edit the newspaper Iskra (The Spark). In London in 1903 she rejected Lenin and became a Menshevik. She took part in the 1905 Revolution but turned against socialism after that and opposed the Bolsehvik revolution.

ACTIVITY

You have looked at various opposition groups and activities in the reign of Alexander II. Try to assess which you think was the most important and why. Try listing them and awarding each a mark out of ten. Think of the justification – involving large numbers of people; having important new ideas; offering a real threat to the Tsar; influencing future developments.

The situation by 1905

The nature of revolutionary groups by 1905

There was both continuity and change between the opposition of 1905 and the opposition groups of Alexander II. However, the greatest change was the emergence of groups who looked at the industrial workers as the basis of popular revolution rather than the peasantry. This was to have profound consequences. Generally, though, similarities abound. Revolutionary groups were relatively small. Like their predecessors they took ideas from abroad and were often in exile. They faced heavy repression from the state; their leadership depended on a small class of rootless intellectuals. They split easily and were still divided between the advocates of violence and those who saw revolution either emerging from propaganda or from the inevitable processes of history. An almost irrational belief in community was also an ongoing feature. Like the revolutionary efforts between 1856 and 1881, the attempts at change in the next period to 1906 were hampered by divisions and lack of communication between different elements of opposition.

The revolutionaries

The direct heirs to the Populists were the Socialist Revolutionaries. Founded in 1900 as a distinct party, they took their ideas not from **Marx** but from Alexander Herzen. Their aim was for an overthrow of Tsarism and an instant socialist society not dependent on the development of capitalism, as in Marxist theory, but based on common ownership of land. What characterised the group was terrorism. Under the command of a police double agent called Azev a battle Group organised assassinations and betrayed the killers to the police. This bizarre campaign claimed the lives of leading officials and generals and even the Minister of the Interior, Plevhe. The leader Victor Chernov was sceptical about violence but it gave the group a high profile.

2 The nature of government

Marxism

The first Russian Marxist party was formed in 1883 in Switzerland by a former member of Land and Freedom, Georgei Plekhanov. The Emancipation of Labour movement joined the tradition of Russian exiles and from Geneva sent propaganda into Russia. Tiny discussion groups formed in Russia itself, but the groups remained separate from actual strikes and unrest. More like a religious group in their arguments about doctrine and what Marx really meant, they were fragmented. In 1895 Vladimir Ulyanov (Lenin) and Julius Martov formed the fighting Union for the Liberation of the Working Class. For the first time pamphlets were produced to incite workers and contacts were made in factories to stir up strikes. In 1898 a small number of Marxists formed the Social Democratic Party and set up 'The Workers' Gazette'. The Marxists took over some positive elements from the Populists – idealism, the experience of veteran revolutionaries like Vera Zasulich, theoretical justifications for revolution and experience in organisation. They also inherited some negative elements such as internal arguments and divisions.

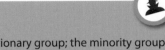

BIOGRAPHY

Karl Marx (1818–1883) Marx was a German philosopher, historian, economist and revolutionary. He believed that it was a law of History that the industrial working classes (proletariat) would overthrow the middle classes in advanced industrial countries and establish after a period of dictatorship an ideal and unchanging society governed by the principle 'From each according to his ability, to each according to his needs' in which property would be held in common for the good of all, ending the injustices and contradictions of capitalism. Marxism came into Russia in the 1880s, but the Marxist groups split in 1903. The majority group (Bolsheviks) led by Vladimir Ulyanov (Lenin) believed in a tightly knit revolutionary group; the minority group (Mensheviks) believed in a mass party and was led by Julius Martov. Later the Mensheviks became the majority of the party; a formal split occurred in 1911.

In 1903 the party split between Lenin's group who favoured a small tightly organised revolutionary party entirely independent from other groups, and Martov's group who were prepared to work with non-Marxist groups to achieve a democracy which would then later become a Marxist state. This was more in accord with Marx's views that a bourgeois phase would have to come before a socialist phase of revolution. Lenin was much more in the conspiratorial tradition and believed in a total sweeping away of the old order. Lenin achieved a temporary majority in a conference in London, after a meeting in Brussels in 1903 had to be abandoned because of police activity. His group – the majority men became known as Bolsheviks (from the Russian word for majority). Martov's group were the minority (even though numerically larger) – or Mensheviks (from the Russian word for minority). The split became permanent in 1911.

58

What was remarkable about the opposition in the period before 1905 was not the numbers involved – not more than 10,000 SR members in the whole of Russia and fewer Social Democrats – but their influence through printed propaganda, the sensational assassinations and the growing number of strikes and peasant disturbance.

Both groups were strongly linked to Russian opposition traditions. What was new was the scale of discontent they could exploit and the impact of Marxist theory. There was a thin tradition of desire for constitutional change going back to the Decembrists admiration for some of the doctrines of the French Revolution in the reign of Alexander I. Alexander II had created elected local bodies which gave some training in politics and government to liberal nobles and educated middle class Russians. These Zemstvos had wanted a national parliament and had shown their potential for government in relief work in the famine of 1891. The Zemstvos allowed like-minded people – doctors, teachers, businessmen and landowners to meet together. In 1895 they agreed to meet for an annual conference. This was forbidden but different professional groups – doctors, lawyers, accountants, engineers and other experts met together in conferences and discussed political reform as well as matters concerning their professions. A Union of Liberation was organised secretly and a newspaper: Liberation was smuggled in from abroad. But like the other reform groups there were splits and disagreements about what sort of constitution should be formed.

ANALYSIS

The situation by 1905 was that there were probably more similarities than differences between the opposition under Nicholas II and that of his predecessors.

- There was little mass support and little party/movement organisation.

- There was dependence on written material smuggled in from abroad.

- The groups were bitterly divided among themselves.

- With no concept of legitimate opposition, their very existence posed a risk to the opposition members.

- There was a greater interest in theoretical discussion than practical organisation.

- The frustrations turned the radicals onto terrorism which tightened the hold of the state and made opposition more difficult to develop.

What had changed was the context. Massive industrialisation had created a restless urban working class unknown in 1855? Population growth has pressured the countryside making it more susceptible to radical ideas than had been the case in the populist campaign in the 1870s. Russification programmes had alienated the nationalities within the Empire to a degree unparalleled in the days of Alexander II.

The revolution of 1905

The background was the defeats in the war against Japan waged since February 1904. The war increased prices and disrupted trade. In January 1905 the famous demonstration of workers led by Father Gapon appealed to the Tsar directly. This was not really opposition, but was seen so by the troops at the Winter Palace who fired on the crowds. The massacre provoked a general strike in the capital. There were waves of strikes notably at Ivanovo (an industrial town 300 km north-east of Moscow) and at Łódź in Poland. They were met with repression.

In June 1905 the crew of the Battleship Potemkin (pronounced Patyomkin) in Odessa mutinied and sailed for Romania. At the same time there were large-scale peasant disturbances in Latvia and the Black Earth regions.

The Revolutionaries met to discuss events – the SRs in Russia; the Marxists in London; the Mensheviks in Geneva. All called for armed resistance, though not for joint action. Lenin was for links with the revolutionary peasants; the Mensheviks for alliance with the middle-class liberals. These met in Moscow in May 1905 organised by the Union of Liberation and by October there was a united liberal party – the Constitutional Democrats or Kadets. The peasant groups formed a Peasant Union in May and called for land nationalisation in November. In October the moderate reformers formed a group known as the Octobrists who argued for moderate constitutional change.

Reform proposals by the government in August were so limited – with a very narrow franchise and a restricted parliament – that disturbances broke out more strongly. There were peasant riots and strikes and street fighting in Moscow. A railway strike paralysed the national network. October 1905 saw a general strike in the capital. The universities became centres of radical activity. On October 13th the first Soviet or workers' council was formed. This saw the emergence of the leadership of Khustalev-Nomar, the Menshevik, Lev Bronstein and Trotsky who urged armed workers insurrection – in vain.

1 On October 17th the government announced freedoms of press, opinion and association and announced a legislative assembly on a wider franchise.

2 This allowed the Bolsheviks to emerge openly and publish its newspaper 'New Life' and Lenin came back to Russia in November.

3 The Petersburg society called a general strike for an 8-hour day. There were naval mutinies at Kronstadt, Vladivostok and a serious military uprising in Sebastopol.

Throughout the empire there were nationalist disturbances – far greater than those of 1863 – in Poland, the Ukraine, Armenia, Georgia, Central Asia (Moslems) and Yakutia and Mongolia. In Finland there was a new Diet which gave votes to women.

The most serious outbreak in the west of Russia was an armed uprising in Moscow on the 8–20th December organised by the Soviet. The government had to use artillery fire which left 1000 dead. Repression spread through the countryside and many revolutionaries went once again into exile, while the liberals found that the Dumas were manipulated by the government of Stolypin.

In March and April 1906 the first national elections offered a chance for more regular opposition but the SDs ands SRs boycotted them. The Kadets gained a majority, but when demands were made for land reforms, the Duma was ended. The opposition of the Kadets and the non-revolutionary Trudoviks – the peasant and workers party – amounted to withdrawing to Finland and calling for cooperation on a refusal to pay taxes or accept military service. But the SRs waged a terrorist war in the countryside with 1500 murders in 1906 alone. An attempt on Stolypin's life cost 27 deaths. However the balance swung to authority once more. By 1907 the Duma elections showed a growth in conservative groups – 150 conservative deputies to 120 leftists. The Social Democrats were officially split in 1912 and the SRs found agrarian reform reduced their support in the countryside.

The Revolution of 1905 contained elements of many forms of modern unrest but like the previous attempts at change faced terrible problems in uniting the different elements.

- The unrest among military and naval units was not a general mutiny and could not be exploited enough by the revolutionary groups. Thus the Tsar's forces continued to suppress riots as they had done since 1856. This is in contrast to the situation in 1917 where the failure of the military to back the Tsar in March and the Provisional Government in October was a key element.

- The educated elite was split, but not permanently. The liberal middle classes, noble critics of the Tsar, nationalist nobles and industrialists did not make lasting links with worker and peasant malcontents. The promises of October 1905 divided them from the revolution.

- Attempts to fight the regime by Civil Disobedience, (i.e. by a sort of passive resistance of not paying taxes or accepting authority) was ineffective in 1906 when the regime was recovering and engendering support again.

- The revolutionary groups came out into the open but lacked the ability to coordinate unrest. The belief in the general strike without armed action by workers proved to be an illusion. The relative lack of urbanisation made these strikes less effective than they might have been in Germany or Britain.

- The Soviets were a striking development but though capable of the most organised resistance yet seen – and a huge advance on the Populists, or the peasant rioters or the nationalist guerillas – did not have the confidence or the means to bring about a revolution on the model of October 1917.

- Peasant disturbances were powerful, but the peasants aimed at land redistribution rather than a revolution inspired by a distinct ideology, despite the efforts of the SRs. Despite Lenin's speeches, there was in practice little coordination between urban and rural unrest.

- The widespread nationalist upheavals took advantage of the weakness of the regime but were again not coordinated and varied in aims and success. Religious differences were evident for example between the Polish Catholics, the Jewish Bund, and the Moslem separatists of Central Asia. Also nationalist revolts, as in 1863, tended to move mainstream Russian opinion back to the Tsar as a unifying influence.

All this having been said, the Revolutions were more serious instances of opposition than anything that had been seen in the previous century and drove the Tsar to greater concessions than any of his predecessors.

Why had these upheavals been so much greater than anything seen previously?

- The war with Japan was particularly humiliating in a way that even the Crimean War (*see* Chapter 5) had not been because it was not a conflict with a more modern and advanced nation, but one which the Russians despised as inferior and more like the Asian people who the Russians ruled as part of their Empire.

- The industrial development had given rise to a great deal more potential discontent. The strains of rapid industrial growth were evidenced in city slums which were breeding grounds for socialist propaganda and which erupted in 1905. The increases in strikes since the late 19th century culminated in the extensive and well-organised industrial unrest which was a vital part of 1905.

- Population growth had put more pressure on the land than had been the case in the disturbances of 1856–61. There was significant land hunger in the countryside.

- All over Europe nationalism had grown and every country with national minorities was finding it difficult to avoid conflict. When central government was weakened it was no surprise that different groups within the Empire, much more developed in their view of national identity than they had been previously should erupt. In 1863 this had only really been true of the Poles. By 1905 cultural changes meant that this nationalism was more of a problem and previous Russification policies – themselves the result of growing Russian nationalism – had provoked unrest.

- The organisation of opposition had been very limited in earlier years. Its ideology had been quite vague. With the development of a scientifically based Marxism, the intellectual confidence and appeal of the Social Democratic groups increased. Rural unrest also gave the SRs more opportunities, while the growth of the Russian middle class gave a chance for a better organised liberal movement to appear. So while the Russian state had faced limited, underground and scattered movements in the 1860s, 1870s and 1880s, in the period from 1890 to 1905 it faced much stronger opposition.

- In some ways it coped with this by developing more of a police state. But the revolutions of 1905 were just too much for this apparatus. The sheer scale and variety of the unrest was too much for the state. But this diversity in the end was the great weakness of the opposition.

> ### ANALYSIS
> **Consider this analysis**
>
> The scale and range of discontent – social and political as well as geographical – showed the Tsar that massive change was necessary. It could have reappeared, but in fact the success of opposition in 1917 did not depend on a repeat of 1905. There were important elements of similarity in the mass demonstrations of 1905 and the situation in February 1917 (and indeed in the fall of the Russian empire in 1918) but the October revolution – the most significant and lasting success by an opposition group depended on different factors.

Point of comparison: Poland

Poland was a major area of rebellion in 1863 and again 1905–1907. To see what had changed is to understand the development and limitation of opposition in Russia as a whole. In Poland industrial discontent was far more important in 1905 than it had been in 1863 when economic development was much less advanced. Over 400,000 workers in Poland went on strike. The city of Łódź was a major centre for revolt in 1905 when Tsarist forces fired on strikers. The so-called June days in this city saw 200 dead and 2000 injured. There were also demonstrations in other urban centres – 30 people were shot in Warsaw on May Day 1905.

An independent socialist state was set up in Ostrów in December 1905 to January 1906 and industrial disturbances continued into 1907 in various regions. Unlike 1863 the liberal nobility were not the centre of the revolt. However, as in 1863, there was little effective organisation. At one stage gunmen from the Polish socialist party and the rival National Democratic Party were shooting at each other in Łódź as well as at the Russians. There was little coordination between urban unrest and peasant attacks in the countryside and no unified central coordinating committee emerged. As with 1863 the loyalty of the Russian forces proved too much.

The success of opposition, 1917

The failure of 1905 meant that opposition became harder. The divisions within the groups and between them grew rather than lessened. The lesson of 1905 was that divisions had prevented success, but it was not learnt. Bolsheviks and Mensheviks were divided. Within each group there were factions. An exiled leadership found it difficult to maintain control and unity. There was resort to criminality and terrorism among many splinter groups.

The **Dumas** had divided the liberals from the revolutionaries and posed a difficult problem for the extremists – should they or should they not participate? Another wedge had been driven between the revolutionaries. The liberals found themselves undermined: the association of the liberal Kadet group with a bogus form of parliamentary constitution caused this. Plus, in the Duma of 1907, electoral manipulation by Stolypin's government put the reformers in a minority. Whilst this was going on, there was violent repression in the countryside by the right wing terrorist groups who were attacking revolutionary supporters and Jews. These Black Hundreds anticipated Nazi racist paramilitaries and the death toll may have reached 25,000. Nationalist groups were repressed.

At the same time, the peasant reforms and the growing opportunities that industrial and urban growth gave undermined the revolutionaries' appeal. The revival of support for the dynasty in 1913 on the 300th anniversary of its establishment; the decline in industrial strikes and the support for the World War in 1914 may have been depressing for a divided opposition.

Once again war was the key factor, just as it had been in 1854–56 and 1904–5; this time the scale of the war was greater and so were its consequences. The war offered the chance for the liberal groups to show their loyalty; after all it might, as with the Crimea, reveal the need for the Crown to join with liberals to bring about a national reform programme.

Liberalism and war

The liberal groups in the Duma expressed their support in 1914, but were frustrated by the lack of consultation or ability to get rid of the incompetent ministers who could not organise effectively. A turning point was the formation of the Progressive Bloc – an alliance of liberals and conservatives who pressed for change – in 1915. Their programme was a blueprint for a new Russia:

- a government responsible to the Duma;
- religious toleration;
- civil rights to Jews;
- autonomy for Poland and Finland;
- legalisation of Trade Unions; and
- equality of all before the law.

It was classic liberalism as recognised in Europe and the USA since the late 18th century. But for most Russians it was meaningless. There was no reference to land redistribution or better working conditions. Autocracy was to be reformed but not abolished. However, even this modest plan was dismissed along with the Duma.

However, that did not mean that the liberals lost all influence. They worked together for the war effort in different organisations: Zemstvo unions, Red Cross, employers' associations, and the Union of Cities. But, the failure of the government to work with loyal liberalism created a highly disloyal liberal movement. This meant that the Duma called in 1916 was unrelievedly critical of the government: the elite on which the regime rested was turning against it. Significantly when the royal favourite, the disreputable holy man Rasputin, was murdered in December 1916, it was by a Duma leader Purishkevich, a member of the royal family, Prince Yusupov, and a Grand Duke, Dmitri Romanov. The key elements within the ruling elite had turned to direct action.

Dumas

the name given to the Russian parliaments that met after 1906. The term fell into disuse in Soviet times but was revived after the fall of Communism and the Russian parliament is again called the Duma, though it does not meet in the Tauride Palace in St. Petersburg as did the Tsarist Duma, but in the so-called White House in Moscow.

Why then did Liberals not establish a new Russia?

Stretch and challenge

Up until 1917 the state seemed to have had all the advantages and the opposition groups had faced an impossible task in overthrowing it. Yet in 1917 there were two successful regime changes. What circumstances led to the state losing its advantages?

Develop a thesis that might explain this exception to the general trend of failure by the opposition in the period as a whole.

When the Tsar abdicated in 1917 the only organised body to produce an alternative government was the Duma. Their wartime programme was ready at hand and was put into practice. Many of their radical opponents had distanced themselves from the war effort and made themselves intensely unpopular. Lenin had seen the war as the final phase of Imperialism and from exile he continued his attacks on his fellow revolutionaries rather than proposing any measures to help the Russian people through this crisis.

The fall of the monarchy did not come about because of dedicated revolutionary activity or terrorism but because of mass demonstrations and a reluctance of the authorities and the troops to repeat the bloodbath of January 1905. The Tsar had already been undermined by opposition within the elites and had fatally distanced himself from the capital by taking personal command of his troops in 1915, leaving his unpopular empress in charge. When crisis came in 1917 a ruler who depended a lot on personal rule simply was not there to exercise it.

Opposition in February 1917 was therefore successful. The Tsar abdicated, as did his brother. New assemblies were established and there was the hope of a new constitution.

This is often seen not as the work of organised opposition, but rather of spontaneous demonstrations. This may be only partly true. There was an organisation of workers led by a dedicated group of Bolsheviks established in the industrial Vyborg district of St. Petersburg – led by veterans of the 1905 street fighting – Chugurin, Pavlov and Kayurov among others. There was too an established group of liberals brought together by the 1915 War Industries Committee which went on to plan a virtual overthrow of the Tsar. Mikhail Tereschichenko, Paul Milyukov, Alexander Guchkov and Alexander Konovalov were its leading figures and it was Guchkov who visited the Tsar at Pskov and told him that he had lost the support of the Duma. These groups were taken by surprise at the huge popular support for their planned demonstrations on International Women's Day on 23 February. They had not planned the mutiny of the troops or the huge scale of the demonstrations. They had not planned the hasty creation of the Soviets – largely by the Mensheviks. The Duma group however was ready for an alterative government – something they *had* planned since 1916.

However, for all the challenge to the idea that the Tsar fell by spontaneous action by considering the impact of organised conspiracies, the fact is that without massive and unexpected popular demonstrations on a par with those in Berlin in 1989, the opposition by itself would not have been successful, It does seem that opposition had not made huge strides since 1905, but the Tsar had failed on a much larger scale than either 1904–5 or 1854–56 and the results were therefore more dramatic.

ACTIVITY

Further research

There is some debate about the 'spontaneous' nature of the demonstrations and the events which brought about the abdication of the Tsar. You may wish to investigate this further, but you will not be expected to evaluate interpretations in the context of this unit.

The opposition to the new regime remained fairly divided and chaotic. The only 'legitimate' government was the Provisional Government. But the problem was to find where its legitimacy lay. Only by establishing a new constitution and having elections could that really be established. This failed to materialise for a vital period. During the interim period there were two possible forms of government. The Provisional Government came from the Duma opposition. The Soviet emerged from the more radical opposition groups. Opposition to these interim arrangements soon developed. The Vyborg workers were dismayed at the way 'their' revolution had been taken over by the bourgeoisie and a Soviet in which they were in a minority. The peasants reacted as in 1905 by a wave of direct action against the estates encouraged by the SRs but not legitimised by the new government. The Bolshevik leaders returned and offered a radical programme. Menshevik leaders hoped that a democratic Russia in which they played a role would evolve into a socialist state. The Bolsheviks were uncertain whether to wait for a revolution by the bourgeoisie or to act in a sudden take over. Lenin believed in a sudden take over but faced considerable opposition. Meanwhile the nationalities were taking advantage of the sudden disappearance of the Tsar to assert autonomy. The Empire stood on the verge of collapse. Much of this seemed a repeat of 1905. The Tsar had gone, but the possibility of a military dictatorship with allied help was not impossible. However, once again opposition was successful – for the last time before the fall of the Berlin wall in 1989 there was decisive change.

Why were the Bolsheviks more successful than their revolutionary predecessors?

The Bolsheviks, led by Lenin, a remote intellectual hardly known in Russia and having a theory of revolution based on a class of industrial workers which was largely irrelevant to Russia, were nevertheless successful. Why?

Did the Bolsheviks have a more realistic programme than the Narodniks or the revolutionaries of 1905?

Not really.

1 They promised peace, but this was not universally desirable and there were substantial pro-war demonstrations as well as anti-war demonstrations in 1917. When they gave Russia peace it provoked huge opposition as many felt the huge losses of the war had been in vain.

2 They promised land, but the peasants had already been taking it and the SRs, the largest of the revolutionary parties had also promised it.

3 They offered 'all power to the Soviets' but Lenin had little time for them; Soviets were not a major influence in Russia as a whole.

4 They offered 'bread', but there was little indication of how this was to be delivered. Also Lenin had not even got the backing of Marxist theory but had plunged off into theories of his own which argued for immediate take over without waiting for the vital development of bourgeois society.

In this the more popular Mensheviks were more moderate and realistic. So the other revolutionary groups were seemingly better placed in the key centres of revolutionary activity – the Soviets in the cities and in the countryside.

Were the Bolsheviks more united than the revolutionaries of 1905 or the Narodniks?

Lenin was not the undisputed leader even when he returned in 1917. Trotsky, the organiser of the Revolution was distrusted as a formed Menshevik. The Bolshevik central committee had not accepted Lenin's wish for immediate revolution at all unanimously. Lenin had had a setback in July when a premature rising seemed to discredit his ideas and had been forced to flee rather humiliatingly disguised in a blond wig.

Did the Bolsheviks offer greater national autonomy?

Not really though this was a result of the breakdown of central authority. Nor did they offer a credible promise of peasant landownership – a study of their writings reveals a long-term desire to control the countryside not to allow it control over the land.

In themselves the Bolsheviks did not offer more chance of success than their predecessors, so it was the circumstances that took them into power. Liberalism, given its chance, simply failed.

- The war went badly.
- The peasant land seizures were neither recognised nor opposed.
- Food supply and inflation remained a problem.
- There was no solution offered to the nationalities problem.
- The constitution did not emerge in time.
- Opposition was not channeled into parliamentary form nor effectively suppressed.
- The Soviets remained a rival to the government and the issue of Dual Power was allowed to persist.
- The danger of a military coup in September made the government reliant on organised workers and helped the Bolsheviks to regain the position weakened by the July Days.
- There was also evidence of popular support swinging to a Soviet type of government which the Bolsheviks seemed to support.

Lenin and Trotsky offered effective organisation of a take over and effective propaganda, so in that sense they did provide perhaps the best-organised opposition of any in the period. But that alone would not have led to success, and after taking over Petrograd on 9 October 1917 they were faced with massive opposition and survival could not be taken for granted any more than the brief successes of the Opposition of 1905.

ACTIVITY

Why was the authority of the State maintained in the face of opposition before October 1917, yet not after October 1917?

Opposition to the new Bolshevik regime

Lenin inherited the power of the Russian state. The opponents became the rulers. Just as with the Tsars and in contrast to the Provisional Government, opposition to the new regime failed.

Once having even nominal power, Lenin had many of the advantages of the Tsarist regime in 1905–6 and during the reigns of Alexander II and III. Basically these were the divided aims and limited organisation of their opponents and the repressive power of the state. The ex-opposition showed a remarkable ability to learn from their former oppressors.

Lenin and his successors overcame opposition from the following elements.

1   The White armies formed of a variety of opponents from Tsarists to Liberals, together with foreign assistance from Britain, France, America, Japan and the Polish army.

2   They faced nationalist resistance from elements within the Empire which had broken away and peasant armies. They also faced local peasant resistance to requisitioning of agricultural products.

3   They faced a so-called workers' opposition by 1921 and an uprising in the naval base of Kronstadt

4   During the 1920s there was internal criticism of the NEP by members of the so-called 'left opposition' and when the policy changed after 1927 there was criticism in the party by the 'right opposition'. However, after 1921, opposition was more like the 'loyal opposition' of a democracy. The critics of policy did not want to see basic regime change, as had been the case of much of the opposition under the Tsars. However, Stalin did not accept the concept of 'loyal opposition' and criticism was dealt with in the same way as if it was the more deadly opposition of the Civil War period.

5   More direct opposition to policy came from peasant resistance to 'requisitioning' and collectivisation and one of the biggest internal struggles of Russian history resulted.

6   The sheer scale of upheaval provoked some criticisms within the party but these were dealt with brutally after 1934.

7   The Second World War brought some opposition from within in terms of groups and individuals hostile to Stalin collaborating with the Germans

8   Opposition also came from parties opposed to communism in the USSR's satellite states in the west after the take over by Red Army forces from 1944. After the destruction of opposition in 1944–49, opposition flared up again in Berlin in 1953, in Hungary 1956 and, just after the end of the period, in Czechoslovakia in 1968.

The only success achieved by any of this internal opposition was the removal of Khrushchev in 1964 by his rivals in the party. This did not bring dramatic changes to the regime or the levels of repression it exerted over the USSR. It was a 'palace revolution' comparable to those seen in Tsarist times.

KEY IDEA

Certain key themes emerge:

1   the divided nature of the opposition and the lack of a unifying ideological element; and

2   the strength of the state and thirdly,

3   the failure of foreign support.

Stretch and challenge

1   Taking a broad view, why was opposition between 1921 and 1964 so unable to achieve the success of 1917?

2   What parallels, if any, exist between post-1921 resistance and the years of futile resistance between 1855 and February 1917 and why?

Unity and division 1918–1964

The divisions among the White armies during the Civil War, which broke out in 1918 as the implications of the Bolsheviks' take over were realised, are a key reason for Red victory. The Whites had an uneasy coalition with a considerable diversity of aims.

- There were opponents of the **Treaty of Brest-Litovsk**, the very unfavourable peace treaty which Lenin accepted from the Germans in March 1918.

- Also there were those who resented the rapid dismissal of the elected Constituent Assembly in January 1918.

- Then the military leaders – Denikin, Yudenich, and Kolchak – were not in agreement with their political allies and the intervention of foreign armies made the command structure even more disunited.

- The Japanese forces seemed more intent on expansion of territory than in pursuing ideological aims or keeping Russia in the war; so even among the allies there was little unity.

- Added to this was the emergence of nationalist movements whose aim was to break from the Russian Empire and peasant forces eager to defend their gains from the land seizures of the summer of 1917.

The Treaty of Brest-Litovsk

This was signed between the new Bolshevik Russian state and Germany, Austria and Turkey on 3 March 1918. Trotsky was forced to sign away to Germany Poland, the Baltic Provinces, Finland, the Ukraine and the Caucasus. Finland, Georgia and the Ukraine were made independent. There were large reparations. Russia lost vital manufacturing and food producing regions. Lenin agreed because he thought that world revolution would make territorial changes meaningless.

There was geographical disunity too. The Whites faced huge problems in communication as they occupied the areas around central Russia. Whereas the Reds had the advantage of interior lines of communication for their armies which occupied the most industrially and agriculturally advanced areas of Russia; they were unified by ideology and the clear aim of defending the socialist revolution, not replacing it. The Whites would not have agreed easily, even if they had won, on what form a new Russian state would have taken. The Bolsheviks could rally supporters round the reforms already announced, particularly the Land Decree of November 1917 (*see* page 89). Peasant support for a policy which seemed to confirm them in the lands taken was a major factor in securing unity.

Therefore the unity of the party was vital to Red victory during these very dangerous years of Civil War and the war with Poland that followed. Lenin stressed it with his 'Ban on Factions', strengthening the authority of the party in 1920.

Socialist unity

It was this emphasis on unity as the ultimate goal of socialism that made opposition difficult. An assassination attempt against Lenin (the attack was admitted to by Fanya Kaplan, an SR terrorist, though it has been suggested that the person who fired the shots was a man called Protopovov) removed the dissident so-called Left SRs, as there was a backlash against internal opposition. After the **NEP** in 1921 there was a determination that

NEP

The New Economic Policy was where Lenin allowed private trade by the peasants and by smaller manufacturers in contradiction to Marxism. This was seen by many in the party as a retreat to Capitalism in order to maintain power.

economic diversification should not lead to political diversification. So in the name of unity, political control was tightened.

After Lenin's death in 1924 it became increasingly difficult to offer criticisms of the party policy *without* threatening unity. The tradition of the party – secretive, conspiratorial, in theory reliant on discipline, and seeing its aim as destroying enemies – now became a major problem for those who criticised. The Civil War had made unity a necessity, but it was easy to see that Russia was still at war through the 1920s and 1930s. Lenin's vision of world revolution had not happened:

- Western states were hostile to communism.
- The new states of Eastern Europe clamped down on left wing political activity.
- The Chinese communist party was persecuted.
- Russia was in relative isolation and, as in Tsarist times, the concept of loyal opposition was not well-established in the party any more than it had been in the Russian Empire.

In the discussions about policy after Lenin's death, the critics of NEP, Trotsky, Zinoviev and Kamenev, were not able to sway the Politburo and in the name of unity, they lost their positions (*see* Fig. 2.3). Despite their key roles in the history of the party, they lost power and Trotsky was forced out of the country. The so-called Right Opposition fared little better. Nickolai Bukharin (Fig. 2.4), the Bolshevik intellectual, and friend of Stalin, who had supported NEP was in his turn forced out. Power became concentrated as once again the party saw itself at war – this time not with foreign powers and White armies, but with its own peasantry.

Figure 2.3   A 1927 cartoon image ridiculing the United Opposition. Trotsky is the organ-grinder; Zinoviev is the singer and Kamenev is the parrot.

Figure 2.4 Nickolai Bukharin 1888–1938. This leading Bolshevik intellectual, wrote the *ABC of Communism*, 1920. He supported NEP and Stalin's policy of *Socialism in One Country* and opposed Trotsky's demand for rapid industrialisation. But when Trotsky was exiled, Stalin turned on Bukharin and the Right Opposition, expelling him from the Politburo in 1929 and subsequently having him tried and executed.

The strains of the battles for requisition of supplies and then collectivisation were so intense that the strictest unity was needed. There was opposition from the peasantry – but there was no political leadership to organise it and localised resistance was crushed. Within the party there was unrest about the methods and results of this massive campaign, but here again the party traditions and the need to show solidarity were overwhelming barriers. The 1934 party conference was the nearest to actually opposing the leadership or expressing criticism until 1956, but Stalin's supporters were more united and could use the considerable power of the party against them.

Stalin's power increased so vastly partly because of the fragmented nature of opposition to him within the party and USSR. Political opponents could hardly link up, as Lenin had done so cleverly, with agrarian discontent. After the Second World War, opposition within the new USSR faced similar problems. The different political groups in the **Satellite states** experienced similar issues to the Whites in the Civil War, as well as facing the overwhelming military power of the Red Army.

Also, the external situation – this time the Cold War – meant that unity was once more needed. The USSR could never relax its efforts and a solid front was needed. This benefited those in power and meant that opposition could not be tolerated or built into any political system. It had to be crushed. Protests such as those in East Berlin in 1953, which were more about economic conditions, were seen as a threat to revolutionary unity and met with the overwhelming force which Russia could bring to bear on opponents. The same was true of the **Hungarian revolt in 1956.**

Satellite state

was the term given to countries dominated by Russia in Eastern Europe but who were nominally independent. These were Poland, Rumania, Bulgaria, Hungary, East Germany and Czechoslovakia, collectively known as the Eastern Bloc.

The Hungarian revolt – a point of comparison, Budapest

On 23 October 1956 police fired on demonstrations in Budapest against Gerö, the secretary of the Hungarian Communists. Demonstrations grew and troops joined the opposition who reinstated the former premier Nagy. Soviet troops, which had occupied Hungary since 1944, were forced out. Russia then sent in more troops in November 1956 and the revolt was suppressed with 3,000 deaths and 200,000 Hungarians fleeing to the West. Khrushchev had been uncertain about using force, but was fearful of a split in the Soviet Politburo and among the leaders of the other satellite nations. He was also aware that the west was distracted by divisions about the Anglo–French invasion of Egypt. Without foreign help the Hungarians, who were divided and militarily not a match for the Russians, could not win. There is a parallel with the Polish revolt of 1863 (*see* page 47).

Had the discontent in the Eastern bloc been coordinated or as widespread as it was in 1989, then the situation might have been different, but the revolts remained confined to individual areas. Discontent in Poland never linked to that of Hungary or East Germany.

It could be said that Khrushchev both benefited from the need for unity and also suffered. His rift with the Chinese Communists (1958) was seen by some as dividing the Communist rule and is one of the reasons for the 'coup' among the top leaders which removed him in 1964.

The strength of the state

Before 1918 the Russian State had offered considerable obstacles to opposition. Censorship; the use of spies and informers; the existence of a secret political police, and in the end a massive army and bureaucracy. Also the church offered spiritual support for autocracy. Lenin inherited a lot of this in 1918 and war offered opportunities to increase repression. State action against opposition became *more* violent, not less. The Tsarist state had resorted to executions, but a good many of its opponents faced exile rather than death. Lenin and his successors were less restrained. The activities of the Cheka exceed those of the Tsarist Okhrana and its predecessor the Third Section. Under Stalin the state came to have an unprecedented repressive apparatus which attacked not only real opposition, but also imagined or potential opposition. This was applied to the new empire after 1945 and, though the apparatus was reduced after Stalin's death (1953), it was still a well-established element of Russian life to 1964 and beyond.

The lack of foreign help

The only time that foreign powers intervened to assist opposition movements was during the Civil War. The Polish revolt got no help in 1863; the Hungarian revolt of 1956 got to help. The German invasion of 1941, which could have come to liberate opponents of Stalin, instead oppressed and tyrannised; regarding all Russians as slaves or surplus population to be killed off. Foreign powers were adept at expressing disapproval of Russian tyranny, in the press if not officially. The Tsars had bad overseas reputations, but foreign capital supported them – especially French loans after 1905   because Russia was needed as an ally. This rather than any humanitarian or deep ideological conviction motivated the allied interference in 1918. Foreign help had an adverse effect on the Whites. It made them seem disloyal and unpatriotic. It allowed Bolshevik propaganda to show the Reds as Russian heroes standing against foreign tyrants. The peasants feared that foreign armies would restore the landlords. Japanese incursions into the east of Russia, as far as Lake Baikal, encouraged the view of the homeland being under attack and gave the Bolsheviks, hitherto

seen as internationalists in the pay of Germany, a different image as defenders of Mother Russia. This was very similar to the effects of the German invasion in 1941. Stalin could be seen as another Ivan the Terrible or Alexander Nevsky – a Russian patriotic leader – making opposition to him even more difficult.

The anti-Communist propaganda common in other countries both before 1941 and after 1945 offered more problems than opportunities for opposition. Opponents were often accused of being foreign spies. Foreign powers did little to assist opponents, apart from sheltering émigrés and arguably increased the likelihood of tyranny. Russian participation in international affairs might have acted as a restraint on persecutions at home, but apart from a brief period between 1934 and 1939 Russia was not really part of an international community. It was not cultivated seriously as an ally against Hitler which increased isolation and distrust.

The exception to this trend was 1941–45 when Russia's reputation stood high in the West among some leaders and among some of the general population. Ironically, this too led to problems for opponents. In 1945 the Yalta agreements were made to return those who had fought against Stalin on the German side, sometimes for strong political or ideological reasons, to imprisonment and death in Russia. Churchill was prepared to concede a considerable Soviet influence in Eastern Europe to Stalin; territorial changes in Poland made resistance there to the imposition of Soviet rule difficult. There was little inclination to use Western military power to insist that agreements made about free elections in Eastern Europe were actually kept. Opposition to the Soviet imposition of power was not given effective support and by 1947 the Americans had shifted to merely containing Russian expansion – nothing had been done to actually stop it before 1948.

Anti-Communist rhetoric and policies like the **Truman Doctrine** strengthened Soviet control over any potential opposition. Again possible opposition within the party in Russia – the party offered the only outlet for criticisms of policy even in a limited way – was crushed in the Leningrad affair of 1948 (*see* page 52). Even oblique opposition such as artistic expression, that failed to have the correct political content, was crushed.

The Truman Doctrine

On 12 March 1947 President Harry Truman announced that the USA would support free peoples who are resisting attempted subjugation by armed minorities or outside pressures. This was accompanied by aid to Greece, then fighting a civil war against Communism. It was a clear message that the US would 'contain' further communist take overs.

Stretch and challenge

The beginning and the end of the period.

In a unit that encourages a synoptic approach, it is often helpful to consider the situation at the beginning and end of an extended period: to look at continuity and change. Before you read the analysis (page 73), which you may or may not agree with, consider what *you* think had changed between 1855 and 1964 in making opposition easier or harder and consider what had changed or remained the same in the power of the Russian state to deal with opposition.

The West had failed to use its nuclear monopoly to exert pressure in support of opposition in Eastern Europe and lost that advantage in 1949. Having done nothing when action was possible, it was not likely to offer support to resistance in Eastern Europe when action might have led to nuclear war. The East Berlin protestors of 1953 gained Western sympathy as did the Hungarian rebels of 1956 and later the resistance in Czechoslovakia, but as with Poland in 1863, nothing was offered. The West sympathised with persecuted churchmen; it welcomed defectors; it offered Cold War rhetoric, but this strengthened the hold of the

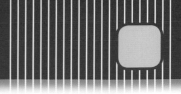

Soviet State over its enemies in rather the same way that the Tsars had been strengthened in their determination to suppress opposition by the willingness of foreign countries to accept political refugees and to criticise autocracy.

ANALYSIS

An analysis to consider

In 1855 Russian political opposition lacked an effective unifying ideology. Liberal ideas deriving from the French Revolution appealed to a limited number of people; revolutionary ideology did come in from exiles but was fragmented. A desire to end autocracy was stronger than any consensus of what to replace it with.

In 1964 this had not changed. The revolutionary certainties that had inspired opposition in 1917 had gone. The regime seemed stagnant and corrupt, but the consumerism of the West and the Cold War rhetoric had not made western liberal democracy an attractive proposition for opponents. There was a desire among exiled opponents and those who had been driven underground for an end to the restrictions of the system, but no real consensus, again for a Russian replacement – this became very evident when the events of 1989 brought an end to the regime but no real agreement of what should follow.

In 1855 there was little practical possibility of opposition bringing substantial political change. The autocracy was firmly founded and had a strong ideology – divine right. Opposition was fragmented and the repressive power of the state well established.

In 1964 this was still true. The Lenin and Stalin eras had established the power of the state even more successfully than the era of repression under Nicholas I. The ideology was all-pervasive and even stronger than the Tsarist ideology because of modern techniques of propaganda and repression. In 1964 as in 1855 opposition had been driven abroad or was underground.

In 1855 there were some forces for change within the Tsarist establishment, though they found it difficult to effect change given the largely conservative nature of the main pillars of the regime – the army, bureaucracy and church. In 1855 there were reforming impulses – some in the party saw the need for incentives, such as greater consumer goods and there had been a relaxing of repression. However, just as liberal elements in government had no wish for democracy or to destroy autocracy, no one in the Communist party wished for free elections or an end to the Communist power monopoly. There were too substantial conservative forces, as in 1855, within the party bureaucracy and the army. The church was no more, but the Communist state was a sort of religion for many which acted against possible opposition.

Lastly, in 1855 opponents within Russia and its empire might expect change as a result of war against foreign powers, but not from the direct influence of foreign powers on the Tsars. No Napoleon would emerge to bring liberal reforms to old Europe. Prussia and Austria had a vested interest in seeing a divided Poland. Britain and France were concerned with their interests the Near East, not in reforming Russia. In 1964 there was more opposition to the nature of the regime from abroad than there had been in 1855, but little indication of any attempt to do more than restrict the spread of communism where it affected the interests of the West.

In 1855, despite the weaknesses and instability of the regime and its reliance on outdated political concepts and a backward and restrictive economy, opposition to it faced huge problems. In 1964 the situation was much the same. Behind the façade of Soviet power, the regime lacked a modern economy and had fallen behind the West in a similar way to 1855. What had changed was that the opposition ideals of 1855 had been tried out and found to be seriously problematic in a Russian context. Perhaps the exiles and opponents of 1855 had more hope.

ACTIVITY

Summarise this analysis, listing your points in one column of a table with your own judgements in the next column.

- What facts support or refute the points made.

- How far do you agree with the judgements?

Conclusion

In this chapter you have moved from a general overview to more specific consideration of the state and opposition and how the state's relations with its subjects changed over the period. You should have developed your skills in comparing different periods and considering a theme over a longer period. It is important to have formed clear judgements, even if you change your mind when you revise the major topics in preparation for the A2 paper.

The impact of the dictatorial regimes on the economy and society: Russian agriculture

3

The impact of the dictatorial regimes on the economy and society is the focus of this chapter which will concentrate on agriculture and rural Russia. The State made a huge impact on the living and working conditions of the mass of the people in this period, and changes decided by rulers had huge implications for the personal, political and religious freedom of millions of Russians

Geographical continuities

Agriculture was a major part of Russian life in this period. The changes and their impact on rural society were enormous, but there were certain underlying factors that ran through the period. Firstly, the climate: with long cold winters, a sudden and vibrant spring and hot wet summers, there were limitations imposed on Russian farmers. The large expanses of waste land; the unsuitability of much of Russia, whether under Imperial or Soviet rule, for cultivation and a limited urban market all had their impact. Generalisation is difficult because Russia remained the only one of the great Empires not to have disintegrated by 1964 and there were huge regional variations. A photo album of the late 19th century reveals scenes in Russia's outlying provinces that had not changed for centuries (*see* Fig. 3.1 a, b).

(a)

(b)

Figure 3.1   (a) Women and children harvesting (Russian Collective Farm, *c.* 1930). (b) Moujiks of the Black Earth district of Yurieff, Ukraine, before the revolution of 1917.

Nomadic tribes yet to adapt to fixed agriculture were not uncommon in the Far East whereas in the Black Earth region there was a much higher degree of agricultural sophistication. Where urban markets and development in transport acted as agents of change, then the generalised picture that is sometimes given of a backward peasantry lacks truth. However, there were plenty of areas where farming was primitive in 1855 and even by 1964 productivity was still low by Western European standards. Certain aspects of peasant life exerted pressure against change throughout the whole period; but the state was a considerable force for change. The ability of farmers to avoid change was far more limited

75

in this period than it was, say, in France to the west or India to the east. This gives rise to the big question of whether the Russian peasants were better off under the Tsars or the Commissars as well as the extent of continuity and change through the period.

> ### Key Questions:
>
> - Did Tsarist or Communist Russia have the greater impact on the peasantry?
> - Were the farmers better off under the Tsars or the Commissars?
> - Was the continuity more significant than the change during the period?
>
> These are important questions and may well be best considered by looking at the problems which led to changes and the impact of the changes. Policy towards the peasantry was to a large extent dictated by the analysis of problems of production in a large country with severe restrictions on the land able to be cultivated. Other influences – political and ideological – were important, but at the root of the choices facing Russia's rulers during this period was the need for the land to feed the cities, support industrial progress and sustain a great military power. Doing nothing was rarely an option for Russia's rulers when it came to the land.
>
> In this chapter you will be invited to think about the changes to the living and working conditions in agriculture between Tsarist and Communist rule. You will also be encouraged through exercises to practise the skills of thesis development and essay-building.

An overview of the period

> ### ACTIVITY
>
> What follows is a general overview of the period. After reading it:
>
> 1 Draw up a time line of the main changes in agriculture 1855–1964.
>
> 2 Frame an initial thesis about whether change in agriculture was greater under the Tsars or the Communists 1855–1964.
>
> This thesis may not be one that you stick to after further reading and thought, but it is a starting point, and will help you when you read the rest of the chapter and look at more sources of information.

The peasants, who had been technically unfree, were emancipated by the Great Reforms of **Tsar Alexander II** (1855–81). This reversed a policy of personal serfdom that had been in force since the 16th century.

However, the reforms while ending personal serfdom did not end many aspects of Russian agricultural tradition, particularly the Mir or commune. Much as the black slaves in the USA were technically free after their emancipation of 1863 but in practice tied to their former owners by sharecropping, so redemption payments following the Emancipation Act of 1861 restricted the individual enterprise of the peasants. Productivity and investment were low and famines such as the horrifying one in 1891 remained a constant of Russian life. There were major changes in the reign of **Nicholas II** (1894–1917). A new approach was attempted after the 1905 revolution in which the countryside had erupted under pressure of land hunger. Stolypin attempted a modern solution to the land question by encouraging land purchase. The Mir (commune) had been abolished and peasants were freer to migrate and encouraged to consolidate holdings and make improvements. It was not unlike British policy in Ireland, and the revolutionary leader Lenin for one saw it as a major danger to any potential revolution if a conservative peasantry could be created, loyal to Tsar and Church. Whether the war interrupted a development towards capitalist agriculture and a new class of wealthier peasant – the so-called **Kulak** – or whether the idea had limited appeal to a peasantry traditionally wedded to communalism and temperamentally unsuited to private enterprise can be debated. By 1915 peasants were returning to the commune. They suffered huge losses in the war, but there is little indication that they were any more wedded to the state than they had been as serfs. The state was seen as an alien institution taking men and horses for the Tsar's war. The great desire was for land. When demand rose for agricultural products during the war, much was withheld to ensure a good price. The larger picture of a national cause was not much in evidence. When the Tsar abdicated in March 1917 it was as a result of urban discontent, failure in war and divisions among the governing classes. The peasant masses looked for land – something offered them by the Social Revolutionaries and, after April 1917, by Lenin.

When **Lenin and the Bolsheviks** took over in October 1917 the peasants faced another ruling group with whom they had little in common; their support was won by a decree redistributing land and by fears that the White forces would restore the landlords. In many areas during the Civil War peasants formed their own forces to fight off both sides and hold on to their newly gained land.

The Bolshevik state proved more ruthless in taking the resources needed for war than the Tsarist state. Resistance was met with violence and the countryside was ablaze with burnt crops as peasants defied requisition. By 1921 Lenin was ready for compromise and the New Economic Policy reversed the requisitioning and attempts at collectivised agriculture that had come about under pressure of war. Between 1921 and 1928 the Russian peasantry at last farmed their own land for profit. However, there was little large-scale investment, low productivity and a tendency to small-scale agriculture. There were still poorer peasants resentful of richer neighbours.

The Bolsheviks, like the Tsars had to engage with the problem of an agriculture that was too backward to provide for urban needs and generated too little capital to allow for industrial growth. Like the Tsars they had little sympathy for peasant aspirations and regarded peasant policy as the means to wider political ends. Under **Stalin** there were major changes. In 1928 there began the second Russian Revolution. The disparity between agricultural and industrial prices because of the failure of large-scale industry to grow quickly enough necessitated a massive seizure of grain. This had to be used for foreign currency to finance industry and also to ensure food supplies. It was resisted violently. The policy developed into a full-scale Collectivisation of agriculture.

Not only was this the biggest change in Russian agriculture since the imposition of serfdom, but also it was the greatest change imposed on any country in the history of the world. Because of the policy of ruthless modernisation that he pursued, Stalin was called 'The Engineer of Human Souls', although masses of the Bolshevik party activists were also unhappy about NEP and its compromises. The Soviet state had developed a great repressive apparatus since 1917 and it was turned with full force against the bulk of the Russian population with short-term results which were so catastrophic that it is difficult to grasp their scale. In Tsarist times the peasants had tried to go to war against the state; now the state was going to war against them.

Kulak

peasants who owned their own farm and as a result were strongly opposed to communist Collectivisation. The term 'kulak' literally meant 'fist' – the idea was to encourage a sturdy Russian peasant middle class to stand between the state and the masses. Under Communism it came to mean 'tightfisted'.

The Red Army and Communist party activists descended on the countryside and resistance was met with repression. Richer peasants were denounced by their poorer neighbours and deported or killed. Crops were burned; seizures of grain were so extreme that a man-made famine was created in the wealthiest regions. Cities starved and cannibalism was once again noted in some regions, as it had been in 1921. Despite a halt in 1930, the process was remorseless. Perhaps it had to be.

In some form or other the bulk of Russian agriculture was collectivised by 1935. The loss of life, crops, and animals was still being felt in the late 1930s. The battle was reflected in a growing inwardness in Russian life and is connected intimately with the political purges of the later 1930s.

The Russian peasantry had barely recovered from these upheavals when the German invasion swept into western Russia. Millions were drafted into the forces, millions were killed: in German occupied areas there was huge damage. After the war, Stalin saw his pre-war policies vindicated by victory and the three-pronged policy of political repression, massive industrialisation and collectivised agriculture was exported to the new empire in Eastern Europe. The Russian peasantry having endured massive burdens to support the military and bureaucratic apparatus of the Tsarist state now had to support an even bigger establishment, as Russia became a Super Power. But being a Super Power did not mean its lands were any more productive or that Russian agriculture became much better. Central planning could not solve its problems and by the time of Stalin's death in 1953 even within the party the need for change was seen. The model of the 1930s was simply not working.

Much was expected from **Khrushchev** as the first peasant-born Russian leader. It was almost as though there had been a full circle return to the 1860s offering the peasantry more freedom in economic terms while retaining the power of central government. Like the reforms of Alexander II though Khrushchev's reforms shied away from the political changes that would have created the freedom in which agriculture might have prospered. Instead, despite the reforms in the running of Collectives, central planning remained the dominant philosophy. The Virgin Lands scheme, a huge plan to cultivate marginal lands in Kazakhstan, was testament to the folly of imposing grand plans on the countryside. When Khrushchev fell, the state of Russian agriculture still remained a major problem to be addressed.

The Russian peasant, 1855–1964

The position at the start and end of the period

In considering a long stretch of history, it is sometimes a good idea to look at the situation at either end of the period. In 1855 and 1964 there were a considerable number of *similarities* in Russian agriculture.

- In contrast to more developed economies, land was extremely important relative to other forms of production and lifestyle. Well over 90 per cent of Russians were rural in 1856 and still by 1964 over 40 per cent lived and worked on the land. In both cases this was higher than Britain, France or Germany.

- The inhibiting factors to farming prosperity that existed in 1856 were still there by 1964. The short growing season, the high levels of wet weather; the arid conditions on so much land in the south and east and the waste lands of the north.

- Both in 1856 and 1964 individual enterprise was restricted by communal forms of agriculture – the traditional peasant communities and the large estates of Tsarist Russia and the expanded Collective farms of the Soviet era.

- In terms of modern technology and methods, Russia was relatively backward in both 1856 and 1964. Its market opportunities were limited by the organisation of society as a whole which in neither case was free either politically or economically.

- The personal serfdom of 1856 which affected millions of people had been replaced after 1861 by a political serfdom which restricted the ability of the rural population to organise, move, express views, buy and sell property, and operate an economic free market.

- In both 1856 and 1964 the rural population were forced to support a top-heavy civil service and military; both bore the burden of the Russian state wanting to maintain a large empire and to be a world power.

- What seems likely is that in 1964 as well as 1856 the state was seen as alien, oppressive and predatory. In 1856 its police and army reinforced the power of the landlords; in 1964 its police and army reinforced a system that offered little to the peasantry.

However, there were considerable *differences* as well. The experience of rural Russia between 1856 and 1964 was so astonishing and so terrible that there could not be complete continuity despite the similarities of climate, geography and the organisation of peasant life.

- In 1856, before the Great Reforms of Alexander II, there was a level of lack of personal freedom that even the greatest excesses of the Soviet era could not match. Whatever talk there can be of a serf state under Stalin and his successors, this is a figure of speech not a reality – the household serfs in the estates of 1856, the 'souls' bought and sold, the personal bonds that linked the 'little men'; to the landlords, the church and state were not the same as the political and economic tyranny exercised by the Soviet state.

- In 1856 there was more variation in rural life than was true by 1964. There were huge cultural differences within Empire. There were variations in landowning and obligations; the distinction between 'state peasants'; the serfs of the monasteries; the private serfs of landlords; the household serfs. The different systems in western Russia meant that the conditions of serfdom varied far more than the regulation of the Collective system thanks to years of the most brutal centralisation by Communism.

- In 1856 the bonds of religion were far greater than in 1964; though in 1964 the influence of political ideology was much greater. Illiteracy and superstition characterised peasant life to a far greater extent than in 1964.

- In 1964 electrification, mechanisation, greater communication and far more links with the urban centres had reduced the isolation common to peasant life in 1856.

- What may have been a major feature of 1856, however, was less prevalent in 1964 – hope. The Tsarist period as a whole saw some expressions of hope for a better life: for land, for modernisation, or at least for eternal salvation. The experiences of the 20th century may well have undermined that hope. By 1964, with the failure of the only leader of Peasant origin that Russia had had, the prospect of nuclear warfare, the seeming inevitability of continuing Communist rule, and with the degradation of traditional religious life continuing, the only hope rural communities had of self-betterment lay in the channels offered by the Soviet system. These centred on a move from rural life to urban centres; on technological progress and growth and an escape from a depressed and depressing lifestyle.

The Russian Orthodox church and rural life

Figure 3.2   Religious Life Picture: A Religious Procession 1861 (Vasily Perov).

The Russian Orthodox church was one of the state's greatest supports and a key feature of rural life. In the later 19th century there was a major religious revival. The church had not been helped by being firmly under state control since the reign of Peter the Great (1689–1725). However, there was a movement for more 'God Seeking' at all levels of Russian society in the later Tsarist period. In the cities it took the form of more religious writings, meetings, discussion and prayer groups and an interest in spiritualism. In the countryside it took the form of a revival of pilgrimages and interest in holy places, mystic occurrences, speaking in tongues and apparitions. Monasticism revived and despite the growth of science, urbanisation, industry and literacy, there was little evidence of religious decline. There were 1000 religious houses with 95,000 monks and nuns in Russia by 1914 and over 80,000 churches and chapels. The state did not recognise other religions such as Buddhists, Muslims, Catholics and break away Orthodox groups, but apart from outbreaks of anti-Semitism, other religions were tolerated.

The events of 1917 had a major impact on religious life. Many of the revolutionaries resented religion which was seen, rightly, as being one of the mainstays of the Tsarist regime. The church was also a major landowner and so a class enemy; it stood in the way of progress through industry and was a supposed enemy to modernisation. However, the major factor that made it a direct political enemy was the church's support for the Whites. In the Lenin period perhaps 1200 priests were executed; church lands were nationalised and properties confiscated. Practising Orthodox Christians were excluded from the Communist party and there were educational campaigns against the church, equating it as an enemy of the people.

The 1920s, though a period of concession to the rural population, did not see political or religious freedom. There was a special section of the OGPU (secret police) devoted to undermining religion. As Collectivisation was imposed on the countryside, there was an intensification of religious persecutions with perhaps 130,000 priests arrested and 95,000 killed. Churches were requisitioned or demolished and by 1939 only 500 existed.

It has been suggested that traditional religion was replaced by the religion of industrial growth, with great new factories as its cathedrals. So, when the famine of the early 1930s devastated rural Russia, the peasants were deprived of the consolation of support from organised religion. However, religion was not entirely stamped out in the way that alternative political activity was. Religious life was possible; traditional worship was still possible. There was a greater degree of continuity here than, say, in political or economic life in the countryside. The church accepted the regime in 1927 when the acting head of the Metropolitan Sergeus Stragorodsky issued a declaration agreeing that church and state, though separate, should cooperate. When Russia was invaded by Germany in 1941, the state turned again to the church. Many churches were reopened, priests were allowed to hold processions, weapons were blessed and, for the first time since 1925, the church was allowed in 1943 to elect a Patriarch (the official head of the church). Though much less than in Tsarist times, the church's support for the state and people in time of war was a feature of Russian life. By 1957 there were 22,000 active churches. Considerably less than 1914, this was nevertheless higher than in the 1930s.

Case study: Changing attitudes to the Russian Orthodox church

The Church of Christ Saviour, Moscow

Under Khrushchev (1956–64) there was a renewed persecution which was by and large maintained by his successors. Not nearly as severe as the period 1917–41 it nevertheless reduced the number of churches. to less than 7000 An interesting case study is the Church of Christ Saviour in Moscow. This huge cathedral was built to celebrate the victory over Napoleon in the reign of Alexander I. It was destroyed in 1931 and Stalin's plan was to build a new Soviet Palace. The war prevented progress and the site became an open-air swimming pool. Then after 1997 it was totally rebuilt and reconstructed and is now one of Moscow's major tourist sights.

2 The projected Palace of Soviets

1. The destruction of the original Church of Christ Saviour

3 The swimming pool at the same site in Moscow

What was special about the peasantry in this period?

Firstly, their relative size – they were for most of the period the bulk of the Russian population. Secondly, the way that they were the subject of state-inspired change, massive social engineering, huge reform programmes and massive interference by the state-characterised Russian agrarian life; far more than that of any other European country. In many European countries economic change affected the farmers; this was also true of Russia. In many European countries, there were significant state interventions, but not to the scale of those of both Tsarist and Communist Russia. In the 1950s and 60s Communist China was to offer policies which affected more people because of the sheer size of the rural population, but the Russian peasantry is probably unique in being the subject of so much change in this period as a whole.

Problems and solutions

The problems facing Alexander II in 1856

What was Serfdom?

The 51 million serfs in Russia in 1856 were not citizens, but property. They were allowed to live in exchange either for rent or service, but had no rights to the land they worked or to any personal freedom. If they worked directly in the manor house and lands of their owners they were little different from slaves and were often mistreated. But most were not in this category. Most were tenant farmers who paid rent either to private landlords, monasteries or the state. The Census of 1858 shows the following.

- Privately owned serfs – 20 million.
- State peasants – 18 million.
- Serfs of the Imperial Family – 2 million.

The privately owned serfs lived on large estates – 80 per cent on estates of over 3000 acres. Thirty per cent of privately owned serfs paid rent while 70 per cent performed service in return for land.

The state peasants were not legally free – in theory all land and all people belonged to the Tsar. They were bound not by service to the state but by a poll tax and rents. A government department imposed restrictions of movement and occupation, and they were closely supervised. In practice, their position was not very different from the many privately owned serfs who did not do personal service to their masters but paid rent.

Serfdom was not a declining institution in the mid-19th century. Nor was it centuries old. It reached a high point not in the 16th century where it had its origins, but in the late 18th century when the alliance between serf-owning landlords and the state became stronger. As late as the 1830s and 40s landlords were active in taking over former royal lands and enserfing peasants. In the 1830s in Simbirsk province alone 350,000 people became privately owned serfs with greater burdens.

So Alexander II did not face merely legalising a decline that was already in progress. What he faced were a number of linked problems. First, state peasants – those who owed obligations, usually rent, to the Crown – were deeply in debt and could not bear the burden of taxes and rents. Second, there was a great deal of discontent among private serfs about obligations and conditions which had resulted in increased disturbances. The Crimean War had seen a big increase in rural unrest. The government had called for peasant volunteers which aroused hopes that a general emancipation would result. Rumours of freedom led to mass migrations of serfs. Even in prosperous areas where rent and not feudal obligations were common there were mutinies, riots and mass flights of serfs (Table 3.1).

Table 3.1 Police records show the following growth in peasant unrest.

Year	No. incidents
1826–29	85
1830–34	60
1835–39	78
1840–44	138
1845–49	207
1850–54	141
1854–58	245
1859–61	180

Armed force was employed 185 times between 1856 and 1860 which makes the situation akin to a peasant war. The peasants were often reacting to increasing oppression by landlords in increasing duties and rents and transferring land from peasant use to the direct cultivation by the landlord.

However more was at stake than law and order. The Crimean War had shaken confidence in the monarchy. A poorly-led foreign expedition had managed to land in Russia and take a major fortress. Russian counter attacks had not dislodged the French and British. Though Russia had destroyed the greatest army in history in the French invasion of 1812, it had not been able to avoid a humiliating defeat by much smaller forces in 1853–56. The conclusion was that modern states with developed industry supported by modern agricultural methods had been superior. The critics of serfdom, who saw it as keeping Russia in a sort of mediaeval state of decay, now seemed to be justified. Not that the bulk of landowners shared the view, but the Tsar reluctantly did. The emancipation of the serfs was carried out unwillingly. The Tsar stated to the nobles in April 1856,

> 'It is better to abolish serfdom from above than to wait until it will begin to abolish itself from below.'

What measures were taken?

In July of 1858 a Royal Decree freed the serfs owned by the Imperial family in their own right. Then in February 1861 the Emancipation Act abolishing serfdom on private estates was signed. It was issued in March 1861 and came into force in 1863. State peasants were emancipated in June 1863 and the final legislation was issued in 1866.

The main principles of the Act were:

1 the freed peasants were to become the proprietors of land;
2 they were to be allotted land to enable them to support themselves and their family and to pay taxes to the Imperial state;
3 the state compensated their owners at a fair price, and
4 in return received payments from the liberated peasants (Redemption Payments).

So reform came as a response to a near-crisis situation, but also as a response to distinct ideas about modernisation. A slave society could not provide the industrial base that a modern state needed; it could not provide the thriving middle class that would ensure well-educated administrators, engineers, soldiers that would keep Russia as a great power. As well as the reform of the land, there would have to be reform of education, administration and law. This would be pointless in a slave society. So the reform of the land was the key to much wider changes.

What were the effects of emancipation?

In practice, the allocation of land to the new peasant proprietors who were former private serfs often meant a reduction of existing holdings. Many families were left with less land or much poorer land to work as 'free' peasants than the land for which they paid rent as 'serfs'. Seven hundred thousand former manorial serfs or military serfs got no land at all. Though former state peasants did better, all peasant farmers were hit by a rapid population growth. The 50 million rural population of European Russia in 1860 had reached 86 million by1900.

There was a massive grievance about land loss or inadequate distribution. The new holdings often consisted of the poorest land and did not contain the balanced elements necessary for successful farming – pasture, water, forest and arable land. The sustained redemption payments – spread over 49 years were a burden and by 1870 only 55 per cent of peasants had even been able to start to pay to redeem land. The value put on the land for redemption purposes was generally higher than its market value. So the peasant payments were seen as too high.

Taxes on the peasantry both indirect and direct continued to be high. Tax collection was often brutal and forced peasants to sell grain quickly and too cheaply in order to meet payments. This depressed peasant incomes and reduced the amount available for investment. There was a big increase in arrears (debts). For the taxes and payments made, the peasants gained little in state benefits. The bulk of taxation went on military expenditure. Industrial growth did not begin to offer consumer goods until the 1880s and the state exploited the peasants.

The peasants did not gain free title to their land. This was given to the peasant organisations set up to oversee the cultivation of the land and to collect taxes and payments. The **Mir** dominated peasant life. Free physical movement was restricted by a passport system. Collective decisions were made about crop growing. The only way to change holdings to adapt to circumstances was through the Mir. Not individual cultivation but *household* cultivation was the norm. The Mir was a collection of households, not individuals. The peasants were not even full citizens and so had their own courts. The individual was restricted by his family, then the communal organisation, and then the state.

The reign of Alexander III saw a tightening of authority with Land Captains established to oversee the Mirs. With restrictive controls, low levels of investment, a great deal of subsistence farming still done in traditional strips, and with heavy pressure from population growth, it is not surprising to see evidence of hardship. The long-term problems of agriculture needed more resources to be put into farming if a larger population were to be fed. Instead there was famine. That of 1891 was particularly brutal. Famine reappeared in 1897 and again in 1901.

Source

An agricultural conference of 1902 received this analysis from Saratov province:

The low productivity of peasant farming shows the general economic sickness of the peasants. There has been chronic starvation and there can be no question of peasants financing agricultural improvements. Taxes, year in and year out, suck out of the peasants an enormous share of income and the state does nothing towards economic progress.

ANALYSIS

Since 1855 the Tsars had freed their peasants, and the abuses of personal slavery had ended. However, the nature of the 'liberation' had resulted in low levels of progress. The state continued to oppress by taxation and redemption payments.

The bulk of the food and raw materials for the market came from the landlord's own estates. Industrial growth could not rely on a mass peasant market; the peasants faced land hunger, resentment and increasingly frequent famines. If the Russian state were to be able to sustain economic growth and expand its military capacity, and if it were to avoid massive peasant protests, then a reconsideration of its peasant policy would be essential.

The causes and consequences of Agrarian Reform after 1905

These also parallel the changes in 1856.

- War, this time against the Japanese 1904–05, had once again revealed weaknesses and stirred up existing discontent in a similar way to 1856.

- At the last major wave of unrest in 1861–63 there had been 1100 outbreaks. There were over 7000 outbreaks in 1905–07 following a build up since 1902. So major rural unrest was a common feature, but unrest was more significant by 1905 and was also accompanied by major revolts in urban centres which had not occurred at the time of the Crimean War.

- Before 1861 and 1905 there had been calls for agrarian reform, respectively by the radical intelligentsia before 1856 and by the Socialist Revolutionary party, which championed peasant land redistribution, before 1905.

- In both cases there were reforming ministers (Witte and Stolypin) prepared to take the lead; in both cases the Tsar came reluctantly to change.

- In both cases agrarian reform was part of a wider package of measures which nevertheless fell short of total political change. Alexander II did not go as far as a national parliament in his reforms; Nicholas II set up a parliament but restricted it very severely. In neither case did the peasants get a chance for political expression of their grievances.

- In both cases not only violent disturbance but also a concern to increase productivity and to use agriculture as a basis for industrial and military growth acted as a motive for change.

ACTIVITY

What impact did the policies of Alexander II have on the Russian peasants?

Write no more than a paragraph. You will need to compare this with the impact in other periods, so it may be helpful to write your ideas on a card and to begin a series of cards with key ideas for different periods.

The key problems and changes of 1906–10

Witte, the reforming minister who advocated the creation of the Dumas drafted a bill to abolish the Mir but it was carried out by his successor Count P. A. Stolypin (Fig. 3.2). Stolypin hoped that a new enterprising class of peasant farmers would emerge. However, after Stolypin's assassination in 1911 rural reform continued under Kokovstov and credit should also be given to agriculture minister Krivoshein for measures usually solely attributed to Stolypin.

1   Redemption payments were ended in 1905.

2   1905 saw an end to peasant passports and the peasant was seen as a citizen for the first time.

3   The Imperial Land Decree of November 1906 became a full law in 1910.

4   Any member of a Mir could demand that legal title be transferred to him and he could consolidate his strips into one holding.

5   He could pass the property freely to his heirs.

6   Where Mirs had not re-divided the holdings since 1861 they were dissolved and land distributed to the farmers as individual holdings.

7   The head of the household, not the household as a whole, now owned land.

8   Some 2.8 million households out of 12 million converted their titles to private ownership (though lands could still not be sold except to another peasant and could not be mortgaged).

Figure 3.3   'The government has wagered on the strong and the sensible.' Count Stolypin on the Imperial Land Decree of November 1906.

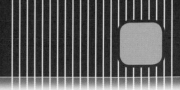

In addition there were:

- grants for new agricultural schools and research stations; loans for improvements;
- the power of the Land Captains of 1889 was reduced;
- migration to new areas of settlement was encouraged and over 2 million migrated 1906–09;
- the crop area of Siberia and Kazakhstan doubled from 12–24 million acres in 1906–14, and
- the Peasant Land Bank was extended in 1905–6 (*see* Chapter 4, page 109).

What were the effects of these changes?

The effects were uneven: they favoured the better off peasant able to take advantage of state loans and an expanding urban market. Migration was far less after 1909 and new farms tended to be smaller with the move towards private ownership peaking in 1908 and falling off subsequently. Large estates still provided the bulk of food actually marketed and there was still an attachment to collective agriculture – as shown by the growth of peasant cooperatives.

The political power of peasants was restricted by electoral changes to the Duma. There was continuing rural unrest and the growth of the Socialist Revolutionaries as the largest revolutionary group, largely because no move was made by Stolypin to redistribute the large noble, church or Imperial estates – the peasants were essentially redistributing their own land. Increased population still meant land hunger and larger profits made the lack of land even more frustrating.

So was this bout of reform more successful than that of 1861?

- There was an increase in production of some 27 per cent between the late 1890s and the period 1909–13.
- Russia became the leading world grain exporter.
- Agricultural prices rose which provided incentives for growth while the wages of hired labourers rose at a higher rate – encouraging a greater rural market.
- There was a growing use of farm machinery. Factory production of farm machinery grew from 13 million roubles in value in 1900 to 60 million in 1913.
- The census of 1910 found a big increase in iron ploughs in place of the less effective wooden ploughs.
- There was a significant reduction in illiteracy. Fifty-one per cent of men could read and write in 1897 and 82 per cent in 1920 (the figures for women are lower at 22 and 47 per cent). This somewhat neglected figure may show one of the greatest changes ever in rural Russia.

The very considerable increase in both industrial growth and military growth in the period may indicate that Tsarist Russia was able to use its main source of wealth without preventing agricultural growth. The greater amount of industrial goods available provided an incentive; there was a developing rural market; there was a growth in both production and productivity.

The debate – an analysis of the success of the policies – must be seen in the light of an ongoing debate about whether the reforms of late Tsarist Russia were limited and illusory or real and extensive. The agrarian reforms seem to have brought real improvements and

ACTIVITY

To build up an overview of the period, do a card similar to the one on the reforms for Alexander II on the changes after 1905. This time, on the back, try to summarise elements of continuity and change.

there is a case for the peasantry being better off in this relatively short period than in any other time between 1856 and 1964. There was a lack of political freedom but there was at least the hope for greater development. Lenin saw Stolypin as one of the greatest practical barriers to immediate revolution while at the same time creating a sort of capitalist farming which in the long run would build up a Russian middle class which would form the capitalist society that the proletarian revolution was destined to destroy. In terms of comparison, the 1861 change was more fundamental in ending serfdom, but the impact on prosperity, productivity, development and potential were probably greater in the 1905–10 changes. As war interrupted the development so much must be speculation. But in a sense the greater confidence that economic change gave to the Tsarist regime was a cause of the war, so perhaps the reforms brought disaster.

The revolution: the Land policy of 1917–21

ANALYSIS

Consider this analysis in light of the information below (pages 88–89) and how far you agree with it.

The November 1917 decree was the greatest change so far to Russian agriculture. 1861 had brought freedom; 1905–10 brought the possibility of efficient development; 1917 brought a massive redistribution of land and was the starting point of subsequent tragedy. No modern industrialised state could be sustained on the basis of an agriculture organised on the basis of the 1917 redistribution; no modern state could maintain a defence capability on the basis of the 1917 arrangements; no Communist state could be based on small-scale peasant proprietorship. The changes of 1861 and 1905–13 promised more beneficial developments whatever their shortcomings. The massive land grab of 1917 offered little chance of long-term development given the circumstances that Russia was in after 1917.

Why was change needed in 1917?

Again change had emerged from war, but this time war had not just thrown up the need for modernisation. Instead war had brought the fall of the Tsarist regime and the institution of an extreme revolutionary party whose philosophy was based on the theory that the industrial working class led by its vanguard representative should dominate Russia and, indeed, the world. The war, by its disruption of transport, its demand for men and horses, and the loss of 10 per cent of Russia to foreign occupation, had disrupted agriculture. But external circumstances, not necessarily the inadequacy of farming, had led to shortages of food.

With limited numbers of workers to offer support, Lenin adapted his theories and took over the Social Revolutionaries programme. Without peasant support he could not stay in power so one of his earliest decrees was the 1917 November Land decree.

What was Bolshevik policy?

It was unashamedly practical. Lenin wrote,

> 'We must follow life itself; we must give complete freedom to the peasants to proceed with agrarian revolution in their own way.'

Wholesale land seizures and attacks on landlords followed by a sort of primitive redistribution at village level were *not* in line with Marxist theory.

In the summer of 1917, as had been the case before the reforms of 1861 and 1905–10, there had been massive disturbances on a much bigger scale. In practice, there was little Lenin could do but to acknowledge land seizures with the decree of the 8 November.

The decree of 8 November, 1917

- Private property in land was abolished.
- Land could not be sold or leased.
- There was to be a massive reserve of land from which farmers were entitled to a share provided they farmed the land themselves.
- The form of land tenure was to depend on the peasants themselves, and so varied from area to area.
- So the peasants farmed the land, but they could not own it – the land was the property of the people and in a people's state that meant that it was administered for the people by the state.

In 1916 28 per cent of Russia was owned by large private estates, 2.5 per cent by the Crown, 64 per cent by the peasants and 7 per cent in public domain. In 1917 the state kept 3–4 per cent of the land for experiments in communal farming and the rest went to the peasants in practice if not in theory. Though there had been a lot of peasant-leased land before 1917, the revolution ended these payments. This, rather than increased size of holdings, was the key factor.

Another key factor was the smaller size of holdings: 43 per cent of farms were under 5.4 acres, 72 per cent under 10.8 acres. Most households had few livestock; for example, 60 per cent had only one horse.

Given that most commercial agriculture before 1917 had been undertaken by the large private estates, given the huge cost of the war to horses and transport and given the relative backwardness of Russian farm machinery and scientific knowledge before 1914, it is difficult to see the developments of 1917 as anything else but disastrous for food supply. Within months the government was resorting to confiscations of food, fixing prices, controlling trade and conscripting peasantry. Class war erupted as government-created committees of poorer peasants began raiding the supplies, personal property and equipment of richer neighbours. If all property can be distributed, then it follows that those peasants with more land were as vulnerable as the dispossessed nobles. Requisitioning under the so-called 'War Communism' often went as far as confiscating seed grain as the Communists tried desperately to defend themselves in the Civil War.

By 1921 the crop area had fallen by 20 per cent of the 1917 level. Armed units of up to 45,000 men were battling with the peasants for supplies as regular market distribution had failed.

Lenin produced a more socialist policy in November 1918: collective farms and a model charter had been drawn up. In 1918 975 were set up, a further 2000 in 1919 and only 156 in 1920. By 1921, 600,000 out of 100 million peasants worked in collectives. But the organising principle and the very name –**Kolkhoz** – had been established. State run farms (**Sovkhoz**) were also established: there were 4,400 by 1921.

Kolkhoz (kollektivnoe khozyaistvo)

or collective farm. These were distinct from the pure state farms (Sovkhoz) in that peasants pooled their holdings, livestock and tools and worked and lived communally, but were still peasants. They had some land of their own, though the farms were managed by state officials and the state provided machinery through the Machine Tractor Stations.

What were the results of these changes?

- Peasant farms were more equal than ever before.
- Large-scale private farming had largely gone and there were efforts to replace this vital sector by state run communes or farms with limited success.
- The peasants had achieved their ambition or land but state intervention was again a barrier to their full enjoyment of it: requisitioning, taxes, heavy political control were features ranged against them.
- Productivity was low and production had fallen. The decline of industry or its diversion to war production had reduced farm machinery; there were few incentives to do anything more than grow enough to support the household.
- There was a huge tension between actual practice and Marxist theory. The party had waged war on the peasants to get food.
- The peasants had shown a remarkable ability to organise armed resistance in some areas with the so-called 'Green' armies which resisted both Red and White forces.

Why was further change necessary?

By 1921, Lenin faced very similar challenges to Alexander II and Stolypin.

- There was widespread peasant disturbance – more organised and well armed than before.
- Productivity was low.
- Food supplies to the cities were too low and there was a strong workers' resistance campaign.
- The agrarian sector could not support the industrialisation and military development needed – again war had brought that home. The Reds had won the Civil War, but only just. Defence needed to be developed as it had been in 1856 and 1905.
- The major difference was that Lenin was much more constrained by ideology than his predecessors, but like them he had to sacrifice theory to necessity. It was hard for Alexander II to tackle traditional beliefs; it was hard for Stolypin to try to create a sort of capitalism outside Russian tradition; it was harder for Lenin to be forced back to incentives, private development and free trade when his heart lay with Collectivisation.
- In addition there was the problem of the virtual disappearance of a money economy and the actual decline of industry and urban population.

What was the New Economic Policy (NEP)?

It was the decree of 21 March 1921.

- The State stopped requisitioning grain and other agricultural products.
- A tax in kind, i.e. a previously agreed proportion of what the peasants produced, was taken instead.
- This tax was to be reduced as production increased to provide incentives.
- The rest of what the peasants grew they were free to sell.
- The Land Code of 1922 legalised the peasants' title to the land they occupied while affirming that land as a whole belonged to the people as a whole.

This was similar to the proposals put forward by the Mensheviks in 1920. As Stalin was later to show, a total change of direction could always be justified by reference to Marxist theory. Lenin claimed that the decision was not a retreat but an advance towards the conditions that Marx had laid down for the coming of socialism. Given that NEP also allowed smaller scale workshops to produce and trade manufactured goods, it is difficult to avoid the view that Lenin needed individual enterprise. However this too could be seen as helping to create the conditions of capitalism which should precede a socialist revolution.

What were the results?

Immediately the change could do little to offset the effects of a terrible drought which led to famine on an unprecedented scale, but 1922 saw a turning point. Statistics indicate progress. Acreage sown increased from 192 million acres in 1922 to 291 million acres by 1929. There were modest increases in livestock numbers.

Peasant cooperatives grew from 14–18 million members indicating greater efficiency in marketing, using machinery. The years 1923–26 saw quite high increases in the rate of grain production over the low point 1921–22. Enterprising farmers were allowed to lease land and hire labour more freely and there is evidence of more scientific knowledge being applied.

CONSIDER THIS ANALYSIS

How does this compare with the results of previous changes?

The most direct comparison is with the other period of encouragement of individual enterprise after 1905. But there were more problems. After 1905 the large private estates were still there to provide exports and to ensure production for market (i.e. that grain and other crops would be produced on a big enough scale to provide food for the cities). This was not the case after 1921. By the late 1920s grain exports were falling off; grain production actually fell in 1928 and increasingly the peasants were not bringing their produce to market, but rather turning to self-sufficiency – growing food for their own families. The limited growth of consumer industries and the much higher prices of industrial goods compared with agricultural products meant in simple terms that there was no point in earning money from crops as there was not the possibility of buying much with it except at highly inflated prices. This was the so-called *Scissors crisis* – prices expressed in graph form showed a big gap between agricultural and industrial prices, so individual peasants were to some extent better off.

In the mid-1920s they were not facing the heavy repayments and taxes of the period 1861–1905; they controlled their land in a way they had never done under the Tsars; they did not face famines; surplus population found work in the growing cities and industries.

They were better off, too, than in the period 1917–21. Taxes were reduced and requisitioning squads and civil war were behind them. However, it is doubtful whether they were as well off as they had been after 1905. Industrial growth was greater and markets were better; individual enterprise was discouraged and now looked at with suspicion. Many in the party disliked the kulaks or more prosperous and enterprising peasants in a way that had not been true under the Tsars.

With the growing power of Stalin, with fears for Russia's security and with important sections of the party demanding that peasant produce finance greater industrial growth, the NEP period was based on very insecure foundations.

ACTIVITY

Summarise the changes to agriculture under Lenin on a card. On the back compare changes in 1917–24 with changes before 1914. You are keeping a sort of running total of changes and their impact which will help you to write an essay.

Collectivisation, 1928–41

From 1928, Stalin introduced two major initiatives: the Five-Year Plans (*see* Chapter 4) and Collectivisation. This refers to a number of different elements where Lenin's Collectivisation model was taken up and imposed by force. First was a renewed period of requisitioning. If the peasants would not bring their goods to market, then party activists and armed units would take the goods. Then there was a class war against the kulaks (*see also* page 120, Chapter 4) who were blamed for the problems of low production and shortages. Finally after what amounted to a full-scale war between the party and the bulk of the Russian people, a sort of revived NEP restored limited private trading and some incentives for production for profit, though on a much more limited scale than before. Even these concessions were restricted in 1939.

The key points are the party conference of October 1927 which called for 'a decisive offensive against the kulaks'.

- The fundamental land law of December 15 1928 confirmed this.
- The winter of 1927–28 saw a determined renewal of requisitioning.
- The 16th Party Conference in October 1929 established the Five-Year Plan which set a goal for 46 million acres of land to be collectivised (leaving 300 million in individual holdings).
- Stalin set out more extensive goals in November and December 1929.
- There were extensive procurement raids 1929–30.
- In December 1929 an army of 30,000 activists led a campaign against the peasantry to take grain, destroy kulaks and collectivise farming which went far beyond the party targets. Decrees of January and February 1930 confirmed the policy.
- Possibly 240,000 kulak households were deported. The number of collectives went from 57,000 in 1929 to 110,000 in 1930. By 1933 there were 244,000 and by 1938 242,000 collectives contained 93.5 per cent of peasant households. A limited halt to the process was declared in 1930 but Stalin and many in the party were determined. The greatest change of all in Russian life, which amounted far more than 1917 to a revolution, had taken place with the utmost violence, death and disruption.

What had brought this about and are there parallels with previous reforms?

There are many possible explanations for Collectivisation, but a distinction has to be made between the decision of the Party in 1927 to expand Collectivisation and the first requisitions on the one hand and the subsequent events. The first is squarely in a line of decisions made in response to the problems of providing enough food for the urban population and enough resources for industrial growth and defence. There is considerable continuity of purpose with earlier decisions. For example, the emancipation decision was taken because Russia needed to modernise. The decisions of 1927–28 were taken for similar reasons. The NEP decision was taken to encourage produce to be taken to markets; so were the 1927–28 decisions. The problem was still that Russian agriculture was more backward than that of the West and that small farming units lacked investment and sufficiently high productivity. However, the massive campaign against the kulaks and the breakneck Collectivisation suggest a motive hitherto unknown – the relentless use of power, paranoia and a naked hostility towards the peasantry. Here the parallels end. Stalin's war against the countryside; or as some see it, the Party's assault on the countryside represents agrarian policy on such a huge and violent scale that it is difficult to comprehend, justify or relate to rational policy making.

What was unique?

- The sheer scale of the enterprise and the death and destruction involved.
- The callousness of the regime to the suffering caused. For example the millions of deaths in the Ukraine and the richest parts of Russia's farmlands caused by requisitioning alone which provoked a man-made famine which exceeded that of the Tsarist period of 1921–22.
- The irrationality of labeling peasants 'kulaks' and 'enemies' and restarting a class war in the countryside which took away the most productive elements.
- The belief that somehow large units would emerge as efficient without preparation, sufficient machinery or the cooperation of the farmers.

What were the results?

In some ways, the policies were based on a sound analysis and had beneficial results. The NEP farms were under capitalised and lacked machinery. The only way to supply this was by creating larger units. Tractors were supplied; there was more electrification and Russia did not drift towards low-level subsistence agriculture.

There is no doubt that Industrialisation was a priority. The shortages had created an imbalance between industry and agriculture. Both Bolshevik theory and the practical needs of a growing population for more industrial products demanded greater industrial growth. As it turned out, Russia was threatened by external forces – an expansionist Japan and a resurgent Germany. Without change there would have been danger. The only source of foreign equipment was from food exports and these were maintained in the face of starvation and suffering at home.

The large private estates that had been the basis of commercial agriculture before 1917 had to be replaced and collective farms were the only way. There had been some spontaneous movement towards cooperatives in the 1920s and it had always been society policy to create them. Statistics, such as are available, suggest some recovery by the late 1930s of production to 1928 levels. Grain seems to have exceeded 1928 levels and enjoyed a 9 per cent growth rate between 1939 and 1941.

More negatively, the period most resembles that of 1861–1904 when the state bore down heavily on the rural population in the form of sheer exaction. Procurement prices (the price paid by the state for products it took for sale) were low. Discipline was severe; the farmers bore the brunt of a very large bureaucracy, as in the Tsarist period, and a big military establishment, again similar to the military expansion of the Tsarist period. There was heavy indirect taxation and high levels of control – freedom of movement, occupation, association, expression was curtailed even more firmly than under the Tsars.

The deaths incurred in the campaigns against the kulaks; reprisals by the peasants against the collective farmers; the costs of the famines; the loss of animals and crops destroyed in protest all meant that this was a period of huge human and economic loss.

After 1936 the great purges took their toll on the people who might have helped the peasants most – local officials, experts, academics, scientists, agronomists. The horrors of the **Purges** also affected the peasants themselves.

Purges

The Purges were large-scale arrest and imprisonment, sometimes execution, of a wide range of Soviet citizens thought to be enemies, or potential enemies of the State.

The model constitution for collectives and an easing of restrictions on farming private plots seemed to ease the situation but by 1939 these freedoms been reduced. Even though private production had been important and efficient it was reduced drastically and the peasants were forced to return livestock to the kolkhozes.

Planned cultivation often resulted in inefficiency, especially as skilled managers were in short supply. Mechanisation lagged behind what had been promised. There was little incentive to produce and the sense of loss of land and freedom was overwhelming.

> ## Source
>
> ### A complaint from a member of a collective farm in Smolensk in 1930
>
> This deals with the party records in Smolensk which fell into Nazi hands in 1941 and then into US hands in 1945. This is a record of a 'middle peasant' overheard and reported to the OGPU who kept a record of it.
>
> *'This year it will be bad to live in the Kolkhoz; by spring there will be no grain. If in the future we sow crops according to the plans of the party we will perish from hunger. The workers are increasingly moving to the cities because in the Kolkhoz it is not worth working. We work all year and get nothing. We have no bread and will not get any because they do not allow us to sow what we need and instead give us flax.'*
>
> Merle Fainsod, *Smolensk under Soviet Rule*, pp. 266–67. 1958.

ACTIVITY

On a card outline the main impact of Collectivisation on the Russian peasantry. On the back compare this with Lenin and the Tsars. By now the comparison will be quite extensive, but keep to the main points.

This complaint from a member of a collective farm in Smolensk in 1930 is typical. It is difficult to see the experience of the peasantry in the period after NEP as anything but tragic or to see this as the blackest period for the rural community in the whole of the period. Especially as it was crowned in 1941 by an invasion by a brutal German army whose actions Stalin and his cronies had failed to foresee.

The reforms which followed Stalin's death

The wars since 1854 had been engines of change but the Great Patriotic War apart from bringing huge destruction to a much larger area than had been the case in the First World War did not bring a reappraisal of Soviet agricultural policy (*see* Chapter 5 for the impact of Wars). Heavy industry was a priority. Collectivisation was established in Stalin's new lands and the USSR's satellites. Private farming was tightened and the regulations of 1939 enforced. Labour shortage, a shortage of animals and equipment, low prices for agricultural produce and high prices for consumer goods all added up to conditions in which production and productivity were depressed. In 1945 the total crop area was 281 million. This was lower than 1940 by nearly 100 million acres. The 1940 level had not been reached by 1950 and not equalled until 1953. Though there was recovery, it was relatively slow. The problems were:

- ■ labour shortage;
- ■ excessive resources devoted to heavy industry;
- ■ the low prices for products and heavy taxes amounted again to a levy or tax on the peasants to fund re-industrialisation and a growing military power needed in the Cold War; and
- ■ the failure of ambitious schemes, often based on insecure scientific information.

There was a vicious circle –low prices meant that kolkhozes could not pay their members enough to buy expensive and scare goods; labour was directed more to individual plots whose products sold far more profitably. This left the Collectives lagging behind in production and earning even less. The kolkhozniks (members of the Collective Farms) who could not produce enough on their private lands were driven to supplement their income by outside jobs in an unofficial economy – again reducing the output of the Collectives. Stalin's plans to grow more grasses, to make the collective farms even bigger and more centralised and to plant vast forests in practice made little difference and wasted resources.

ANALYSIS

This was the situation that Khrushchev faced after Stalin's death. The severe repression meant that unlike Alexander II or Nicholas II or Lenin he did not have to face active peasant resistance; but the similarity is the alienation of the peasants and their failure to 'buy into' Soviet aims. Low production remained a problem as it was for Alexander II, Nicholas II, Lenin and Stalin. Unlike these leaders, Khrushchev came from peasant stock and had firsthand experience of village life. Like all these leaders, he was constrained by his outlook. He could not dismantle the Collective System any more than Alexander II could create a really free peasantry or Nicholas II and Stolypin could create a real democracy in which political freedom and economic freedom could feed off each other. Unlike Lenin he was not pragmatic enough to abandon his dogma and boost the one area of the agricultural sector that was effective – private plots. Unlike Stalin he did not take a radical new course to pursue the aims for greater productivity. There is more parallel with Stolypin. He relied on changes within an existing system, but in contrast, the level of success was not as great as the late Tsarist reforms.

The main elements of agricultural change under Khrushchev

- The Collective Farms were made larger. In 1950 there were 121,000 Kolkhoz and 4988 Sovkhoz farms. In 1960 there were 44,000 Kolkhoz and 7,375 Sovkhoz farms. The tendency was to greater central management and the distinction between the communal Kolkhoz and the 'farm factory' Sovkhoz was eroded.

- Higher prices were paid for produce and there was an effort to eradicate rural poverty.

- The distinction between the Machine Tractor Stations and the Collectives was ended in 1958. Machine Tractor Stations had their origins in 1927. They came under the control of the Agriculture ministry in 1930 and controlled all mechanised farm machinery. They developed a large staff and the collectives had to employ the machines and their operators for use on the farms. MTS became a sort of directing force with specialist agronomists and political commissars. They grew from 2,500 in 1928 to 8,000 by 1957 employing 1.7 million workers. These were all transferred to the Collectives to give more decision making and local control to the kolkhozes.

- There were national initiatives – a massive campaign to grow maize and the famous Virgin Lands scheme announced in 1954. Grain production was to be increased by a third by cultivating unused land in Kazakhstan, Siberia and the lower Volga regions. A campaign rather like Stalin's mobilisation of workers to descend on the countryside in

1929 was launched. But here the scale was larger. 500,000 volunteers went west (akin to the size of Napoleon's invasion of 1812!) with huge mechanised resources.

■ Village life was affected by a campaign against the Orthodox Church waged after 1957.

What were Krushchev's successes and failures?

Unlike previous rulers, Khrushchev sympathised with the farmers, visited them and talked knowledgeably with them. The standard of living improved though not to the extent of Khrushchev's promises – four bed-roomed houses did not appear and roads continued to be bad. Procurement prices rose and peasant consumption of consumer goods rose as the state made more effort in that direction. To that extent this era can be compared with the 1920s and the period before the First World War. However, what linked Khrushchev more with the Stalin era was the continued belief in central planning and the 'big idea'. Stalin's Collectivisation, then his extensive 'mega projects' such as the Forestation plans are an example of these large-scale schemes. Khrushchev also believed in big farms and he had the biggest of big ideas: the planting of the Virgin lands (Fig. 3.4).

KEY ///// Area of Virgin Lands

Figure 3.4 The bulk of the Virgin Land cultivation was in Northern Kazakhstan.

The scale of cultivation exceeded anything that the Tsars could have contemplated, but it was based on inadequate knowledge. While investment was needed in transport, it went into the Virgin lands which did boost production in the short term, but not in the long term. In 1956 the Kazakh harvest yielded an impressive 16 million tons of grain. But it was not the success that was hoped for. Huge investment had to go into infrastructure and the soil was not good enough for sustained good harvests. In 1963 there was harvest failure in

Kazakhstan and in the traditional grain growing areas. In the longer term there was some recovery but Khrushchev's enemies saw the bad harvests of 1963 as evidence of failure.

Through the Khrushchev era there was still the gap between rural and urban income that had been a characteristic of Soviet economic life for the entire period. Also the benefits enjoyed in terms of pensions, social security, housing, travel and access to cultural opportunities remained unequal between town and country. Though the farmers did not suffer anything like the violent impact of Soviet rule that had been the case under Stalin, nevertheless the reorganisation of the Collectives and the greater control by the state was unsettling and demoralising.

ANALYSIS

The issue of reviving private plots and establishing incentives remained a talking point after Khrushchev and one of the great unresolved themes of Russian rural policy was how much production should depend on private peasant cultivation and how much on some sort of communal structure. Put simply, the Tsars from 1856–1905 could not be parted from a communal model because it offered a form of control; they feared the peasantry who were deeply alienated from the whole concept of an orderly modern state. After 1927 the Communist rulers came to the same conclusion, whatever the evidence to the contrary, they preferred to see the economic and political necessity of communal control of the peasantry.

For a brief period between 1905 and 1927 individual peasant farming had its chance – but the chance was very restricted by a number of factors. First, the lack of political freedom as a context in which to develop a healthy free economy; secondly the disruptions of war and revolution; thirdly the problems of climate and geography that were constant enemies to production in the period as a whole, and lastly rulers whose ideas of progress depended on using rather than supporting the peasants. A constant feature of the period as a whole is that the rulers of Russia, both Tsars and Commissars were essentially isolated from the rural community, they did not understand its needs, and they distrusted it.

ACTIVITY

On a final card consider the impact of post-1945 agricultural change and on the back compare it with the main periods of change before 1945. *Remember* you are not summarizing the entire changes, but making key points.

KEY IDEA

Turning point

A turning point is an event or circumstance this is such an important change that it is irreversible.

Stretch and challenge

From your cards and from the information and analysis in the chapter you could now attempt three things.

1   Go back to your original thesis framed after the overview of changes. Do you still find this convincing or do you want to change it?

2   Plan an essay based on the cards you have drawn up as you have been reading the chapter. Assess the view that, in the period 1855–1917, the Russian peasants were better off before 1917 than after 1917.

3   Consider which of the periods studied here might have been the greatest turning point.

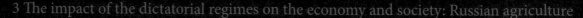

Conclusion

This chapter has dealt with economic and social developments that affected most of the people of Russia. It has considered possible turning points, comparisons between policies and the extent of change and continuity. It is important for you to keep considering these elements rather than seeing a narrative of part of Russian history. It is also important that the developments in this chapter are seen in the wider context of Russia and its Rulers and the changes in government outlined in the first two chapters.

The impact of the dictatorial regimes on the economy and society: Russian industrial development

This chapter deals with one of the major elements of the period 1855–1964, industrial growth and its impact on the conditions of Russian people. Industrial growth brought considerable change to living and working conditions to Russia's urban population in this period; urbanisation brought considerable change and economic developments were strongly linked to issues of personal freedom.

An overview of the period

During this period Russian industrial development transformed the country (*see* Fig. 4.1). Yet some of the changes that industry brought about in other European countries did not occur in Russia. In the West alongside the hardships, particularly of early industrialisation, came diversity of opportunity, a developed consumer market, and a transport revolution which unified the country. Social and political change followed in the wake of industrialisation in Britain, where public policy had to adapt to the needs of an urban and

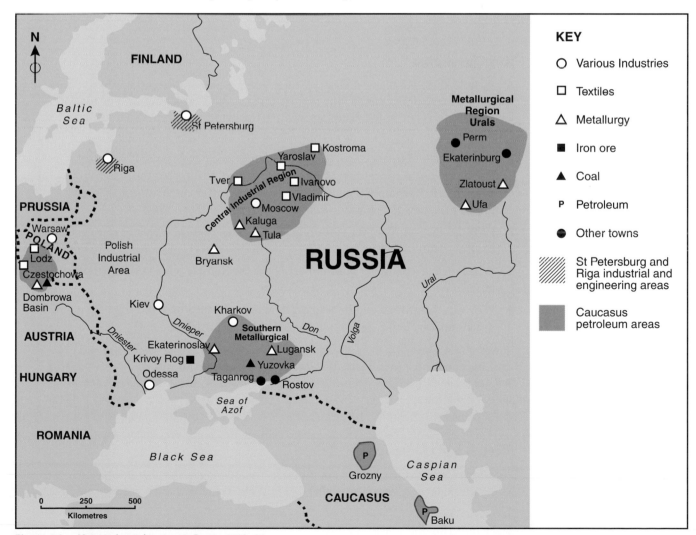

Figure 4.1　Major industrial regions in Russia, 1900–14

industrial society. In even in more authoritarian states, which experienced industrialisation, such as Germany, the SPD (Socialist Party of Germany) a mass political party representing the workers established itself and put pressure on the state for political change. This sort of development did not happen in Russia where working class revolutionary groups, at least until 1905 had no chance for legitimate political activity.

In other ways, Russian industrialisation did have similarities with that of other countries. For instance, the creation of urban slums and industrial areas with considerable health and social problems. There was also the creation of social and political tensions arising from a big growth of an industrial working class.

The recognition by the state of new urban and industrial needs was a feature of Russian industrialisation as well as that of other countries. There was also the impact of growing industrial power on the state's military capacity and its use in war. So Russia's industrialisation did have marked similarities with the experience of industrialisation of other societies.

However, given the practical problems of rebuilding the economy and the theoretical importance given by the party to the industrial working class, it is not surprising that economic development was at the heart of the Soviet regime. The costs in human terms were immense.

Key Questions:

As a whole, then, Russian economic growth gives rise to important questions about whether it met Russian needs. The rapid growth of the Tsarist economy made Russia, along with Italy, one of the fastest growing of the world economies in the late 19th century.

1   What was the significance of this growth for future development? A major discussion point concerns the likely development of Russia if the First World War, the 1917 revolution and Civil War had not intervened? Would Tsarist Russia have developed into a flourishing liberal capitalist state?

2   How did the impact of the second major industrialisation which began after 1928 compare with the first?

3   Which period of industrialisation benefited the Russian state and its people the more?

4   Why was the growth and impetus of industrial development in both the late Tsarist and the Stalin period not sustained in the post-Stalin era?

In this chapter you will be invited to think about the changes to the living and working conditions in industry between Tsarist and Communist rule. You will also be encouraged through exercises to practise the skills of thesis development and synoptic thinking.

Stretch and challenge

Form a thesis about the workers in industrial Russia. Were they better off under the Tsars or under the Communists after 1917? Why? What was the turning point, if any?

Make notes on one side of A4 only.

What marked the characteristics of Russian economic growth under the Tsars?

- Initially it came in large units in a limited area of the country.
- It was not generated from relatively small-scale enterprises by enterprising businessmen using capital generated from a wide variety of private investors.
- It was not sustained by a flourishing and diverse home market.
- It proceeded very rapidly in spurts generated by the state.
- It was very linked to state policies.

What was unusual in Russia in the period as a whole from 1855 to 1964 was that the process needed to be engendered by the state. The developed industrial economies suffered terrible crises and depression as a result of the First World War and the subsequent slump. However, because the disruption in Russia was made worse by a Civil War and because industrialisation had relatively shallow roots in Russia, the nature of industry and the economy changed decisively. There was a decline in industry and trade and the economy became more dependent on agriculture. By the late 1920s it was clear that if Russia was to be a major industrial country again then another phase of industrialisation would be needed. Economies such as the USA, Germany and Britain had not had this experience. There was more state intervention in the 1930s, particularly as these economies prepared for war, but not on the scale of USSR. The divergence between the Russian experience of industrialisation and that of other European countries became considerably greater after 1929.

The impact of this particular history of economic growth separated out the economies of Russia together with those of her post-war satellites (Poland, Bulgaria, Romania, the Baltic States and Czechoslovakia) from the economies of the West once more after 1945. Russian economic losses in war had been considerable – but so had those of Germany. Britain's economy had been strained by war, but had suffered less direct damage. The US had seemed to show that the free enterprise model could supply a modern war with enormous efficiency. However Russian rulers were more influenced by the view that the pre-war industrial changes had allowed the Russian state to survive a long war and emerge victorious. Thus the massive planned industrialisation continued through the remainder of the period. The crucial points were that the economy could not supply consumer needs and sustain the huge demands for weaponry made by the state and that it fell behind in terms of science and technology compared to western economies which experienced high rates of growth. What had seemed modern and forward looking in the 1930s came to seem old fashioned by 1964.

Why was Russian industrial growth so delayed?

There were inhibiting factors about the development of Russian industry which still applied in the beginning of the period. Why was there no full industrial revolution in Russia before the 1880s?

The British Industrial Revolution which had its origins in the late 18th century and was in full swing by the 1820s and 1830s had had all sorts of preconditions that were not present in Russia.

- The availability of capital from developed overseas trade and a strong improving agriculture that grew crops for a growing market.

Industrial revolution

This is when economic growth becomes so powerful that the nature of the economy is changed permanently and there is a self-sustaining industrial growth leading to mass urbanisation.

- The ready availability of coal at various sources throughout the country for power.
- A well developed transport system including coastal shipping, river transport and road links.
- A freedom to develop industrial enterprises, with weak guild control and government interference. Taxes were low and credit available in a developed banding system.
- A developed middle class out of which entrepreneurs emerged and who provided investors and markets.
- An interest in science and engineering among an element of the elite which could provide support for industrial growth.
- A sympathetic attitude from the state.

Instead in Russia in the first part of the 19th century, there was a serf economy with a top-heavy bureaucracy and severe geographical restrictions on transport development which *prevented* a flourishing internal market. Russia had only a restricted number of urban centres and an aristocracy more interested in its landed wealth than in industrial development.

There may have been no full-scale industrial revolution involving a decisive shift in the balance between agricultural and industrial production and urban and rural population, but there were elements of growth in the reigns of Nicholas I (1825–55) and Alexander II (1855–81). This period is sometimes referred to the Free Trade era and could be said to extend from the 1840s to the 1870s.

Relatively limited attention is given to it, but it is worth considering as a sort of base line for the period 1855–1964 as it gives a model for economic development that was not sustained in the Tsarist period.

The Free Trade era – a 'might have been' of Russian history

It is characterised by a good deal of foreign investment in Russian businesses. British industrialists established textile factories in the St. Petersburg and the Baltic regions using exported British machines and management techniques. Engineering works were set up in Moscow. British capital went into establishing major shops. German expertise went into banking and finance. Overseas loans financed the first major railway building in 1842–52 with the Moscow–St. Petersburg railway. By 1861 some 2000 miles of track was laid and this was extended by a further 11,000 miles by 1878, opening up market opportunities in Russia's most fertile agricultural lands in the Ukraine and the north west. Exports rose by 60 per cent in the 1870s offering the chance for capital accumulation. Careful control of imports allowed a native Russian railway industry to develop. Modernisation of machinery in Urals iron and Moscow textiles built on foreign expertise and abundant raw materials. Benefiting from population growth for both labour and markets the industrial and commercial/transport sector expanded to employing, at least for part of the time, 20 per cent of the population and producing 10 per cent of Gross National Product (GNP). By and large this had been facilitated by relatively limited control over imports, by allowing entrepreneurial freedom and by moderate taxation under the finance minister **Mikhail Reutern** who was in office under Alexander II from 1864–78. Seen in conjunction with greater personal freedom for the peasants; a growth in local improvements with the elected Zemstvos or councils; greater academic freedom and more links with European 'progress' after the Crimean War, this period could be seen as one of quite encouraging economic and social development, despite the somewhat 'colonial' reliance on imported machinery,

BIOGRAPHY

Count Mikhail von Reutern (1820–90)

Reutern oversaw Russia's finances during the Great Reforms. He was born in Poreche, Smolensk; helped oversee the emancipation of the serfs in 1861, and was Minister of Finances 1862–78. He disapproved of the Russo-Turkish war of 1877–78 and resigned in 1878.

capital and industrial expertise. It stands in contrast to tendencies in the economy after the 1880s, which showed greater continuity with the Soviet era.

The late 1870s saw Russia hit by a general European economic downturn, by a resort to tariffs in most European countries, including Russia and by the effects of the war against Turkey 1877–78, all of which led to a financial crisis, and the collapse of the rouble. There was also a run of bad harvests in 1878–81 that was to recur in 1885 and 1891.

The state and industry – a pattern emerges for the future

Out of this period of downturn came a determination by key elements in the Russian state to force the pace of industrial change that has a parallel in the late 1920s and 30s. The freer progress of the economy was more apparent after 1905 and after 1921, but the dominant theme of industrial development after 1881 throughout the period was the role of the state.

The changes from the 1840s had not amounted to a real sustained industrial 'take off' such as had been seen, say, in Britain in the late 18th century. This had not been possible in a society where the communal ethos in agriculture rather than developed farming for profit dominated. The Tsar's abolition of serfdom (*see also* page 54, Chapter 2) had not produced an individualistic capitalist agriculture. Urban growth had not produced a strong middle class. There had been a remarkable growth in Russian science in the 1860s but not in the managerial class needed for large-scale industry. Though there was a stock market and there had been a reasonable increase in joint stock companies – 256 registered in the 1870s and 350 in the 1880s – this was not an indication of huge independent entrepreneurial activity, compared to say the USA or Britain. Capital was not being generated on a huge scale from overseas trade, from a flourishing home market, or from agricultural enterprise or exports. The industrial labour force was very much 'part time' and regarded themselves as peasants at heart, sending money back to the farms and having their hearts in the countryside.

Yet external pressures indicated the need for Russia to compete and to be a great power; here is the major comparison with the 1930s. In both periods, the security of the country depended on military developments at a time when rivals were expanding their forces and military technology was rapidly increasing. The wars of the mid-century had showed the economic basis of military power. In the Crimean War of 1853–56 Russia had failed to defeat an invasion of southern Russia by France and Britain. The more advanced economies of these countries had resulted in their being equipped with better weapons. In the American Civil War of 1861–65 victory had gone to the northern States who had a much more developed industry and could supply their armies more easily. The wars which unified Italy (1859) and Germany (1864–71) had shown the very destructive power of modern rifles and artillery and the crucial role of railways. All this depended on a strong industrial base.

Prussia had used its mass produced needle gun against Austria in 1866 and its rifled artillery against France in 1870 to powerful effect. Railways had been the key to Prussian economic leadership of Germany and then to successful movement of forces against Austria and France. Its rise to power owed as much to 'coal and iron' as to 'blood and iron' and now, in any case, it was a question not of iron but steel. The modern economy lay behind a modern army. The fleets were becoming not only iron clad but also steel clad. Russia's navy needed modernisation. Its forces had not swept away the less well-equipped Turkish forces. War once again had revealed inadequacy.

Pressures on the Russian state to boost industrialisation

Russia's need to modernise was not just about defence; it was Russia's mission to be a great power that was felt keenly. Like Britain it had great imperial possessions. Imperialism and a sense of mission was very much a feature of late 19th century Europe. The Far East called; there was the possibility of domination in the Near East and the Pan Slav feelings in court circles meant that Russia had a duty in the Balkans. To fulfill these missions it needed a modern army which could only come, as the 1860s and 1870s experience in Europe and the Civil War in the United States had shown, through a modern industrial economy.

So much of this – a sense of mission, a fear of more advanced countries, a need for modernisation and modern defence seems to project forward to the Stalin era. Common with the Stalin era too was a realisation that 'normal capitalist development' would not provide this growth, or at any rate not at a fast enough pace. What dominated the thinking not only of Witte (*see* Fig. 4.2) but also of Trotsky and Stalin, both of whom advocated rapid economic growth after the 1917 Revolution, was the need for the State to provide a sort of shortcut. For Witte the miracle was to be based on railways; for Stalin the miracle was to come from collectivised agriculture. The difference lay in the theoretical justifications after 1917 and the more practical approach in the 1880s, but Witte was just as committed to maintaining the ideology of an autocratic state as Stalin was to preserving the ideology of the Revolution.

Figure 4.2   Finance Minister Witte, a major promoter of industrial growth under Alexander III and Nicholas II.

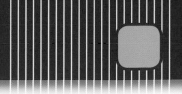

The Witte era

The **'Great Spurt'** is inextricably linked to the policies of Sergei Witte. From a Baltic-German background, Witte was in a sense the product of the previous economic development. He was a successful promoter and builder of railways. Railways were seen as the key to all other developments, but would not be able to be financed from private internal capital on the scale that Witte envisaged.

What emerged in the 1890s when Witte was made Minister of Finance in 1891 was an interlinked financial and economic strategy. However, Witte was more than a financier and economist. In 1893 he wrote,

> *'Russia is destined to dominate not only the affairs of Asia but of Europe as well, with a mission of cultural enlightenment based on those principles which have given to her a special character – orthodox religion, autocratic government and strong nationalism.'*

He told the Tsar in 1899: 'He who does not go forward will, for that very reason, fall backward as compared to those countries which do move forward'. He thought that the different elements of Tsarism might be held together by 'a grandiose economic transformation and by the interests it would foster and create'.

Witte had no wish however to create the same sort of free society that had, perhaps, actually created economic development in Britain and the USA. He had in mind taking the capital, expertise and technical knowledge of the advanced world and using it to promote entirely traditional Russian values and aims. He did not seem to foresee the consequences of modernisation. The later industrialisation was more focused on conscious promotion of *social* change, but shared a desire to retain an essentially Russian value system.

The main elements of economic and industrial growth in the 1890s

Almost all economic indicators show firstly a considerable rate of growth between 1890 and 1900 and secondly that this was sustained up to the First World War (Tables 4.1 and 4.2), indicating that there was take off followed by continued development which are characteristics of an industrial revolution as seen by economic historians and analysts. There is more disagreement about the nature and strength of the developments.

Table 4.1   Some indications of economic growth, 1890–1913.

Indicator	1890	1895	1900	1913
Pig iron production million puds	56.6	88.7	179.1	283
Coal million puds	367.2	555.5	986.3	2,200
Raw cotton million puds	8.3	12.3	16.0	25
Railway building 000 km	30.6	37.0	61.1	70
Imports 000 roubles	406.650	526.147	636.087	1374.0
Exports	692.240	689.082	716.217	1520.1

From a Soviet source in 1950 (quoted in Munting, *The Economic Development of the USSR*, 1982).

The results, in terms of Witte's aims in 1913, can be seen by a comparative table (Table 4.2). The USA's output was far greater, but at this time the aim was to bring Russia closer to her European rivals.

The 'Great Spurt'

was the name given to the considerable growth of industry under Count Witte's guidance. The average growth rate in the 1890s of 8 per cent and the rapid rise in heavy industry, railways and textiles seemed to contemporaries to be more than just normal development and more like an exceptional and sudden 'take off' – hence the term 'Great Spurt', redolent of the spurt of oil from a well.

Table 4.2   Key indicators of economic performance of Russia and other major powers, 1913.

1913 Production	Russia	France	UK	Germany	Austria
Pig iron 000 tones	4635	5311	10 425	19 312	2435
Steel	4841	4687	7787	18329	2685
Cotton spindles	8,990	7,400	55,633	11,186	4,090
World machines (%)	3.5	1.9	11.8	20.7	3.4

From a Soviet source in 1950 (quoted in Munting, *The Economic Development of the USSR*, 1982).

In a way that would not have been true in 1880, Europe saw Russian economic power increasing and the real threat of Russian domination. The German Chancellor Bethmann Hollweg said in 1914,

> '*The future lies with Russia. She grows and grows, and lies on us like a nightmare.*'

He even advised his son not to bother to plant trees on his north German estate as they would only be taken over when the Russians advanced (quoted from Sergei Podbolov, *The State Form and Russian Entrepreneurs* Centre for Russian Studies, University of Ankara).

The growth was much less after a major crash and downturn 1899–1901, but revived after 1905 with a huge alliance between Russian industry and Russian rearmers from 1908.

So what were the main elements of the most dramatic stage of growth in the 1890s?

In terms of a grand strategy, Witte was influenced by the writings of the German economist **Friedrich List** whose *National System of Political Economy* urged the influence of the state to promote and protect growing industries. Witte had no time for the free market and imposed a heavy tariff; he did not think that industry would grow without a considerable intervention from the state. The 'kick start' was to be large-scale railway construction. The capital for this was too great for private enterprise so the state provided it. Witte's most famous railway project was the Trans-Siberian railway– the first plan for a rail link between European Russia and the Far East. However, most of the railway building was in European Russia. The immense scale demanded steel mills for the rails and the equipment; coal and iron would then be stimulated by the demand. As these industries grew so would a host of supporting industries – brick works, cement, and carpentry. The growth of this heavier industry would stimulate consumer industries as wages went into the heavier industry. There would not only be a demand for industrial goods but also for agriculture. The railways would also open up markets for the farmers and this would in turn generate spending on industrial products which could be carried to consumers by the new railways.

BIOGRAPHY

Friedrich List (1749–1846) was a highly influential German economist who recommended the 'National System' in which the state protected industry and helped its development, mainly by putting import duties on goods from other nations. He was the main theoretical influence behind high tariff policies introduced by many countries in the later 19th century and opposed the Free Trade ideas of the economist Adam Smith. But his personal economic management was poor and he killed himself because he went bankrupt.

On the basis of this industrial expansion the state would gain more in taxes and be able to provide better services, modernise its army and pay its debts. Unlike previous expansion this growth would owe much more to state intervention, growth would be on a much larger scale and there would be greater modernisation.

However, unlike previous expansion, Witte's developments involved finding capital for the state to invest. The Russian state was already a demanding one with a large military and administrative burden. On top of this now came railway development on a grand scale. The burden fell on the mass of consumers as indirect taxes were raised; the wealthier classes were spared direct taxation, as their wealth was needed for private capital. Tariffs protected native Russian industries but added to the cost of living. The benefits of railway expansion were long term; in the short term the mass of the Russian people suffered a squeeze on their living standards and thus their ability to purchase goods. Also the state simply could not find the money for spending on this new scale, so Witte turned to foreign capital. Foreign loans came into Russia at an unprecedented rate, but there were problems. The interest had to be paid in a secure medium – foreign currency and a rouble that was firmly based on gold reserves. This meant that grain had to be exported even when, as in the famine of 1891, it was needed at home. It also meant that Russia needed her balance of payments to be in credit. This meant a high tariff on imports. This made vital imported goods expensive. It also led to foreign markets imposing tariffs which restricted income. The imposition of the **Gold Standard** was bitterly resented by the agricultural sector.

Gold Standard

A common belief in the late 19th century was that currency issue should be directly related to gold reserves. Thus gold coins really did have a value (unlike modern coinage) and paper money was printed in strict relationship to the amount of gold. This was to prevent inflation and link currency issue directly to the performance of the economy. It also meant that investors could be happy that the currency was stable. Many countries, including Britain, saw the Gold Standard as the bedrock of international trade, payments and respectability. Witte was signing Russia up to the group of advanced nations, but at the expense of an over-valued currency.

The plan rested on the state stimulating enterprise but with guaranteed state orders. A limited tradition of business enterprise and a workforce lacking skills did not result in a flourishing capitalist economy. The productivity of Russian industry (that is the amount produced per worker) remained much lower than that of the West. The state exerted a greater degree of control than in the West – railways were regulated; there was factory legislation: to earn contracts and subsidies, firms tended to have to be large. So unlike the British experience small-scale business enterprises were not generating a new class of active businessmen, engineers, and salesmen. At the top end, there were few Russian equivalents to the great German industrial firms. There was heavy reliance on foreign expertise and investment and the development of a skilled workforce was inhibited by a lack of technical education. The lack of development within agriculture, thanks to the communes, prevented the development of a broad home market; the industrial workforce tended to regard itself as part of the peasantry.

What was the impact of large-scale economic development on Russian society?

However, the opening up of Russia by railways, the creation of great new industries, the remarkable levels of growth did have a huge effect – but not what had been expected. Greater communication and contact with the West spread political ideas; the sudden influx of workers into the cities without adequate housing and services created huge discontents. The relatively low wages and the high taxes together with poor management resulted in large numbers of strikes. There was no plan to offer political freedom alongside economic growth, and no fall back plan to deal with a possible reduction in foreign markets and trade. The depression of 1899 showed Russia's dependence on overseas investment and it hit the relatively recently developed class of urban workers.

As with all large-scale industrial developments, the new Russian proletariat had to face:

- ■ New work disciplines alien to the rural world.
- ■ A concentration of workers in poorer areas of the big cities.
- ■ Periods of hardship and unemployment.
- ■ Cultural disruption as they adjusted to urban-industrial life.
- ■ New health problems linked to the pollution and the dangerous machinery of the factories.

A fall in trade and lower national income reduced the flow of capital from the state. Progress came grinding to a halt and there was a prolonged depression for which Witte was blamed. He was dismissed by the Tsar in 1903.

ACTIVITY

Compare the account of life in Moscow given by Alan Monkhouse in 1911 and the account he gave in 1932. This is not a document-based paper, but Monkhouse's Book (*see* Sources **A** and **B**) offers an interesting view of change over time.

Sources

 Monkhouse visited Moscow in 1911

'The sanitary conditions existing in these districts were appalling. In these working class suburbs of the cities typhoid and infantile diarrhoea took their toll. As I drove to work daily I seldom saw less than four or five pathetic little processions. Two children usually took the lead carrying an ikon, the other the lid of a small coffin. A bereaved parent plodded behind holding the little open coffin. A weeping mother dragged her feet along the hot and dusty cobbles. Not surprisingly, Woodhouse found drunkenness endemic. On the more positive side are the effects of state factory legislation and the much better conditions among railway workers, but the picture is fairly grim.'

 Monkhouse visited Moscow again in 1932

'Great changes had occurred. The low two-storey buildings had given place to a modern city of six- or eight-storey blocks of workers' flats. There was an eight hundred acre park where tens of thousands of citizens enjoyed relaxation on summer evenings. Planned new factories in eastern Moscow will employ 60,000 workers for all of whom adequate and good accommodation is being built in large apartment houses. A central bakery, schools, factory kitchens and communal dining rooms, clubs, crèches and theatre are already completed.

During the early years of the revolution the city became overcrowded; 30 per cent of population found themselves five in a room and 83 per cent lived eight to a room. Since 1925 large sums have been spent on building modern housing. In 1932 an exhibition was held in Moscow showing plans for housing 5 million people. The city is to be encircled by a green belt beyond which there will be residential districts. There has been an extensive central heating installation. Electric railways leading out to the suburbs are being developed and there are plans for a new underground 'metro'. Compared with 1911 colour has gone from the Moscow streets. The effect of the Five-Year Plan on the people is obvious. No money has been spent in the USSR for many years on good clothing, but there are no longer the beggars on the streets. Good restaurants are little used by the people for fear that the OGPU (secret police) would ask questions about where they find the money.'

Source: *Moscow 1911 to 1933*, published Gollancz, 1933.

The British engineer Alan Monkhouse went to work in Moscow in 1911. He was also employed in the Soviet period and his memoirs of Moscow 1911 to 1933 provide a fascinating analysis of the impact of economic change. By 1911 some 4 million people were employed full time as workers, 2 million in industries, the rest in mines and transport. In addition there were 3.5 million in small workshops linked to village industry. When Monkhouse first went to Russia he confirmed the view that the bulk of the 'workers' were really peasants, retaining their plots of land and sending earnings back to their villages. There would be a labour shortage in the cities in peak times for sowing and reaping the harvests. Monkhouse, who was building Moscow's tramways, was shocked to take on workers at a contemporary British rate of £2 a month, but became aware that rural wages were even lower. Monkhouse was impressed by a well-regulated and large engineering works which employed 35,000 men at Kolomna, near Moscow, even though there was an 11 and a half hour day. Elsewhere he found workers living in crude two-story wooden buildings, overcrowded and without drainage and water supply.

Later Tsarist development

Witte had achieved a huge amount and Russian industrial development was not halted. The infrastructure created during the 1890s was there for subsequent growth. Changes made after 1905 were able to build on Witte's work.

- Agricultural development built on the railway network for the greater marketing of produce. It also built on Witte's policy of a **peasant land bank** and encouraging peasant enterprise.
- After Witte Russian industry was better able to meet problems by diversifying its products. The low taxes on the rich meant that there had been some build up of capital for investment which continued even when foreign capital was less available in the early years of the 20th century.
- There was an available workforce. Despite all the problems, urban wage rates, particularly in the south, were higher than agricultural incomes and were generating markets.
- The financial ministers after Witte, particularly Vladimir Kokovtsov, managed to avoid excessive taxation, even after Redemption payments ceased after the Revolution of 1905.

There had been a severe financial crisis in 1901 and a huge disruption of the economy in the revolution of 1905–06. The government had not devalued the currency and kept the rouble on gold, which had restricted overseas trade, and there had been a large number of bankruptcies in these years.

What is striking is the ability of manufacturers to respond to crises. When railway construction slowed in the 1899–1906 period, a leading Riga firm turned to motorcar and aircraft development. The great rubber factories developed motor tyres and medical equipment. There was a renewed influx of foreign capital to take advantage of a growing home market which was boosted by agricultural reforms and transport developments after 1905. A good example of this is the company 'Harvester', the agricultural machinery company, establishing factories in Moscow. There was an also an expansion of consumer goods, like the gramophone. The urban centres were providing flourishing markets for more consumer goods; the greater market economy in the countryside was offering more market opportunities for a range of products.

> **Peasant land bank**
> This was a special state-funded bank which lent peasants money for improvements at reasonable rates. The idea had been tried with some success in Ireland by the British government.

Russia was developing more of a business and enterprise culture; greater home markets and more diverse foreign investment. In the wake of 1905, when France needed a stable Russia as an ally against Germany, there was a great deal of French investment. However, the major impetus came not from a 'natural' growth, but once more from the state. The Russian fleet, destroyed at Tsushima (*see also* Chapter 5 pages 137) by the Japanese navy, had to be rebuilt – this alone amounted to 900 million roubles of state investment into major industrial enterprises in the St. Petersburg naval building yards. This in turn regenerated the Ukrainian steel industries which had not been able to diversify so successfully. This was also stimulated by a great renewal of railway construction and a lot of building in urban centres. A decline in cotton sales at home was remedied by state subsidies directed towards building up exports to the near and Far East to earn foreign currency.

During the period, additional income tended to be spent more on imports than native manufactures. The domestic market was not providing the stimulus for the continuing growth – instead the state was playing a leading role in:

- railway construction;
- foreign loans;
- a huge rearmament programme – not only the rebuilding of the navy but also a great expansion of heavy artillery and equipment for a growing army, and
- subsidies both to agriculture and industry.

Indeed, Russian manufacturers had come to accept the state plan as a natural part of Russian economic life. The Russian Association of Trade and Industry, which was founded in 1906, did not call for deregulation, but for greater planning. It proposed developing the Magnitogorsk iron deposits, digging a canal between the Volga and the Don Rivers and developing the Turkistan deserts by irrigation. This looks forward to the Soviet era in a remarkable way, as does a proposal for a central planning organisation based on the gathering and analysing of data. This was later the basis of the Communist **Gosplan**.

Where was the economy by 1913?

In 1913 Russia remained predominantly agricultural (Table 4.3).

Table 4.3   National Income in million silver roubles.

Agriculture	4960
Industry	2587
Trade	790
Government generated income	870

Industry had accounted for 10 per cent of national income in 1850; by 1880 it was 30; by 1914 40 per cent. However, industrial rates of growth had not been as great as the statistics for production might suggest.

The proportion of income taken from the very top of society had increased rather than decreased. The aristocracy, the top 1 per cent of the population controlled 6 per cent of national income in the 1850s; in 1905 it was 12 per cent and by 1914 15 per cent. There was little sign of a significant income redistribution which might have put the economy and society as a whole on a firmer footing.

Gosplan

State Economic Planning Organisation, an extension of the overall planning commission set up after the Revolution which made economic decisions and collected data during the Five-Year Plans after 1928.

The finance minister Kokovtsov in his memoirs *Out of My Past* in 1935 saw growing agricultural wealth and a strong industry growing together in harmony,

> '*On these firm foundations, had it not been for the Bolshevik catastrophe, Russia would have continued its swift and powerful developments with the growth of public prosperity.*'

What was the human impact of the change?

First, Russia was on the move: 3.5 million passports were issued in the 1880s and 7 million in the 1890s. Some moved eastwards to new agricultural areas. Most joined the industrial labour force; between 1881 and 1897 some 15 per cent of the population migrated. By 1897 15 per cent of Moscow's population and 33 per cent of St. Petersburg's were immigrants from the countryside. Other industrial centres like Łódź and Ivanovo saw a massive influx from the Baltic regions.

There was some variation in wage rates. In Moscow the average in the 1890s was about 175 roubles per year; further north in St. Petersburg and the Baltic the figure was 230. In the south, in the Donbas region where there was a greater scarcity of labour, the average was 340; in Baku oil workers could earn 360. Within industries, too there were variations – miners did less well than oil workers or engineering workers.

However, growing immigration into the cities pushed down wages; it also created huge problems from lack of appropriate accommodation and services. The Tsarist state made some provision for medical insurance in the 1890s but did not plan effectively for the results of industrial growth.

A survey of 1896 revealed urban overcrowding with four to six people in a bed not uncommon; hasty basic dormitories housed incoming workers. Poor sanitary conditions led to a cholera outbreak in 1896. As with other fast growing areas like Berlin, where poorly equipped tenements housed workers, medical services were inadequate as was the water supply.

In factories, there were harsh disciplines that were hard for peasant workers to adapt to. Fines and beatings were common. The state had to back up factory discipline with increasing numbers of workers coming under the state factory commission.

Harsh living conditions were a feature of many European countries in the period and though the evidence left by observers and writers makes harrowing reading, there must be some balance.

First, Russian population was growing rapidly. The population of St. Petersburg grew from 1 million in 1900 to 2.25 million by 1914. Urban population trebled in the 19th century: the total population grew from 60 million under Alexander I to 140 million by 1914. If industry had not expanded, then the results could have been disastrous.

The Russian state struggled with adapting to a new world of industry, but it did do a lot to encourage industrial growth even if it did not cope with the massive social demands of a new work force. Limited measures of social reform were put into place, but few other European countries produced a massive amount of reform. Workers' strikes were more brutally suppressed in Russia than other countries, but repression of industrial action was common in other countries.

ACTIVITY

Compare economic development in the Free Trade era with that of economic development in the Witte era.

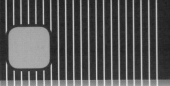

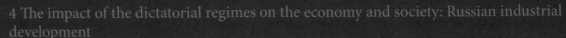
Industrial growth was producing more opportunities and a more diversified culture than had been true of the opening period in 1856 – for the limited numbers able to access it, the late Tsarist period was a golden age of literature, music, theatre, and ballet. It was also a time of intellectual expansion with scientific and technical achievements. The cities offered gardens, galleries, museums and fine buildings as well as squalid industrial slums.

War and the economy

The Russian economy was already strongly influenced by state demands before 1914, so there was not the transformation that affected the economies of some other countries as the state ordered vast amounts of war supplies.

The sectors that were most affected were trade and agriculture. Overseas trade was badly affected – some 90 per cent of pre-war trade had gone through the western frontier which was now closed by war. Exports of grain fell. Imports of machinery fell. The Russian economy fell back on itself; the State had the challenge of balancing resources between purely military needs and the need to keep production and distribution of supplies going. It did not rise to this challenge. Huge numbers of peasants (10 million) and factory workers too were caught up in the great sweep of young men taken into the armed forces– 40 per cent in all. The whole make up of the work force changed.

The appropriation of horses, vehicles and railways for the war effort provided a severe strain on a transport system which was not really well developed before 1914. There was a virtual break down in the market by 1916 with peasants returning to self-sufficiency, transport bottlenecks, and stockpiling of grain. The results were severe inflation. Urban workers experienced food shortages, a fall in real wages, and increased demands to meet the war effort. On top of this were the emotional strains of war and the worsening living conditions in the cities with growing fuel shortages.

The loss of over 5 million men by 1917 also had a huge effect on the labour force in both industry and agriculture.

Pre-war Russian industrial expansion allowed Russia to sustain a huge effort and even to enjoy some success – particularly against the Turks and in the summer offensives of 1916. In this respect it is possible to compare Witte's industrialisation with that of Stalin's, which also allowed Russia to sustain a war effort after 1941. Russia had an industrial workforce of 3 million by 1914 and the impact of industry had made it possible for Russia to take on Germany, Austria and Turkey in a sustained war that was in sharp contrast to the previous wars in 1853–56; 1877–78 and 1904–5. Some valid comparison can be made between Witte's and Stalin's industrial policy here. However, few anticipated the sheer demand for arms.

Russia was capable of making 13,000 shells a day in 1914, but even the early campaigns needed 45,000. The shortfall continued into 1915: 2.4 million rounds of ammunition were being fired, but Russian industry could only supply 320,000. By the summer of 1915 there were complaints about ammunition shortages.

The shortages had to be made up by very large orders abroad and the importation of supplies from Russia's allies. Foreign investment and technology had underpinned Russia's industrial development since the 1840s and this continued to be the case. Even recently industrialised Japan offered to supply a million rifles that Russia could not provide. Neither was the Russian government able to organise arms production effectively and private organisations like the War Industries Committee of 1915 had to step in. However, by 1916–17 the situation had improved (both world wars saw an expansion of industrial production). The industrial work force expanded to 5 million; more weaponry was produced. For example, to meet air raids an additional 149 batteries of anti-aircraft guns were produced in 1917 and Russian aircraft production was able to make 4 engine IM bombers. The distorted image of Russian troops going into battle without rifles was not true by the later stages of the war.

What could not be made up though were deficiencies in transport. Large-scale rail construction, with the exception of the line to Murmansk built by prisoners of war, stopped; resources could not be diverted to make up for what had not been completed before the war. Also the losses in the 500 km retreat of Russian armies in the west in 1915 left valuable resources in enemy hands.

ACTIVITY

It is possible to underestimate the role of industrial production in the First World War. Military expenditure had grown at an unprecedented rate from 5 million roubles in 1908 to 44 million in 1912 and 75 million in 1913. Indeed it probably helped to bring about the war that it was preparing for. What restricted its effectiveness was a lack of infrastructure in transport and a failure in government use of resources.

How far do you agree?

The post-revolution economic development

How far was Communist policy more effective in promoting industrial development and prosperity than Tsarist policy?

Lenin faced similar problems to the Tsarist regime from 1918–21 in that he was fighting a war for survival. Whereas the Tsar began the war in 1914 with an accumulated build up of military power and industrial growth, Lenin faced war with depleted resources – of labour, of capital investment, of valuable resources handed over to the Germans in the peace treaty and with a peasantry whose land seizures had reduced the flow of agricultural goods and raw materials to the market. Unlike the Tsar he could not rely on foreign loans and supplies which instead went to his enemies. The huge industrial resources of the allies were not, however, applied to the defeat of Bolshevism in a way that they had been applied to the defeat of the Central Powers and the decline in industry affected the Whites as well. Unlike the Tsar, Lenin did not rely on empty edicts controlling resources and an alliance with private economic organisations of industrialists. The Bolsheviks ruthlessly controlled the economic resources of the central areas of Russia they ruled. The policy of War Communism could not expand industry but it made sure that its resources were used as fully as possible, while the farmers' products were taken by the state on an unprecedented scale.

By 1921, though, the Russian economy was in a worse state than at any time in the late Tsarist period.

Possibly 9 million had died in the Civil War and the famine that accompanied it. There had been a decline in the number of industrial workers – by 1919 the factory workers were 76 per cent of the 1917 figure and building workers fell to 66 per cent and railway workers to 63 per cent. The industrial population went from 3 million in 1918 to 1,240,000 in 1920. The population of Petrograd fell from a high point of over 2 million to 600,000 by August 1920.

The fall in industrial production was enormous. Oil managed to achieve 41 per cent of its 1913 production, but coal, iron ore and heavy industry fell well below this. Manufactured goods generally were 12.9 per cent of their 1913 value. There were large-scale drop offs in the manufacture of raw materials like hemp, flax and animal fodder. The peasantry fell back of subsistence farming, but even that declined with wheat being 43 per cent of pre-war levels.

On top of these basic economic indicators came disasters which affected labour supplies, demand and the quality of life. Typhus, cholera and scarlet fever were rampant. Pre-1914 medical care in Russia had not been strong; by 1921 medical supplies were in very short supply and disease followed in the wake of malnutrition. The birth rate went into decline while the death rate doubled. The industrial working class, relatively small even in the boom years, was more than halved.

Even Lenin wrote,

> 'The industrial proletariat, owing to the war and to the desperate poverty and ruin, has been declassed and has ceased to exist. Large scale capitalist industry has been destroyed.'(Complete Works, Moscow, Vol 33, p. 65 1920.).

In other words Lenin and his successors faced the unusual situation of having virtually to begin again in the creation of a modern industrial country capable of defending itself.

ANALYSIS

There is a sort of broad symmetry here. From the 1840s to the 1880s, there was an era of Free Trade with limited state control, a greater freedom to the peasantry within a controlled political environment – autocracy, which led to a limited degree of economic development. This was abandoned in favour of a plan for much faster growth rates which involved a greater degree of state intervention, again without political change. From 1921 Lenin embarked on the NEP which did allow a degree of economic freedom, even if the state kept 'the commanding heights' of the economy. Unlike the 1840s–70s foreign investment was not so important, though Lenin once again allowed foreign capitalists and expertise into Russia. Like the earlier period, there was no political change – even though the regime was Communist and not autocratic, there was no question of economic freedom liberalising it. Then when recovery had been achieved – faster than the earlier period because the infrastructure had already been established – a much more radical policy of forced economic growth was put into effect. This was aimed at a faster change, linked to the country's need to defend itself and based on rapid industrial growth not dependent on the slow build up of markets and the capital of NEP. In other words, Communism produced its own version of Witte's Great Spurt.

To pursue the parallel, once again war disrupted the growth. The direct losses of the Second World War were even greater than the First World War. But this time industrial territory, population, and resources were added not lost, and post-1945 Russia recovered more quickly.

The changes brought by NEP (allowing the peasantry to trade privately in return for a payment of tax in kind and allowing smaller-scale industrial enterprises to trade), though the state kept the 'commanding heights' and the infrastructure, for example, electrical power and utilities, unlike the changes in the Tsarist period were brought about by pressure from below. For instance by rebellious sailors at Kronstadt and by the so-called workers' opposition, also by massive peasant resentment and armed revolt. Lenin pointed out that a proletariat working in large-scale industry had ceased to exist and that workers were really peasants and declassed elements rather than a true proletariat. With the stimulus of the market and support from the state there was some industrial recovery. In 1922 production doubled and by 1926 pre-war levels were being reached. However, there were a number of vital considerations.

- Price levels between industrial and agricultural products were very different. Not enough industrial products were being made to act as an encouragement for the peasantry to market crops.

- The most productive sections of industry were too small scale.

- The country faced severe dangers from being isolated in Europe and needed, as before 1914, to boost its defence capacity. This was not possible with the still weak industrial base.

- A party which ruled in the name of the proletariat had to ensure that this class was more numerous than was the case by the late 1920s.

- There was still a shortage of labour in industry, despite huge propaganda appeals for more recruits into the factories.

- There was still a danger that Russia would develop into a peasant country rather than the industrial power which the Bolshevik's view of history saw as the necessary forerunner of true socialism.

Industrialisation was partly a matter of practical economics, partly a matter of survival and partly a new religion – part of the creed of the Bolsheviks. In this way, Stalin's industrialisation had differences from Tsarist industrialisation. It differed in ideological motivation, in scale, in the extent of state intervention, and it differed in the effects it had on Russian life. However, in many ways it was similar in that it rested on the peasantry – in terms of direct seizures of

produce, insistence on agricultural exports, heavy taxes in the form of low official prices for products. The pressure was not so much indirect as in Witte's 'cross of Gold' (the suffering caused by Witte's policy of maintaining he Gold Standard which made imported goods dearer and rested on relatively high import duties and taxation) but direct in the form of confiscation, forced reorganisation into collectives and man-made famines. Industry was being created by accumulating capital from the peasantry: food for the cities and a new labour force by the methods of Genghis Khan rather than Friedrich List.

The Five-Year Plans, 1928–38

The plans had a number of origins, including the hopes of pre-war businessmen for state development of resources and the earlier policies of War Communism. They were originally intended to go to 1942 but were interrupted by the German invasion of 1941.

However the industrial growth they promoted was unprecedented. Industrialisation created a second revolution. They created new disciplines, a new culture and an unprecedented level of disruption to the Russian way of life. They laid the basis for survival in the Second Wold War and post-war SuperPower status. They provided a model for other countries but they also contained the seeds of the destruction of communism. Stalin's industrial policy was unique in the speed and ambition of its changes whilst retaining some characteristics of earlier developments.

Source

In February 1931 Stalin spoke to the Soviet conference of Managers in Socialist Industry:

'The tempo of industrialisation must not be reduced! On the contrary it must be increased as much as it is within our powers and possibilities. To slacken the tempo would mean falling behind. And those who fall behind get beaten. One feature of the old Russia was the continued beatings it got from falling behind. We are fifty or a hundred years behind the times. We must make good this distance in ten years. Either we do it or they crush us.'

Quoted in Munting, *The Economic Development of the USSR*, p. 86, from Stalin CW 1947, pp. 355–56.

Stalin's words can be compared to those of Witte (*see* page 105). Stalin's policy was a remarkable turnaround; in effect he was taking up the policies urged by Trotsky in the 1920s.

What were the features of the Five-Year Plans 1928–32, 1933–7 and 1938?

1 An increase in control and discipline in the workforce. The power of the manager was strengthened and the influence of trade unions and workers committees reduced. Absenteeism and idleness were met with dismissal and loss of housing. The working week was lengthened and Sundays eliminated. Criticism of unrealistic targets was seen as a political offence. The Tsarist workbooks were reintroduced to keep a record of workers' performance. These had to be taken to any new employment.

2   Heavy industry was targeted at the expense of consumer goods until 1938. The aim was to reduce dependence on foreign imports which had been a feature of Russian industry since the 1840s. Large-scale enterprises were encouraged, as in the Great Spurt. However there was a great deal more direct state construction. Some 1500 large-scale industrial enterprises were built.

3   New sectors of industry were developed that had not been strong in the 1920s – machine tool production, car and tractor factories, large-scale aircraft production, chemicals, turbines and generators, high grade steel, synthetics like rubber and artificial fibres.

4   There was development of the East as a metal and oil centre for the first of time

5   Communications, which despite Witte and his successors lagged behind the West, were developed and roads, railways and canals were built.

6   There was a growth in urban centres with existing towns extended and new towns built. There was considerable construction of housing and new public buildings.

7   As had been originally suggested by businessmen in the Tsarist era there was a considerable collection of data and the establishment of a central planning agency to establish norms and check targets.

8   There were changes in working practice such as the introduction of piece-work (i.e. payment merely for items produced), the control of labour, the reintroduction of internal passports and the setting of ever increasing norms. All these forced progress.

9   Propaganda was used to encourage production, for example the **Stakhanovite movement**.

The results of this massive and sustained effort could be seen easily in terms of new factories, electrification, growing cities, a much larger industrial workforce, and improved communications. The posters, literature and party speeches made industry a sort of new religion. The old Russia of the backward countryside was assaulted. There was a continuation of the pre-1914 migration to urban and industrial centres which changed the structure of society. The party united the nationalities with the centre far more by industrial changes. A proletariat was created and the countryside was industrialised by collective farms, so that the justification for Bolshevik rule was established.

The Stakanovite movement

This was one of the greatest propaganda ideas of Soviet Russia. Alexei Stakhanov was a miner in the Donbas region who supposedly produced 102 tons of coal in 6 hours in August 1935. This was used in a campaign and 'shock brigades' of workers called Stakhanovites were established to push up production. Bitterly resented by other workers Stakhanov became a symbol of industrialisation. He died in 1977 at the age of 71 after a career in mine management.

Table 4.4 This shows economic progress under Stalin by looking at key indicators – aspects which economists consider when assessing overall growth an development. (Milliard = 1000 million.)

Indicator	1928	1932/3 plan	1932 real	1937 plan	1937 real
National income milliard roubles 1927 prices	24.4	49.7	45.5	100.2	96.3
Gross industrial production milliard roubles 1926–7 prices	18.3	43.2	43.2	92.7	95.5
Workers in state employment (millions)	11.3	15.8	22.9	28.9	27.0
Electricity m. kWh	5.05	22,000	13,540	38,000	36,000
Coal (million tonnes)	35.4	75	64.4	152.5	128.0
Oil (million tones)	11.7	21.7	21.4	46.8	28.5
Steel (million tones)	4.0	10.4	5.9	17.0	17.7
Pig Iron million tonnes	3.3	10.0	6.2	16.0	14.5
Machine tools (thousands)	2.1		19.7	40.0	45.5
Tractors (thousands)	1.8		50.6	166.7	66.5

ANALYSIS

Statistics, maps, and posters present an image of economic growth that was unreal. However, that was probably the only way to push Russia forward. Of course the targets were not met. Of course a peasant workforce could not acquire the industrial skills developed over a long period in the West in such a short time; of course central planning produced absurdities – inflated targets, bottlenecks, problems of transport and distribution, inefficiency and too much paper work. Of course Stakhanov did not really cut the huge amounts of coal that he was supposed to have done. Huge projects like the White Sea canal could often be disappointing and fail to work in practice. The suffering caused – by the war against the peasants, by the use of slave labour from the prison camps, by harsh discipline and repression – was huge.

Industrialisation depended on myth, propaganda (*see* Figs 4.3 and 4.4), and illusion, but there was probably little alternative. Trotsky was right when he said that 'State ownership of the means of production does not turn manure into gold', but the huge increase in production, in self-sufficiency, in the heavy industry needed for modern war, in the industrial culture of Russia and the opportunities open to its people could not really have come from 'natural' development of capital accumulation from small-scale peasant agriculture, or from a non-existent capitalist enterprise. Nor could they have been allowed to develop over a twenty or thirty year period. The results of that might well have been total conquest by Nazi Germany. The plans of the German state for Russia were clear – a massive reduction in 'surplus population', starting with the mass murder of Jews; resettlement of its richer lands by Aryans and a pool of virtual slave labour in the fields and factories from the racially inferior Slav population. Thus, just as Witte found that continuation of a Free Trade era was an unrealistic option, Stalin knew that a continuation of NEP would not have been possible.

Figure 4.3   Poster: *Civilised life - productive work* (**Gustav Klutsis, 1932**). The message of this poster is directed to members of Komsomol, the Communist youth organisation. They have to set an example of civilised living and productive working. The composition is flatter, more 'socialist-realist' than Klutsis' earlier work. Klutsis has to comply with ever stricter artistic regulations.

Figure 4.4   Poster: *With shock labour we will ensure prompt delivery of the giants of the Five-Year Plan* (**Lyubimov, 1931**). The workers in supply companies, pictured, have to speed up production in order to finish the large factories above in time.

Were the human costs greater or lesser than those of Tsarist industrialisation?

The sheer scale of Stalinist growth was greater as more people were involved in change than had been the case earlier. Also, agricultural changes were deeply linked to industrial development. This had also been true under Witte, but not to such an extent. The massive campaign against the Kulaks (*see* pages 92–4, Chapter 3) which involved up to 5 million people had no parallel in Tsarist times. As far as industrial workers were concerned some distinction has to be made between the first Five-Year Plan and subsequent developments.

The peasants who went into the very rapidly expanding factories of the 1890s faced new disciplines – the set working day, constant application at machines, fines for inefficiency or absenteeism. This was a feature of the early stages of any industrial revolution with a big influx of rural labour used to the changing rhythms of work in the countryside. This was less true of the 1928 period when there was more awareness of industry. Nevertheless there was also a big increase in working disciplines and the part-time peasant-workers that characterised so much of the workforce in the late Tsarist period gave way to a new class of full time workers. The power of the state was deployed more directly in 1928. Punishments were harsher; expectations were higher; failures could be seen as a betrayal of socialism, so the pressures were greater. Workers dependent on state housing, state transport, state rates of pay, and state regulations were more controlled. There could be no easy retreat for part of the year to the village, especially when the villages themselves were being transformed by Collectivisation, hit by famine or the deportation of Kulaks. The secure rural base of the workers of the 1890s had been lost by the 1930s. There was little choice but to adapt to the new world of the factory, especially if workers were drafted into the new complexes such as the famous Magnitogorsk metal works or the new industrial centers in the east.

A more developed proletariat may have developed, but there was a new element in the workforce that had not been significant in Tsarist industrial expansion – a huge element of slave labour from the network of prison camps established by the Communists from their earliest period in power and massively expanded in the 1930s. Already labour problems were being solved by the use of masses of poorly equipped captive labour. The Belomor Canal (Fig. 4.5) was constructed with only the most primitive means – treadmills, picks and bare hands – to make use of this abundant labour and to overcome lack of machinery.

On the positive side, there could be rewards on a larger scale than during Tsarist times. The very basic amenities resulting from an unplanned influx of peasant labour into the Tsarist cities was more a feature of the early stages of an industrial revolution. The workers suffered from severe shortages of food as agriculture was hit by the onslaught of Collectivisation. There was over crowding in cities right through the Soviet era and there was rationing of foodstuffs unknown in Tsarist industrialisation. The gap between Soviet propaganda and an over worked, under fed, harshly controlled, poorly housed workforce was considerable. However, by 1935 bread rationing ended and other basic foods were freed. Food prices fell and there was some improvement in real wages (i.e. what money wages can actually buy). There were more cultural opportunities in the cities and the party offered incentives. The construction of the Moscow Metro while providing employment also signaled to the urban workforce that its needs were being considered. The deliberate high levels of decoration and comfort sent a message that urban life was valued. The greater range of technical sophistication in the industrial development gave opportunities to a wider range of people. The Soviet interest in the arts and cinema as a means of propaganda did not mean that they could not be enjoyed. The barrack-like existence of the urban workforce for many in the

Figure 4.5   Captive labour from Communist prison camps was used to complete The Belomor (White Sea) Canal.

Tsarist era gave way to a more diverse way of life – at least for those not in the barracks of labour camps struggling to survive.

The working class became more skilled and better educated than before, with much higher literacy levels than during the Tsarist era. They were valued in propaganda if not in reality and less of an alien outgrowth regarded with suspicion by the state, as had been the case under the Tsars. The position of women also improved, with their contributions being officially valued and better facilities being provided in terms of crèches and communal restaurants to take away the burden of cooking. Peasant domestic violence was seen as less of a norm when families moved into cities, and the party tried to educate the workforce into more civilised domestic behaviour.

However, the outlets of political and economic protest that had been available before 1914 were not open to workers in the Soviet era. Though the Tsarist police had closely observed, infiltrated and persecuted trade unions, they remained as independent organisations. In the Stalin era they became merely another organ of state power.

Even during the war there had been strikes and protests against conditions. However, the strike was not a feature of Soviet life and worker control of factories was not a reality. The Civil War of 1918–20 and massive industrial growth meant that strict management, not idealistic discussion was the norm.

Tsarist workers often faced chronic instability as trade cycles came and went and there were large depressions, for example in 1901, and big upswings. The diversification of industry after 1905 so admired by economists often brought considerable hardships. The very limited safety measures imposed by the state were poorly enforced and injury could mean starvation. Insecurity was a feature for workers, perhaps offset by the links maintained with the world of the village, but more often by alcoholism and violence. The planned economy of the 1930s offered less dependence on the capitalist trade cycle or the fortunes of individual factories. A developing shortage of skilled labour often meant a degree of

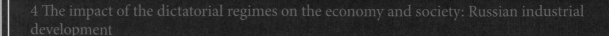
security of employment and enjoyment of better living standards. However, massive insecurity remained a feature of Russian life and must have increased rather than decreased. Rising to any post of responsibility brought the dangers of being blamed for 'sabotage' or anti-socialist behaviour. Prosperity brought with it the danger of envy by neighbours and denunciation to a secret police. Even the police were affected by planning and were eager to achieve their set quota of arrests and deportations in the same way that workers were trying to meet targets.

As workers made their way in the gleaming metro to the impressive new factory past the inspiring posters of hard working Stakhanovites, did they think of what new film they might go to in the evening or how their children might enjoy the latest Komsomol outing? Did they read Pravda, rejoice in the latest achievements of the regime in achieving its industrial targets and hope for promotion? Or did they face an exhausting day struggling with machines for which vital spare parts were not available, watched by their supervisors for any hint of slacking? Did they know that to buy even the limited amount of food in the state run shops they would have to work flat out to achieve the quota on which their piece work pay was based? Did they worry about their families in the countryside trying to cope with the new collective system? Did they remember relatives who died in the famines of the early 1930s and were they concerned that a joke that one of their family had made about Stalin might have been overheard and reported by a neighbour with whom they had quarreled?

Some Soviet comments

Source

(A) From a newspaper article in the Soviet press

Aleksei Tischenko with his wife Zoia arrived in Magnitogorsk in 1933 with all their possessions in a single homemade suitcase. By 1936 the couple owned furniture including a couch and a wardrobe, as well as decent clothes – two overcoats, some dresses, men's suits, shoes. He had a hunting gun, a gramophone and a motorcycle.

(B) Soviet jokes

1 *A worker is taken to the top of the Kremlin wall and asked if he will prove his devotion to the Soviet Union by leaping to what he thinks is certain death. He jumps without a moment's hesitation and is caught in a net specially prepared, and congratulated for this devotion. One of the witnesses asks him why he jumped with so little hesitation.*

   'Oh to Hell with the life we're leading.'

2 *1937. Night. A knock at the door. The husband goes to answer. He comes back. 'Don't worry, dear – everything's all right. It's just burglars come to rob us.'*

ACTIVITY

What are Sources **A** and **B** saying about the quality of workers' lives in the 1930s?

Post-Second World War industry

The losses of the Second World War were staggering. As well as 27 million dead with all the implications that had for work force and markets, steel production had fallen from 18–11 million tons; coal from 166–49 million tons oil from 31–19 million tons. There had been a wholesale shift of industries eastwards, a neglect of consumer goods and a large amount of physical destruction in the occupied areas and in areas of heavy fighting. The difference between the two world wars was the ability of the soviet economy to sustain the war effort and the lack of a major change of direction after the war. This time there was no revolution, no massive change to agricultural and industrial policy. For Stalin the victory had vindicated the methods of the 1930s and state planning, very large-scale enterprises and schemes dominated the Soviet economy and were transplanted to Russia's new empire in Eastern Europe.

How successful was the policy in the changing context of post-war Europe?

Apologists compare Soviet economic recovery favourably with that of West Germany or Japan even though the methods were different. Stalin envisaged 60 million tons of steel, 500 million tons of coal and 60 million tons of oil by 1960. In fact Khrushchev's Russia had by the 1960s produced substantially more and claimed 91 million tons of steel, 609 million tons of coal and 240 million tons of oil.

So in terms of continuity, Russia after 1953 could be said to have been in line with industrial development since 1891 – large-scale state-led enterprise focusing on traditional heavy industry, increasing workforce and production. The change in sheer scale of growth after 1929 was repeated during the 1950s and all this development was driven by the need for heavy defence spending. This was already a huge part of the total state spending by 1913 and it continued to dominate policy as Russia feared the rise of Fascism in the 1930s and then entered into a Cold War with the USA where scientific, industrial and technological development meant either keeping up or fatally falling back with the possible loss of influence and empire.

However, there are differences. Necessity forced quite substantial changes both under the Tsars and also under Lenin and Stalin to economic *policy*. The whole culture had to be changed and there had to be adaptation to changing circumstances. However, after 1953 there were not really very new policies and the stagnation that was feared before 1929 did become a reality. The more modern economies of western Europe and the USA offered a completely different model – more diverse production based on flourishing consumer demand; meeting the needs of a physically and socially more mobile population; balancing consumer production with heavy industry; using new technology and raising productivity. The urban culture that emerged was altogether more alluring for the people of eastern Europe than the world of sacrifice, military discipline, low-level consumer goods and belching factories. In the 1930s the contrast had been with a depressed capitalist world, but in the 1950s the parallel was far more with the 1855–1914 period in which Russia seemed to be backward in comparison with the confident economic development of the Western world. The repression of Russia in the 1950s seemed as backward as that of the Tsars; economic goals seemed to the expressed in old-fashioned terms of heavy industry. The initiative, which was producing ever-changing mass consumption and economic diversification in the West, could not be generated by a very controlled and labour intensive Soviet economic System whose grand projects seemed doomed to fail. The West looked on

The Chinese Great Leap Forward

This was a Chinese project of the mid 1950s to establish a new sort of Commune combining agricultural and industrial planning, based on a massive local production of steel in relatively small blast furnaces. It disrupted both agriculture and industry and was a catastrophic failure.

projects like the **Chinese Great Leap Forward** and the Russia's Virgin Lands scheme (*see* Chapter 3 page 96) with some contempt as unrealistic, highly labour intensive and accompanied by ludicrous propaganda. They seemed as old-fashioned as the Tsarist regime had seemed to progressive Victorians and American businessmen.

The features of the post-war economy were a rapid population growth which put pressure on resources in the same way that population growth had done after 1855.

The economic planners became part of a privileged order comparable to that of the Tsarist officials and gradually corruption ate into the managed economy. Skilled workers gained underhand incentives; managers had to bribe suppliers for raw materials; regular retail outlets faced a growing black market. Class distinctions grew between the privileged party member and the ordinary worker.

Khrushchev attempted to meet possible discontent by relaxing factory disciplines, increasing official wages, boosting food supplies and providing more consumer goods. This may have had some parallels with Lenin's economic concessions after 1921 but were not nearly as far reaching. The growth of industrial workers and urban dwellers continued and, to some extent, the Soviet state met their needs with low rent housing, welfare, education, and cultural organisations. Food consumption, disposable income and consumer sales rose markedly in 1953–64 but nothing like that of the West. The development of a mass market was as unlikely as it has been earlier and overseas trade was inward looking – with over half being with eastern Europe. Ideology was often costly in terms of the cost of military spending and of subsidising allies: for instance, Cuba was paid consistently over the market price for sugar in order for Khrushchev to subsidise Castro's communist government there. The Russians were used to economic sacrifice, but Russia's new satellite states less so and revolts in Berlin and Hungary were comparable to the nationalist risings and unrest in the later Tsarist period.

What was new was the level of spending the Russia was herself forced to embark on. A substantial programme of nuclear weapons and a space race begun with the launching of Sputnik, an advanced space satellite, in 1957 were drains on the economy and in many ways similar to the Tsar's railway and naval building policies which rested heavily on peasant taxation. Though in many ways it was remarkable that Russian economy could rise to high-level scientific and technological projects, economic development as a whole did not keep pace with that of the West. Sputniks and missiles were produced at the expense of, for example, developing adequate cars and everyday electrical goods and improving the housing stock. There was also a continuing imbalance between improvements in certain areas of the economy and agriculture which still suffered from underinvestment.

Continuity and change – a bitter example

How little some things had changed by 1963 is shown by the protests in the city of Novocherkassk in June 1962. Wage cuts, falling food supplies, bad housing conditions, demonstrations, fraternisation with local troops and finally machine guns fired at the crowds by reinforcements with no local connections, arrests and trials. The position in 1962 was similar to that in 1905 and 1917. There had been economic development and growth, but it had failed to meet the needs of many people. Too much had been directed at the needs of the state. Working and living conditions had not grown as fast as industrial production. There were still large numbers of poor people in crowded housing with limited diets. For all the changes of the period, there were depressing continuities.

ACTIVITY

Assess the view that industrial change had more impact on Russia after 1917 than it did before.

Stretch and challenge

Having read this chapter and completed the exercises, go back to your original thesis on the workers. Do you still find this convincing or do you want to change it? If so, why?

Add in further notes on the back of the original sheet of paper and file safely for revision purposes.

Conclusion

In this chapter you will have added to the overall picture of Russian development in this period in terms of the impact of the state on economic and social development and changes in the way Russians lived. The stress is on judging the extent of change and continuity and seeing how far 1917 was a turning point. There is a chance to evaluate the relative importance and scope of economic developments before and after 1917 and to compare them. You should consider which period of economic change was the greatest turning point in the period as a whole and develop your skills in writing synoptic analysis and bringing together material from different periods (synthesis).

The impact of war and revolution on the development of Russian government

In this period Russia fought a number of major wars. In all but one, she was unsuccessful. There was a profound link between war, the development of government and revolution.

It is impossible to argue that war had no effect. It was, as Trotsky said,

> '[war is] *the locomotive of History*'.

It is possible to discuss the relative importance of war compared with other pressures for change and it is also possible to discuss the extent of the changes brought about. However, in this chapter the emphasis will be on how great a **turning point** the wars and revolutions were. There will not be an attempt to give full accounts of the causes and course of these major events. The emphasis will be on their effects on government and the criteria for deciding on how great a turning point each was.

ACTIVITY

Think of turning points in a life. What changes are merely significant and what changes are turning points? For instance, take some of these changes and consider which are really turning points:

- Learning to read
- Going to nursery
- Riding a bike
- Starting secondary school
- Choosing History as an A level
- Getting married
- Having children
- Choosing a University
- Getting a first full time job.

The key is to consider continuity and change – what elements in life remained the same and what altered as a result of these changes?

An overview of the period

War was a highly important part of Russia's development in this period. The wars she fought were of three sorts. Firstly wars against other nations which became increasingly costly and destructive between 1854 and 1945; then there was the Civil War fought between 1918 and 1920. The strangest war, however, was the Cold War; this made huge demands on Russia in terms of military expenditure and the need to compete with the Western powers against whom it was 'fought', but the war was not a conventional one. Unlike the other wars in the Crimea (1853–56), against Turkey (1877–78), Japan (1904–5) and the two world wars (1914–18 and 1941–45), this was not a 'shooting' war. However it had, like conventional conflicts, massive effects and led to internal changes in Russia after 1989 in a way quite unforeseen by Russia's rulers in this period.

The Crimean War 1853–1856

This was the first major European war fought, not only by Russia, but also by any of the other great powers involved since the era of Napoleon. It was what has been described as a 'cabinet' war. Few great interests were at stake and its causes seem almost farcical.

Why did Russia fight?

Russian rulers had long been concerned with the state of the Ottoman (Turkish) Empire which bordered Russia. Seen as the 'Sick Man of Europe' it contained in its Balkan provinces many Slavs who belonged to the Orthodox Church. These Christians were subject to periodic persecution and looked to Russia for protection. The Russian government felt duty-bound to offer protection. There was another major issue: if the Ottoman Empire broke up then Russia did not want foreign powers taking advantage. A weak Ottoman Empire was no threat, but it was important for Russia that other powers did not use this weakness to establish influence or territory in an area so close to Russia.

In 1841 Russia and the other major powers had agreed to close the Straits, the area leading from the Mediterranean to the Black Sea, to warships of any nation. Tsar Nicholas I discussed with the British ambassador a possible division of the Ottoman Empire to ensure stability. The British were concerned that Russia meant to occupy Constantinople and bring her warships into the Mediterranean, threatening the British routes to India via the Near East. There was no such intention, but events seemed to show that Russia did have aggressive ambitions.

These events were provoked by French actions. The nephew of the great Napoleon, Louis Bonaparte, had declared himself Emperor of France in 1851. Napoleon III was anxious to assert French privileges and for no very good reason supported the Catholic monks in the Ottoman controlled Holy Land when they quarreled with the monks of the Orthodox Church over certain rights to the Holy Places in Jerusalem. This obscure quarrel in which France backed the Catholic monks and Russia backed the Orthodox monks led to a war because of the confident and assertive personalities involved. Napoleon III was sure that a Bonaparte-led France would sweep away all enemies; Britain's Lord Palmerston was sure of Britain's naval and industrial power. The Tsar's minister Menshikov was eager to show the power of Russia's God-given autocratic government and to assert control over a weak Turkey. Public opinion in all countries was warlike and ready to support military action.

When Turkey, supported by France and Britain would not give way, war broke out in October 1853 between Russia and Turkey. Russian forces invaded Turkish Moldavia and Wallachia, and superior Russian naval technology ensured the defeat of the old fashioned Turkish fleet at Sinope. However, the danger was now that Russia would dominate Turkey, and France and Britain, with the diplomatic support of Austria, demanded a Russian

withdrawal from Turkish territory. The Tsar did withdraw his forces, but the war went ahead in March 1854 (Fig. 5.1). The allies' objective shifted to ending Russian naval power on the Black Sea by destroying their base at Sebastopol on the Crimea. So the war was between Russia and its Bulgarian volunteers on one hand and Britain, France and Turkey, with the diplomatic support of Austria, on the other.

The war was fought on three fronts – first of all the Crimean itself (Fig. 5.2), then on the Baltic and also on the Pacific. A very large French and British fleet blockaded the Baltic ports of Russia and attacked coastal forts in Finland, but modern mines stopped progress and defended St. Petersburg. There were some naval engagements in the Far East, but the main thrust of the war was in the Crimea. Though Russia raised large forces – 700,000 – the main humiliation was the failure of the Russian army to dislodge the French, British and Piedmontese forces from the homeland. (The Italian state of Piedmont jointed in to gain French and British support for greater Italian unification.) The British were very poorly led but their elderly generals still managed to cross the Alma river and set up a siege of Sebastopol. Efforts by the Russian forces to dislodge them in the battles of Balaklava and Inkerman failed. Though costly, the attack on Sebastopol itself did succeed. The only striking Russian success was when a confused order sent a force of British cavalry in a frontal assault on a Russian artillery strongpoint in the famous Charge of the Light Brigade. Worryingly, even this suicidal mission was partly successful and the Russians were not able to stop the charge reaching its object. Nicholas I died while the war was still being fought but Alexander II brought it to an end and Russia had to agree to continued closure of access to the Mediterranean in the Treaty of Paris in 1856. The war had been fought on a substantial scale with allied forces in excess of 600,000 and Russian forces of over 700,000. Casualty rates were high – 250,000 allied losses to 500,000 Russian losses – but on both sides actual battlefield losses were substantially lower than losses through sickness and the effects of a severe winter campaign in 1854–55.

Figure 5.1   Russian troops at the Crimean war in the 1850s.

The public were far more aware of the war than had ever been the case and both sides suffered humiliations. The British were shocked by the failure of their government to ensure adequate supply and medical treatment for the troops; the military leadership was

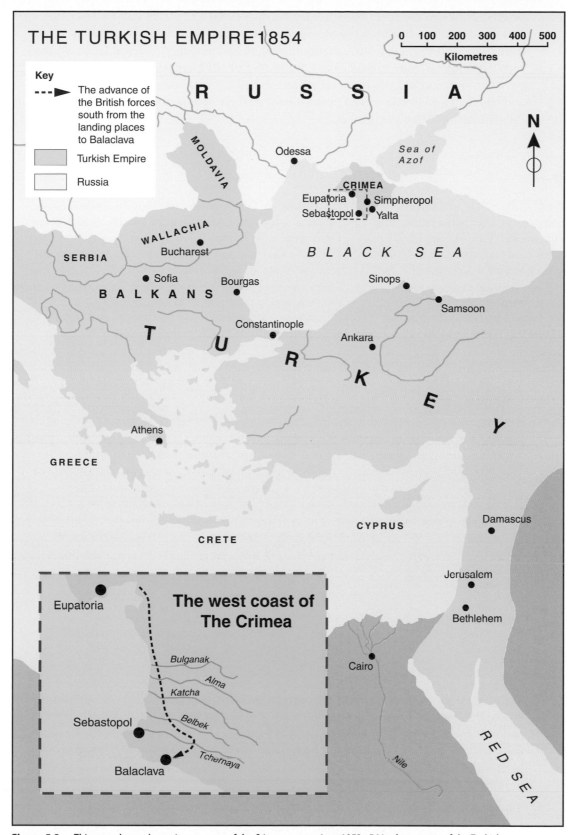

THE TURKISH EMPIRE 1854

Key
- - - ▶ The advance of the British forces south from the landing places to Balaclava

Turkish Empire

Russia

0 100 200 300 400 500
Kilometres

N

RUSSIA

MOLDAVIA

Odessa

Sea of Azof

CRIMEA

Eupatoria   • Simpheropol

Sebastopol • • Yalta

BLACK SEA

WALLACHIA

SERBIA   Bucharest

Sofia   Bourgas

BALKANS

Sinops

Samsoon

TURKEY

Constantinople

Ankara

Athens

GREECE

CRETE

CYPRUS

Damascus

Jerusalem

Bethlehem

Cairo

Nile

RED SEA

The west coast of The Crimea

Eupatoria

Bulganak

Alma

Katcha

Belbek

Sebastopol

Tchernaya

Balaclava

Figure 5.2   This map shows the main war zone of the Crimean campaigns 1853–56 in the context of the Turkish Empire

severely criticised and there was considerable opposition to a war fought for few clear national objectives. In Russia the obvious question was how allied forces fighting so far from home and with huge lines of communication had managed to defeat larger Russian forces fighting on home ground. The great **victory of 1812** over the French by Russia had passed into legend and this time foreign armies had not been swept from the motherland, and had managed to take one of Russia's most strongly defended fortresses and to resist all Russian attempts to drive them out.

Victory of 1812

The great victory over the French in 1812 was when Napoleon invaded with an army of over half a million and was defeated. In reality the Russian army was outnumbered and driven back at Borodino and Napoleon was able to take Moscow. However the Tsar Alexander I sacrificed his capital and withdrew his forces. Napoleon was faced by the two enemies typical of Russia, 'General Hunger' and 'General Winter'. Without enough food and faced by the extreme cold, Napoleon retreated and was harried by Cossack forces, the peasants and the Russian army. So in a sense, Russia's people as a whole united against the French invader. Russian forces went on to occupy Paris; this was the greatest victory for Russia since the time of Peter the Great in the early 18th century. It was commemorated in Tolstoy's War and Peace, an epic novel of the 19th century, and in Tchaikovsky's 1812 Overture and became part of Russian legend. Not Napoleon's misjudgments, but the Russian soul and the Russian land itself had defeated an invader.

ANALYSIS

The Russians were not technically inferior. Their fortifications and mines had defended the Baltic; their superior naval artillery had sunk the Turkish fleet; they were not fighting with muskets against the modern Minié rifles of the allies. However, communications with the Crimea were remote. The Russian forces could not rush by train to meet invasion – they had to march hundreds of miles. The allies arrived in modern steam ships; they communicated by telegraph; they stockpiled in the harbours of their Turkish ally a vast amount of military equipment produced by their modern industries. Their professional soldiers were highly skilled. The infantry endured the hardships and fought effectively when defending against superior numbers. They could act effectively in smaller units and take initiatives that the larger mass of Russian forces could not. The long service serf-based armies were not effective except in mass frontal attacks. For all their dreadful errors, the allied armies could muster the artillery power to finally take Sebastopol. Russian organisation, communication and industry were all inferior; their casualties were higher and their leadership was ineffective. British and French performance was in many ways just as bad, but the impression was of a modern, industrial civilisation with armies of a higher caliber defeating an old fashioned, rural, serf-ridden society.

The greatest shock for Russia was the contrast with the invasion of 1812. By 1855 this had passed into legend. The ineffectual bloodbath at Borodino in which Napoleon's larger forces had inflicted heavy casualties on the Russian forces had been forgotten and the Russian soul and loyalty to God and the Tsar had been made into the main factors which had turned back Napoleon. Yet the much less charismatic allied leaders of 1854–55 had managed to humiliate Russia in a way that Napoleon's vast armies had not.

The New York Times correspondent writing in the aftermath of another defeat by Russia in October 1877 expressed a view which has remained common to most analyses of the impact of the war.

'The fall of Sebastopol caused the fall of the repressive arbitrary and mechanical system of Nicholas I and sided the reform of local self-government and the manumission (freeing) of the serfs. After the Crimean War, there was everywhere the very natural feeling that the thing for which the people had sacrificed liberty and progress had turned out to be an illusion. Their military and arbitrary regimes collapsed just when it was brought to a practical test. All set to work with enthusiasm to correct those evils which had so plainly made Russia inferior to Western Europe.'

However, he noted that fundamental change had not occurred to the Tsar's autocracy: *'Russia is still in the Middle Ages compared with Western Europe'*.

The success of the Western powers was attributed to a number of factors. Firstly, their armies were not serfs. Modern warfare with its technological advances such as the use of rapid firing, long range rifles; the use of railways, steam ships and larger artillery needed modern soldiers not masses of illiterate serfs. Secondly, industrial growth was the basis of improved technology, communication and general modernity in the West. Russian agricultural society had encountered this and been defeated. The arrival of US warships in Japan in 1853 and the collapse of a very conservative, emperor-dominated society in the face of Western military technology might have been noted by thoughtful Russian observers.

Thirdly, the confidence and sheer energy of the West – their support from their civilian populations, their newspapers, photographs, their cables, their modern ships – all seemed in deep contrast to the limitations in the Russian campaign, the remoteness of the regime, its reliance on repression and not consultation. What seemed a major strength in 1812 when old Russia had rallied against Godless foreign invaders now seemed a source of weakness.

So how great were the changes brought by war?

'Alexander II was from the outset wholly committed to the autocratic principle. He was never in the least tempted by constitution mongering. Admittedly his reforms had a liberal element, but that was a reluctant tribute to all-conquering Britain and France; Russia had been brought to defeat by isolationist conservatism. It had to learn from the victor countries; and what had given them their dynamic was liberal-capitalist civilisation, which had created the wealth, technology and élan that had proved unbeatable in the Crimea. The point was to borrow selectively rather than to imitate.'

John Gooding, *Russia and its Rulers*, p. 58, Arnold, 1996

This perceptive analysis emphasises the importance of the Crimea, but also its limitations as a locomotive of change.

Modernisation was certainly sought: in the end of serfdom (*see* page 13) and in the liberalisation of the legal system, in educational change, in military reforms and in government. However, the Crimean war was not the only reason for this; there were liberals within the ruling class and the Tsar himself was more prepared to change and adapt than Nicholas II; but war was a major catalyst. The principal governmental change was the creation of local councils.

Zemstvos (see *also* Fig. 5.3) were set up from 1 January 1864. The basic unit was the district council. This was chosen by election and landowners, townsmen and peasants voted for representatives. From these district councils members were elected to regional councils. The role of the councils was in local matters and they were not seen as political bodies. Their tasks were to look after the building and upkeep of roads, assistance in emergencies such as famine, agricultural matters and aspects of medical care. To do this there was a local tax which they administered and whose income they spent. They could recruit specialist advisers.

Figure 5.3   This fine building constructed in 1870 for the Zemstvo in the small Russian town of Alatyr in Simbirsk, the province where Lenin was born, was commissioned by the local noble Nicolai Krylov who was the first President. It shows that, despite its limitations, the Zemstvo was taken seriously. The building is still the main administrative office in the town.

In order to prevent too much freedom the Chairman of the council was officially approved. The councils were not allowed to act together – they had to stay focused on their particular region. There was no elected local council at the level of individual peasant commune or the administrative unit known as the Canton. And there was firmly no national assembly. The voting regulations ensured that the nobles dominated all these councils. Voting was strictly done along class lines with greater weight being given to the natural leaders – the nobles.

However, in terms of what had gone before, there were some remarkable elements. All classes actually voted. The very idea of representative councils offered an alternative model to all decisions coming from the very top. The process of voting in itself, however restricted, made a statement about the rights of the individual. The specialists employed by the Zemstvos created a class dedicated to improvement and were potentially politically active.

The Zemstvos reforms have to be seen in the context of some liberalisation of education and intermittent relaxation of legal repression. Whatever judgement is made about their significance, the major feature of the post-Crimean government is the continuation of autocracy. Alexander II was still in control of appointments; if he favoured liberals at times, he withdrew his support at other times, when there was fear of political change. There was some borrowing of some key ideas from the West. In this respect the Russia of Alexander II is similar to contemporary Japan during the so-called Meiji Period after 1867. Both countries were confronted with stronger, industrialised Western powers; both countries felt the need to modernise; neither country wanted profound change to its emperor-based system; in both countries old traditions remained close to the surface of modernisation.

ACTIVITY

In this analysis, the failures of the Crimean war raised major issues about the nature of the regime and its ability to compete with modern world powers. However, the extent to which those issues were addressed remained relatively limited.

How far do you agree?

ANALYSIS

Assessing the impact of the Crimean War

In Russia, a key criticism of the changes made were that the links between economic success, technological growth, urban development, social diversity and a freedom of thought and expression and some sort of representative political system were not understood.

In other words, Britain's economic growth and hence her military success in the long wars against Napoleon and now in the Crimean War were closely linked to political development. Gooding refers to this in his analysis of liberal-capitalism. Alexander did not draw this conclusion. The idea was to take some elements from the West – legal reforms, a more modern army, a free peasantry, and intellectual activity in universities, some elections and some representative government to improve local conditions. However, modernisation would not include a free press, a well-educated population able to form political views, a national parliament with open debate on major policies, government responsible to the people or at least its representatives and a questioning culture able to develop entrepreneurialism and develop an urban culture. What was still highly valued was the traditional hierarchical social system with the Tsar at the top, a service nobility, and a church dedicated to the regime. The Empire would continue to dominate its subject people and traditional communalism would continue to dominate rural society.

The Russo-Turkish war of 1877–78

The next war of any significance was the Russo-Turkish war of 1877 (*see* Fig. 5.4). This war, which began on 24 April 1877, had its origins in continuing Russian ambitions to dominate Turkey, but its immediate causes were the massacres in the Balkans by Turkish forces fighting Christian Orthodox rebels against Turkish rule in Bulgaria. A feeling that all Slavonic peoples should be free from Turkish rule and join with Russia was strong. Alexander III had promoted nationalism and there were strong pressures in government and the ruling classes for a strong **Pan Slav** policy.

However, if Russian forces invaded the Balkans to help the rebels then this could mean conflict with Austria and Britain.

Britain regarded the defence of Turkey of major national interest and had supplied the Turkish army with modern weapons. The war took place on two fronts: an invasion of the Balkans led to a long siege at Plevna from July to December 1877 (in which Russian forces were held up and suffered considerably from disease and winter conditions); an offensive in the east in the Caucasus led to a rather similar stalemate around Kars. In both fronts the Russians were eventually successful but at high costs. Their successes were reversed by diplomacy. Russia had wanted to create a large client state in Bulgaria and signed the Treaty of San Stefano in March 1878 with Turkey giving her a victory. This was overturned at an international conference in Berlin when Russia humiliatingly had to back down and agree to dividing Bulgaria. War had exposed Russia's massive inefficiency in supply and medical care; Russian artillery was less modern than the Westernised weaponry of the Turks, even with Finnish, Rumanian and Bulgarian help, and even with the support of public opinion

Pan Slav

The prefix pan means 'All'. Pan slavism was a movement in Russia that thought Russia had a historical mission to bring all people linked racially, religiously and linguistically with Russia together under its protection. Pan-slavism had its modern origins in agitation within the Austrian Empire by the Slav people and there was a pan Slav congress in Prague in 1848. The defeats of the Crimean War led to more official support for Russification policies.

behind a distinctly popular cause. Russian military performance had been disappointing, progress on both fronts slow and costly against an enemy who was generally socially, economically and technologically backwards.

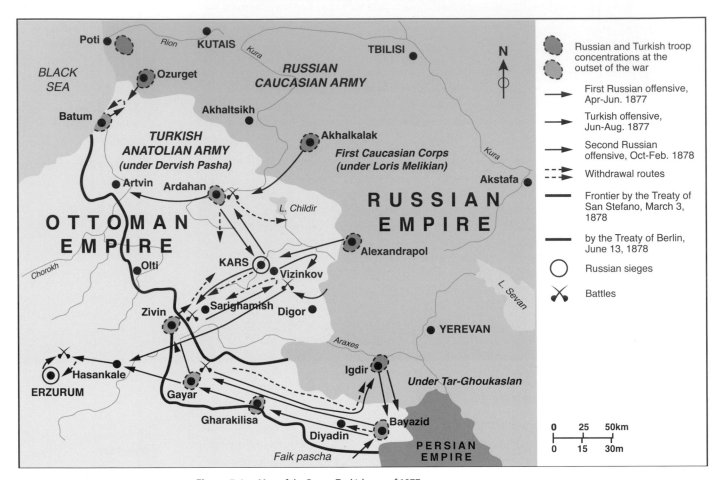

Figure 5.4   Map of the Russo-Turkish war of 1877

The New York Times correspondent was hopeful, therefore, that the war would produce change:

> *'There is no doubt that, like the defeats and losses of the Crimean War, this great disaster will produce an excellent result.'*

What the war brought was a financial crisis and the collapse of the rouble. It was a major factor in the end of the so-called Free Trade era in Russia's economic development (*see* page 102); subsequent economic development was led much more by the state. However, despite once again showing Russia's backwardness, this time there was no major series of reforms and the assumptions made by foreign observers proved wrong (*see* the Analysis on page 135).

The Russo-Japanese War, 1904–1905

Whereas previously, Russia had been concerned about the future of the weak Turkish Empire, by the late 19th century, attention had shifted eastwards to China. The defeat of China by Japan in the war of 1894–95 showed its weakness, and the major powers were eager for control of its trade (*see* Fig. 5.6). The newly modernised Japan took the important

ANALYSIS

Why did War in 1877 produce fewer results?

Possibly it had to do with the nature of the war. Contemporary pictures show the heroism of the Russian forces who were fighting for a popular and widespread cause. The horrors of the massacres of Christians were widely circulated in Russia in pictures and in the growing number of newspapers and periodicals. The Tsar's decision was popular and the fruits of victory were seen to be snatched by foreign intervention. This time there was not a contrast between modern European nations and Russia – the war had been fought against Russia's traditional enemy. Unlike Alexander II, Alexander III did not have liberal tendencies and he would not have interpreted the failures of 1877 having any link at all with greater democracy or changes in government. The war, unlike that of 1905 or the First World War, did not produce massive strikes and demonstrations – possibly it did not last long enough and the mood was generally patriotic and pro-Tsar. For instance, Tchaikovsky's Marche Slave was one of many expressions of the support from artists, the painting below was another.

This wonderfully lurid and emotional picture was produced in 1877 by the popular artist Konstantin Makovsky and is entitled *Atrocities of the Bashi Bazouks*. (These were Turkish irregulars who massacred Bulgarian Christians.) The same outrage led to large-scale ethnic cleansing of Muslims with Russian connivance in the independent Bulgaria between 1876 and 1882.

What the war did encourage was industrialisation, Russification and the prestige of the Tsar as representative of traditionalist pan Slavism. It was of major significance in many ways, particularly in changing the direction of Russian economic growth (*see* Chapter 4) but its political consequences for various reasons were not as great as expected and not as great as those of the Crimean War.

Figure 5.6 Map of China-Japanese war 1894–95.

port of Port Arthur in Manchuria. Russia wanted this port. It was a warm water port and offered trading access throughout the year, unlike Russia's northern ports which froze in the winter. Russia forced Japan to give it up, and then went on to force China to lease the Liaotung peninsular and the Port. Another major ice free port in the Far East offered Russia the chance to dominate the region. When a Chinese rebellion in 1900 led to foreign troops being sent to defend Europeans, Russia occupied Manchuria and did not keep its promise to Japan to leave in 1903. For Japan there was a major issue – would she or Russia be the dominant power in Korea and Manchuria? Negotiations failed and Japan launched a strike on Port Arthur in January 1904 without warning or official declaration of war. The enormous industrial expansion of Russia and its military growth made it seem that victory must go to Russia.

It is important to see Russia as a colonial power; throughout the 19th century it had extended its empire eastwards against technologically inferior peoples. Only Western intervention had prevented more decisive victories against the less industrialised Ottoman Empire. Now the Russian state was again intent in expanding at the expense of a supposedly inferior oriental race. There was little expectation that this war would not be as successful as campaigns in the Caucasus. The Minister of the Interior in a famous letter to the Minister of War in 1903 said,

'What this country needs is a short victorious war to stem the tide of revolution.'

The Russian government had virtually provoked the war, ignoring the advice of Witte and the obvious signs of Japan's military and naval modernisation programme. Russian tactics were largely defensive. The Pacific fleet was unable to break out of the Japanese blockade of Port Arthur and the Russian forces both naval and military waited for reinforcements and endured a long Japanese siege. Attempts to break the siege failed and Port Arthur fell on 2 January 1905. The Japanese attacked the Russian strongpoint of Mukden, forcing a Russian withdrawal in February 1905. The long-awaited rescue attempt by Russia's Baltic fleet which had sailed 18,000 miles to demonstrate Russian naval power turned to bitter fiasco. It was defeated by the Japanese at Tsushima on 27/28 May 1905 (*see also* pages 110, Chapter 4).

The news of the fall of Port Arthur was a sign for growing discontent in Russia, made worse by wartime inflation and shortages, to reach danger levels. The Bloody Sunday massacre on 22 January was the spark. The country plunged into a revolutionary situation with various manifestations of unrest in urban centres, the countryside, and different regions of the empire and among the intelligentsia (*see* Chapter 2). The Tsar responded with the October Manifesto and offered concessions in a way that neither Alexander II nor Alexander III had been forced to do.

ACTIVITY

The end of serfdom and the reforms of Alexander II had not come about directly from concessions forced by defeat in war: they had come about because of a process of reflection caused by a disappointing performance in the Crimean War. Whereas, the creation of a national parliament after 1905 under Nicholas II is much more directly attributable to war revealing weakness in the autocratic system and revolution bringing about a huge pressure for change which the Tsar could not ignore.

How far do you agree?

Why was the Russo-Japanese War more significant in bringing about change than earlier wars?

- Expectations were higher and disappointments greater.
- Russia fielded the largest forces ever assembled in her history with no resulting victory.
- The press coverage of the war was unprecedented; defeats were high profile and consequently highly humiliating.
- The autocracy had developed a view that Russia's interests were best cared for by absolute monarchy under Alexander III and Nicholas II to counter growing opposition. Now it appeared that there was no real reward in terms of efficiency and effectiveness for the loss of political rights. The autocracy was based on military power and that military power had been overcome by supposed racial inferiors.
- The situation differed from the Crimean War because there existed substantial opposition movements – the middle class Zemstvo liberals, the urban revolutionary groups and the Social Revolutionaries who were there to take advantage of any weakness of the autocracy. Neither the Crimean War nor the Russo-Turkish war led to revolution; neither gave rise to such pressure from below for change.

ANALYSIS

How significant was this war?

There is a strong case for seeing this war as the major turning point of Tsarism. Consider the following:

- It shattered the image of Russian power, based on dynamic economic growth, military and naval reform and cultural superiority. This time defeat could not be blamed on serfdom and centuries of backwardness: disaster had come through poor decision-making and leadership. As Nicholas had insisted on the rightness of autocracy, then failure went straight back to him – it was his fault. What was clearly needed was some sort of power sharing.

- The revolutions, which the war brought, were the largest disturbances ever seen in Russia. The serf unrest had been widespread in the 1850s and 1860s, but had not been accompanied by any other political or urban revolution. The activities of the terrorists had been disturbing since the 1870s, but were essentially isolated. Large-scale revolution in Poland had taken a large amount of military power to suppress, but again had been isolated. There had been growing numbers of strikes, but these had not been linked to rural disturbances. What the war did was to unite a number of separate strands of discontent; the unity was superficial and the different elements of revolt did not come together, but nevertheless the fact that they were going on simultaneously offered the Tsar a unique challenge.

- The concessions that this war-induced unrest brought about were the most significant to date. The emergence of a national parliament (the Duma) for the first time in Russian history was, for Nicholas, a massive step. Because it did not develop into a full parliamentary system, there is the temptation to discount it. But the opening ceremony in which the Duma was inaugurated was a grand one – there was the sense of a new departure and a distinct break with the autocracy of pre-1904. The changes in the countryside brought about by Stolypin (see pages 86–88) could be seen as the end of old Russia. For the first time there was a serious challenge to communal agriculture and taken with political and economic change, there is a strong case to be made for the post-1905 years to have been one of the most significant periods of change in the period. If one adds the military rebuilding which followed the defeats and the reorientation of Russian foreign policy once again to the west and the Balkans, then the case for the 1904–05 war being the major turning point of all the wars becomes even stronger.

Source

Manifesto of 17 October 1905

'We, Nicholas II, By the Grace of God Emperor and Autocrat of all Russia, King of Poland, Grand Duke of Finland, etc., proclaim to all Our loyal subjects:

Rioting and disturbances in the capitals [i.e. St. Petersburg and the old capital, Moscow] and in many localities of Our Empire fill Our heart with great and heavy grief. The well being of the Russian Sovereign is inseparable from the well being of the nation, and the nation's sorrow is his sorrow. The disturbances that have taken place may cause grave tension in the nation and may threaten the integrity and unity of Our state. By the great vow of service as tsar, We are obliged to use every resource of wisdom and of Our authority to bring a speedy end to unrest that is dangerous to Our state. We have ordered the responsible authorities to take measures to terminate direct manifestations of disorder, lawlessness, and violence and to protect peaceful people who quietly seek to fulfill their duties. To carry out successfully the general measures that we have conceived to restore peace to the life of the state, We believe that it is essential to coordinate activities at the highest level of government.

We require the government dutifully to execute our unshakeable will:

(1) To grant to the population the essential foundations of civil freedom, based on the principles of genuine inviolability of the person, freedom of conscience, speech, assembly and association.

(2) Without postponing the scheduled elections to the State Duma, to admit to participation in the Duma (insofar as possible in the short time that remains before it is scheduled to convene) of all those classes of the population that now are completely deprived of voting rights; and to leave the further development of a general statute on elections to the future legislative order.

(3) To establish as an unbreakable rule that no law shall take effect without confirmation by the State Duma and that the elected representatives of the people shall be guaranteed the opportunity to participate in the supervision of the legality of the actions of Our appointed officials.

We summon all loyal sons of Russia to remember their duties toward their country, to assist in terminating the unprecedented unrest now prevailing, and together with Us to make every effort to restore peace and tranquility to Our native land.

Given at Peterhof the 17th of October in the 1905th year of Our Lord and of Our reign the eleventh.

Nicholas

The manifesto was proclaimed in one of the grandest rooms in the Peterhof palace, outside St. Petersburg, in a ceremonial way. It was not issued in a furtive manner, however much Nicholas II resented it. Looking at its language – particularly Point 1 – it is difficult not to see the statement of these liberal principles as of immense significance.

Of course, Nicholas did not keep to his word and the actual impact of the Dumas was disappointing, but then this too had significance for the future of Tsarism. Principles had been announced but not kept to; the Tsar could not be trusted and in the event of a future crisis, there could be no more concessions.

The Tsar had survived because of the loyalty of his armed forces and the divisions among the opposition. After 1905 Russian military power expanded at an unprecedented rate. There were to be no more eastern adventures, so the only point of this massive growth would be some military action in the west. This induced extreme alarm in both Austria-Hungary and Germany – really the only countries Russia was likely to fight. Since 1895 Russia and France had been close and France rushed to supply investment to the Tsar's regime, needing Russia as an ally against Germany.

Interestingly the battleship Aurora, which fired the shot that began the October Revolution, was made partly in French shipyards. Millions of francs poured into Russia – to Germany's alarm. Russian railway expansion was a particular source of panic for German military

ACTIVITY

1. What were the disturbances that the Tsar referred to in the first line of the source?

2. Taken at face value how much change does this document represent in Russian government?

3. How far can this change be linked to the results of war?

planners who saw 1915 as the key date when Russian military preparations might make any future conflict impossible. However, there were no signs of Russia rushing into another war – the deaths of between 40 and 70,000 troops in the Far East and the huge naval losses needed to be made up. International crises were settled peacefully between 1908 and 1912 and Balkan wars did not lead to Russian-Austrian conflict. Russia had the alliance of France and the friendship of Britain and was not under any particular threat by 1914. Internal unrest was still a problem, but the formula of a foreign war to calm revolutionary disturbances had lost credibility.

The First World War

Russia entered war in 1914 because she could not stand aside and allow Austria to control Russia's fellow Slavs in Serbia. A Serb-based terrorist had assassinated the heir to the Austrian throne in Sarajevo on 28 June 1914. Supported by Germany, Austria insisted on virtual control of Serbia's internal affairs. The Serbs looked to the Tsar. Virtual Austrian control of Serbia would have been unacceptable to Russian opinion and her interests in the Balkans. On 28 July Austria-Hungary declared war on Serbia. Russia's vast army needed time to prepare so a mobilisation order was issued on 29 July. However, mobilisation could be seen as a threat by Austria-Hungary and Germany. They requested a stand down. Mobilisation, once begun could not be easily stopped. It would seem like weakness. The result was a German declaration of war on 1 August. Like all the powers in Europe, Russia, after being so cautious for years, was swept by a sudden crisis into a war in which she stood to gain little and to lose everything. Russia fought alongside Britain and France against the Central Powers: Austria-Hungary, Germany and Turkey.

The military reforms since 1905 initially paid dividends and Russian forces were able to enter Germany far quicker than expected. The betrayal of Austrian plans led to early Russian victories further south. However, as in 1905, chaotic leadership prevented much exploitation, the highly trained German forces inflicted crushing defeats at Tannenberg and the Masurian Lakes and Russian forces were driven back. By 1915 Russian armies were fighting along 1000 miles of front from Riga in the north to Czernowitz in the south; they also had to face war against the Turks. The supply system was inadequate and Russia was slow to mobilise her total resources. Casualties mounted, but by 1916 there were more encouraging signs. There was more effective war production and better tactics led to some successes in the offensive by Brusilov in the Summer of 1916. The Tsar himself had taken command of the forces in 1915 to no particular effect. The royal family was deeply committed to war – the Winter Palace housed a military hospital. But by the winter of 1916 the situation was bad. Distribution problems had left the cities short of fuel and food; there had been heavy losses on all fronts. Also, the government had been brought into disrepute by the scandal of the influence and murder of **Rasputin** (*see* case study).

Case Study:

Father Grigory Efimovich Rasputin 1872–1916.

Rasputin was a Siberian priest who was introduced to the royal family in 1905 and became trusted by them for his seeming ability to help the Tsar's son Alexei who suffered from haemophilia. Rasputin had a reputation for sexual excess and was popular with women in St. Petersburg's highest social circles. His influence was resented in political circles and when the Tsar went to join his troops in 1915 it was thought that the Tsarina, who had been left in charge, relied over heavily on him. He was murdered by one of Russia's greatest nobles, Yussopov, in December 1916.

Whatever the truth of his personal life or his influence, Rasputin certainly brought the Tsar and Tsarina into disrepute.

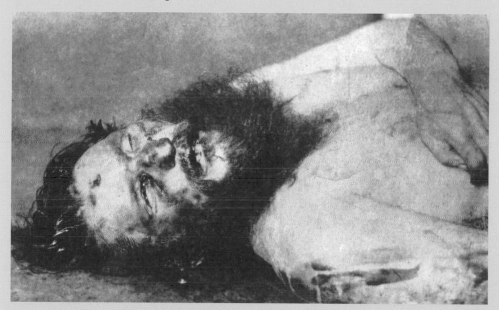

The corpse after the upper class assassins had dumped it in the frozen river Neva.

The loyalty of the elites and of the armed forces could no longer be taken for granted. Having said that, this was not a situation unique to Russia. All the participants in the war had suffered heavily. By 1916–17 there were more signs of discontent in the home fronts. The French army mutinied in April 1916. The very severe food shortages in Germany in 1916–17 provoked unrest. It is questionable whether there was, however, a widespread demand in Russia or anywhere else for peace, rather for food and for a more effective way to victory.

The war had brought very severe conditions to Petrograd (as St Petersburg had been re-named). Already overcrowded, wartime production had swelled the industrial areas. Food and fuel were short. Revolutionary agitators were active in the workers' districts. The troops in the capital were often newly recruited from the countryside. There were some 340,000 reservists stationed in or near Petrograd. These were hungry, under-occupied troops who had picked up political ideas from the civilian population. They were very different from the long-term professional soldiers in the capital in 1905. The Tsar was not physically

present to act as a reassuring symbol. Strikes increased and prices outstripped wages. Also the Duma was not in session from December 1916 to February 1917. So there seemed no way of expressing discontent and casualty lists continued to be high. When street demonstrations grew and grew and troops did not obey orders to clear the streets, then the Tsar's authority crumbled. The Duma would not disperse; a new Soviet, a council of workers and soldiers emerged. Faced with Duma demands for his resignation, without the support of his generals and isolated from his wife and closest advisers, Nicholas abdicated on 2 March 1917.

Was the First World War then a major turning point because of the abdication of the Tsar?

The Crimean War had led to a major social development and the creation of the first elected councils; the Russo-Japanese war had led to the Tsar adopting major new principles and a national parliament, but neither had led to the end of monarchy itself. So it might seem that it is obvious that the very much larger scale war from 1914–18 must have had a very much larger effect on Russian government.

A few statistics might seem to confirm that this war must be the greatest turning point.

- Out of a population of 181 million, Russia raised forces of 14.6 million and suffered 5.5 million casualties, including 2 million prisoners and over 3 million dead, sick and wounded by the end of 1916.
- Wartime inflation ran at some 300 per cent.
- The number of strikes increased from 211 in 1915 to 684 in 1916.
- The Inspector General of Artillery, the Grand Duke Sergei, estimated in January 1917 than 1 million soldiers had deserted

So it seems that this war must be the one which is the greater turning point. However there are some points to consider.

1   If the Tsar had managed to incorporate the Duma into government, then it would have shared the responsibility for war. In England, for example, when the war was being badly run, the political parties made a change and brought in a tougher leader, Lloyd George. The whole regime did not change. In Russia the Tsar failed to share responsibility. This was because of a pre-war failure to develop a constitutional monarchy.

2   The failures of the Tsarist economy to meet the needs for a modern war has a lot to do with the persistence of old fashioned bureaucracy and the relatively limited industrial development of Russia. There had been huge rates of growth before 1914, but in terms of the proportion of industrial to urban population Russia was still relatively backward.

3   Russia's allies were a lot more successful in mobilising public opinion behind war by modern propaganda. Traditional loyalties to the Tsar, to the motherland were invoked, but there was nothing like the more sophisticated appeal of, say, British propaganda or post-war promises. For the vast mass of poorly educated and remote rural dwellers, the war was just another demand from the 'high ups'.

The First World War made huge demands on all countries and it was often the long-term limitations of the Russian state and culture that were exposed by the war that were the crucial areas of weakness. There is an argument that even had the war not taken place; these long-term failings would have resulted in some sort of major change.

Stretch and challenge

Compare each of these wars as a turning point in the development of Russian government. You need to make a judgement about which was the most significant: the Crimean War; the Russo-Turkish War; the Russo-Japanese War, or the First World War (to March 1917).

1   First list the major changes brought about by each war – remember this exercise focuses on government.

2   Now try to frame a thesis.

3   Now go back to the notes you made and defend that thesis by comparing the impact of your chosen war with the other three.

4   Compare notes with others in the class.

5   Can your view be challenged? Try being 'Devil's advocate' and thinking about why your chosen war might not be the major turning point.

After all this, write up your views and keep them as a provisional judgement that you might want to amend after studying the other wars.

The First World War and the Provisional Government

The Duma committee which tried to run Russia until its overthrow by the Bolsheviks in the October Revolution made what seems to be a tragic decision to continue the war, yet at the time it was popular. Apart from Lenin's Bolsheviks who adopted the famous 'Peace, Bread and Land' slogan in the April Theses, all political groups supported the war. Russia's reputation with its allies was at stake; Germans were intensely unpopular and there was little desire for previous sacrifice to be in vain. Too often demonstrations in the Summer are shown in documentaries and even textbooks to be against the war, while their banners actually read not 'Mir' (peace) but 'Voina' (War). Lenin was careful not to say too much about peace while the June offensive was being prepared and rumours of his association with the Germans made him unpopular with the troops. However, the failure of the Kerensky attacks in June ended this period of renewed war fever. It did not however bring Lenin into power. The July Days failed; revolutionary soldiers were disarmed by loyal troops. The bulk of the forces were still loyal to the Provisional Government by August 1917.

So did the war bring the Bolsheviks into power?

It is true that peasant soldiers were rapidly deserting eager to get into the countryside for a major repartition of land. When Riga fell to Germany in August, General Kornilov regarded it as his duty to stop the rot in the army. It was the Kornilov coup of September when he launched army units on Petrograd following Korensky's dismissal of him as Commander-in-Chief of the army that was a major turning point and revived the Bolsheviks. The political failures of the Provisional Government to establish a constitution, to end the problems of the dual role of the Soviet now came home to roost. The attempted coup by Kornilov and the failure of Kerensky at a vital moment to establish clear leadership coupled with the failures in war and the organisational ability of the Bolsheviks all came together. However, it is doubtful if the war alone was the key factor.

Once Lenin had taken power he was determined that world revolution would make any temporary territorial losses irrelevant and so signed away huge amounts of Russia to Germany in the Brest-Litvosk peace treaty. This view was not shared by many for whom peace at any price was not acceptable. Had peace been such a priority then the waves of opposition to this treaty would not have been so tremendous. For many Lenin, the German spy, had betrayed the memories of the war dead. There is an argument that war was more significant a factor in the February Revolution than it was in October.

Civil War and revolution 1917–1924

The nature of the Revolution, really a coup with an element of popular support in the capital rather than a massive nation-wide grass roots movement, and the bitter Civil War which followed were instrumental in forging the system of government of the Soviet era.

The elections held for the Constituent Assembly 12 November 1917 in which 41 million people voted had the following results (Table 5.1).

Table 5.1

Party	No. seats	Votes (%)
Social Revolutionaries	370	38
Bolsheviks	75	24
Left Social Revolutionaries	40	?
Mensheviks	16	3
Kadets	17	5
National Groups	89	?

These figures disguise Bolshevik support in the urban centres. The Bolsheviks had a majority in the armies of the northern and western fronts and also in the Baltic fleet. They also got quite a bit of peasant support where their policies were known.

So their support was rather greater than it seems from these figures, but the nature of the revolution by which they had already taken power had a big influence on what followed. They could hardly go ahead with an assembly which they did not control. So the logical step was to dismiss this elected assembly which Lenin contemptuously did in January 1918. Logically the revolution should have thrown up in its place a Soviet based system – after all Lenin had urged 'All Power to the Soviet'. Again the nature of the Revolution – masterminded by the Bolsheviks and being a take over of key points – led to the actual system which followed: a one party state.

The originality of this concept needs to be remembered since Lenin's model was copied by Mussolini, Hitler, and Mao and has been the type of government for millions. However it had no real historical precedent and Lenin had to make his own way towards the Communist dictatorship. It was partly based on Marx's dictatorship of the proletariat, partly on the nature of the party he had created since 1903 and partly it arose because of the Civil War and the need for total control.

Features of the Lenin state

The Constitution of 1918 was applied to a Federal structure in 1922. It was subsequently modified in 1936 by the so-called Stalin Constitution and changed again in 1977.

1. (VTsIK) – the All Russian Central Executive Committee was set up by the Congress of Soviets with 61 Bolshevik members and 29 left SRs – 101 in all.

2. A Soviet of People's Commissar – the Sovnarkom.

3. The VSNKh or National Economic Committee.

4. The All-Russian extraordinary Commission (Cheka) – to suppress counter revolution.

5. The Constituent Assembly was replaced by a Congress of Soviets.

6. There was a Workers and Peasants Army and Navy.

7. The scope of government was extended by large-scale nationalisation of large-scale industry and trade.

8. The USSR – a federation of Russia, Ukraine, Belarus and TransCaucasia was established in December 1922. The final constitution of 1924 confirmed the elected body would be the Congress of Soviets. There would be a Central Executive Committee with separate representation for the republics and other nationalities. The praesidium would be a collective presidency chosen from members of the Central Committee and the executive government would be the Sovnarkom.

The effects of the changes in government brought about by war and revolution in 1917 were profound, but there is a gap between what the constitutions say and what the real source of power was. In this respect there is deep continuity between the Soviet and Tsarist eras.

ANALYSIS

Consider the ideas which follow: they are certainly open to challenge.

What do you think?

War and pressure for change had brought about important changes involving the principles of government after both the Crimean War and the Russo-Japanese War. The first had brought the principle of local participation in government and the principle of elected assemblies. The second had brought a declaration of liberal rights and a national assembly. In the context of previous Tsarist autocracy these were major changes and could be seen as turning points as it proved impossible to return to the levels of personalised rule of the previous century or to the lack of political opposition enjoyed by the Tsars before Alexander I. However, what characterised the period 1855–1916 was a considerable degree of continuity; in practice representative institutions did not develop because of a lack of tradition, a solid middle class base, the emergence of an educated and electorate and a willingness to make a parliamentary system work. Terrorism and political extremism became more characteristic means of protest. Repression, censorship and reliance on naked authority continued to be strong elements of Tsarism. The promises of representative government and a liberal political system remained just that – promises for some future time.

The Soviet system was in many ways similar. The principles established were genuinely new. Consider this analysis by Martin McCauley (*see* Source).

Source

Lenin envisaged that the Provisional Government would be replaced by a Soviet republic and hence proclaimed all power to the Soviets. Power was handed to the 2ⁿᵈ Congress of Soviets in October 1917 and soviets were to be the vehicles of the dictatorship of the proletariat and the poor strata of the peasantry. The soviets were to be elected at all levels and at the centre would be the Congress of Soviet and its central executive committee. The government, Sovnarkom, would be subordinate to it. This amounted to a commune state, or one which was administered by the population itself. Workers' control, cooperatives, soviets, factory committees, trade unions, revolutionary tribunals and other organisations would represent democracy from below.

Martin McCauley *Companion to Russia Since 1914*, Longman, 1998.

In both this and the Stalin Constitution of 1936 there was a federal structure, quite different from that of Tsarist Russia with agriculture, justice, internal affairs, health and education being the responsibility of the Republics. In 1936 voting was extended to all and not merely the favoured proletariat and poorer peasants of 1918. In neither was the party directly acknowledged as the leading institution of the state. In all three constitutions the Republics had a right to secede from the Soviet Union.

The demands of the Civil War ended any development of what McCauley calls the Commune State. The party needed efficient industrial discipline and food supply not local democracies. The Soviets had little meaning outside the grip of the party that was not officially recognised in any meaningful way until the 1977 Constitution. The huge personal dominance of Lenin, Stalin and Khrushchev had no constitutional justification.

Though crude Russification ended and there were greater efforts to recognise regional cultures, control of policies by the centre dominated the Soviet period. The hugely democratic constitution of 1936 was meaningless when no opposition outside the Communist party had been allowed to develop and even within the Party there was no real democracy. The rights of the individual had been eroded since 1917 and the paper constitutions offered no protection in reality to the property or liberty of Soviet citizens.

Thus what seemed, as in Tsarist changes, to be major changes towards federalism, a new Soviet organisation, and a communal state were, in practice, of little real significance compared with two major developments. First was the unique role of a political party and second was a massive increase in the personal power of leaders whose role was unacknowledged in the official constitutions. The party was new; the power of an autocrat welding life and death authority over a people cowed by police/military power was not. Arguably the war and revolution of 1914–17 had not produced many more profound changes in the practice of government that the wars between 1855 and 1906.

The Civil War

After the resignation of the left SRs in March 1918 in protest at the peace treaty with Germany, these 'Soviet' or 'People's' institutions became one party. The assassination attempt on Lenin by two SRs in August led to the suppression of opposition. The Constitution of July 1918 had hardly been established when violent civil war broke out and the tendency for the centralisation of power and the suppression of opposition by violent means accelerated (*see also* Chapter 2). However, it is difficult to the see the war dictating change as in the case of 1905 or 1914–18. It confirmed tendencies already evident in Bolshevism and Lenin himself.

Russia might have been a truly Soviet state but in fact it was a one party state. The nationalities might have achieved freedom but in fact were tightly controlled. There might have been a socialist if not a bourgeois democracy, with freedom of opinion and discussion within the socialist community; in practice alternative socialist groups were repressed and a 'democratic centralism' established with tight political control by the central body of the party. The party became the state. The state took on a greater role than it had even under the Tsars with higher levels of economic control, higher levels of repression and more direction of everyday life.

Figure 5.7   Map of the European theatre of the Russian Civil War.

Was this a result of the Civil War?

From 1918–20 the Bolsheviks controlled the central regions of western Russia and the main cities. They were surrounded by 'White' armies of political opponents, by foreign expeditionary forces from France, Britain, the USA and Japan (*see* Fig. 5.7). They fought separatist movements for example in the Baltic states and Ukraine and 'Green' peasant forces. There was also a major war against the newly created state of Poland. There was little mercy shown and Russia suffered perhaps an 8–10 million population loss through war, famine, terror and disease between 1917–21. So war and revolution while transforming government had a devastating effect on Russia as a whole.

In a way there was some continuity before and after 1917. Before there was a limited and somewhat dishonest 'constitution' which kept power focused on the Tsar and his ministers. After 1917 the elaborate constitution served only to keep Lenin and his party in power. The sad showing of the Kadets (Liberal party) in the elections of November 1917 reflects the lack of interest and social base for middle class democracy. This was true both before and after 1917. The nationalities' aspirations were not met either before or after 1917. The changes made after 1905 offered more chance of constitutional development, perhaps. After the bloodletting of the Civil War period, it would be highly unlikely that the Bolsheviks would yield any power at all; after Lenin's death dictatorship was consolidated and then increased to incredible proportions.

The Second World War (or the Great Patriotic War)

Soviet Russia, apart from border clashes with the Japanese in 1938–39 and the so-called Winter War in which they were beaten by the Finns, did not go to war again until they were invaded by the German Army in 1941.

From 1933 Russia had to face a hostile regime in Germany with a Nazi ideology totally opposed to communism and which equated the Russian revolution with a world-Jewish conspiracy. Soviet foreign policy could find no allies in eastern Europe and Russia was distrusted by Britain, France and the USA. Stalin's decision to send aid to the left wing Republic in Spain during the Spanish Civil War of 1936–39 made him more distrusted in the West. Ironically, the purges of the 1930s weakened the Russian army at a time when Russia needed to be very strong defensively, but the industrialisation may well have saved Russia by permitting large-scale defence production. Stalin then decided to rely on a direct deal with Hitler and signed the Nazi Soviet Peace Pact in August 1939 leading to valuable oil and war materials being shipped to Germany after the start of the Second World War in September 1939.

The fears and suspicions that Stalin felt towards his own people were not extended to the German dictator despite Hitler making it absolutely clear that he intended a racial war against Russia and its Communist ideology. Incredibly, Stalin was taken aback by the sudden German invasion, ignored all advice and warning signs and was sure that a pact he had signed with Hitler in 1939 would never be broken. He believed that Hitler had accepted Russian occupation of Poland and the Baltic States and that the Nazis did not have any intention of pursuing their ideas of 'Lebensraum' and colonising the Slav world. However, vast numbers of Russian prisoners were taken as German armies hurtled towards Leningrad, Moscow and the south. Then bad weather delayed the German advances which had expected to be in the big cities before the snow and large-scale reserves drove the Germans back from Moscow. Even so, Leningrad endured a 900-day siege whilst the main thrust of the German advance was redirected to the south. Stalingrad held out and inadequate German air forces meant that the German armies could not be saved from encirclement. Mammoth efforts by Russia to produce tanks and equipment led to epic battles in 1943, which drove the Germans back, and the Red Armies then entered the Baltic States, Poland, Hungary, Rumania and Germany. Persistent appeals by Stalin for a Second Front were ignored until June 1944 by his British and American allies.

The Germans had brought vast destruction of life and property and made little effort to work with the Russian population in occupied areas. As a result Soviet forces took their revenge when they occupied eastern Germany and took Berlin in May 1945. After a belated declaration of war against Japan, Soviet forces entered Manchuria and Sakhalin.

What was the impact of the Second World War on Russia?

The scale of this war remains hard to comprehend. In 1939 there were 168,500,000 inhabitants in the USSR. Military deaths may have exceeded 10 million and civilian deaths 11 million. The total per cent of population lost may have reached 13.7 per cent. Over a million people lost their lives in 1941–42 during the siege of Leningrad alone. By comparison total British war dead amounted to 450,000 or 0.94 per cent of the population

Thus war between 1941 and 1945 had a far larger impact in terms of loss of life, the destruction of towns, cities ands villages and sheer violence than any other war in Russian history.

However of all the wars so far, it had the least effect politically, partly because it was the only one of the major wars of the period which Russia actually won. Russia emerged with the losses of 1918 restored to her. All the lands in eastern Europe, which she had been forced to give up, now became part of a new Red Empire. She came to be seen as a Super Power for the first time in her history. Unlike the wars against Turkey and Japan in which countries seen as being backward had defeated a country which was seen as more powerful, the Second World War had shown that Europe's more advanced military power, backed by powerful industry and science could be defeated by a country who had traditionally been seen as backward. The reason was seen as lying in Russia's ideological strength and the ability that communism had to plan and organise the use of resources. It was not seen in the total disregard that Stalin's repressive and blood soaked regime had for casualties that surpassed and exhausted even Hitler.

Unlike the Crimean war, which had showed Russian society, economy and government to be old fashioned, the Second World War seemed to show that Russia was ahead of its time. Its planning, its Five-Year Plans and Collectivisation had ensured victory. In the West there was admiration for Russian planning as opposed to the waste and unemployment of the 1930s which lay behind appeasement and forced Britain and France to be weak. In Britain, the example of Stalin's planning was a strong element in Labour's post-war plans and may have influenced an electorate who admired Russian endurance and victory. Town planning, the role of the state in welfare, perhaps even rationing and hopes for a more equal society, seemed to be shared values with a victorious communism in 1945. So Russia unusually found herself for a while being admired by many in the West rather than seen as backward or unknowable. It was hard for any internal criticism at all to be made – so there was no repeat of the calls for reform which had followed the Crimean war or the Russo-Japanese war of 1904–5. Rather, as with the Civil War, Communist victory led to a hardening of the system, a reaffirmation of its rightness. The Soviet model of the 1950s was applied to occupied eastern Europe. In Russia collective farms were rebuilt, Stalin's cult was reaffirmed; the power of the party, its police, and its economic control were reinforced.

ACTIVITY

In the period 1855–1964, discuss the view that war brought more change before 1941–45 than afterwards.

However, if war were indeed the locomotive of historical change, then this time the engine was going into reverse. Suspicion reached new heights with any foreign contacts even as a wartime prisoner being likely to lead to imprisonment.

In Russian-occupied areas of Germany former concentration camps were pressed into service for repression, ensuring a tragic continuity. There was no attempt to look at the failures and hardships of the 1930s as Stalin's views had been vindicated by victory. Russia became a SuperPower and in 1949 entered the atomic age. All this had been delivered by a communism expressed through the genius of a living god (*see also* Chapter 1, pages 40). Continuity with the 1930s far outstripped any changes that the war brought. The great cities were lovingly restored; there was little review of aims or values as conflict with the West drove Russia back on itself. Stalin was now unquestionable. His image was even more extensively portrayed than in the 1930s and writers and artists glorified him in a way that was even more exaggerated than before.

The Cold War, 1945–1964

The prolonged struggle between Russia and the West known as the Cold War can be compared to the wars of 1904–5 and 1914–17, perhaps even 1853–56. Russia as in these wars found that the strain of war, its cost and its inferior technology led it to question some basic values. Unlike 1941–45 this was a war which could not be won. In Afghanistan from 1980–89; just as with Japan in 1904–5 the might of the Russian army was waged against a people whom the Russians saw as less culturally, politically and militarily advanced. In both cases Russia could not secure victory. The struggle to keep up with US technology meant increasingly heavy expenditure which could not be sustained by a faltering Russian economy. Russia decided to let its empire go as the scenes at the Berlin Wall show in 1989. However, in the shorter term the Cold War had different effects.

Conventional wars had varied effects on Russian government. The Crimea pushed it more towards aspects of a more progressive European model. The war with Japan led to disturbances which extended this to the adoption of a western European liberal democracy, if only in theory. The First World War initially allowed a liberal democracy but then a unique mixture of autocracy and western Marxism. The Second World War confirmed the pre-war tendency for a barely disguised personal dictatorship or even Tsarism and Stalin's hold on the USSR was strengthened further. Increasing tensions with the West after 1945 led to the Soviet propaganda machine creating a mythical enemy. As the USA had atomic weapons and the USSR did not, the threat of American capitalism destroying the Russian homeland was used to instill the need for complete obedience to the Communist Party and its leader. This had been the case during the Great Patriotic War, but the Cold War lasted much longer. Until Stalin's death any change could be seen as weakness in face of the western enemy. War continued to bolster the status quo. Arrests and purges continued, particularly in eastern Europe but also inside the Soviet Union where the party leadership of Leningrad was singled out for arrest and execution in 1948. Cultural control increased as a result of the influence of former Leningrad party boss Zhdanov. Anti-Semitism re-emerged as there were attacks on 'rootless cosmopolitanism': this was coded language for hostility to Jewish culture. A low point was reached in 1949 when to mark Stalin's 70th birthday, the Pushkin fine arts museum in Moscow was given over to a display of his birthday presents. Just before Stalin's death in 1953 there were indications of more extensive purges with the arrest of nine Soviet doctors accused of plotting to kill military leaders.

ANALYSIS

After 1953 it is possible that war pulled two ways, making the Cold War hard to compare with the other conflicts. In one way it pulled for change. Western Europe and the USA were clearly more prosperous and its governments clearly more responsive to its citizens economic and social demands. Stalin's last years and the activities of Beria, the police chief, merely served to reinforce Western propaganda stereotypes of Russia. As Russia needed to extend its influence in the Third World, then some change was needed. Khrushchev's more liberal era was created with one eye on world opinion.

On the other hand the hostilities of the Cold War – with Nato (1949) facing the Warsaw pact (1955) and with an ongoing arms race and a struggle to be the best in new space technology meant that Soviet defence needs had to be defended at all costs. There was no question of East Germans having political concessions despite the demonstrations in East Berlin in 1953 and traditional repression was applied to the revolt in Hungary in 1956 despite the seeming relaxation. So generally the Cold War acted as a restraint on change. Economic, social and political modernisation was difficult because of the need to present to the West a constant and self-confident power.

ACTIVITY

Divide into groups. Each group takes one of the wars of the period. The aim is to establish a case for 'your' war being the most important.

- The first thing to do is to establish a case for its importance. Try isolating at least four major points with supporting examples.

- The next thing to do is to establish arguments that this war was more important than others. This can be done when you have listened to the arguments of the other groups.

The discussion could take the form of a series of power point presentations followed by discussion *or* you could have a balloon debate – only one war can stay in a balloon which is losing height. The others have to jump out!

Conclusion

This chapter has given you more opportunities to consider turning points, an important concept in a synoptic examination paper. It has stressed the importance of looking at the period as a whole and drawing comparisons between different situations. War is an important element in the period as a whole and gives you a chance to consider the importance of external elements in the development of Russia.

When you review the course and re-read the chapters here, it is important to keep an open mind about judgments you made earlier. There are no 'right answers' to very open ended questions involving comparisons and turning points. Don't be afraid to re-think: historians do it all the time. Above all, have the confidence to offer your own views.

ExamCafé
Relax, refresh, result!

Millie

The first time we did an essay under timed conditions, I wanted to put down everything I knew, and I was very interested in Alexander II and the emancipation of the serfs. The trouble was, by the time I'd written about that, I had used up half my time and so I just didn't finish. My teacher was very nice about it, but I didn't get a good mark. It took a while for me to plan my time so as to cover the whole period. It's the first time in my life that I actually knew too much!

Nisreen

I was very used to taking things in order and when I started writing I wanted to write about all the Tsars and all the Communist leaders. I did make some comparisons, but I realised that I was writing a very long essay. When I gave it in my teacher asked me if I realised that in the exam I would only have an hour. That made me think about how I could have got to the key points more quickly.

Tim

I got good marks for my AS essays so I was quite fed up when my friend Lisa got higher marks than I did: she is a lot less thorough and didn't seem to use nearly as much detail. I couldn't really understand why she got higher marks. Then we looked at more examples of synoptic writing and I began to see what she was doing. She didn't write thoroughly about all the aspects but she did lots of comparison and was able to pick out key points better. Anyway, I got her to show me how she planned and now I'm doing much better.

Student tips

Davina

When I started doing the synoptic bit, I wanted to find out the answers to whether industrial workers were better off under the Tsars or the Commissars. I had a lot of information about industry, but there was no book which actually spelled out what I ought to write. I even went on the internet, but I couldn't find much. I got a bit panicky, but everyone in the class felt the same, so we asked the teacher. We got a bit of a shock when she said that the point of the course was that we thought about things like this ourselves. When I got used to it, I enjoyed the freedom to approach the questions in my own way, rather than learning lists of factors.

Julie

I found quite a few excuses not to study, but I regretted it when we came to do the Russia course. If I had done more reading I would have got a lot more out of it, especially when we moved from the outline to doing the comparison between different bits of the themes. You have to really know what happened to pick out key bits and I was a bit out of it during the first term. I needed an A for Southampton so I had to really get down to work over Christmas and then I found the essays got better marks because I could see which information was really important more easily. I began to enjoy the course more.

Getting started – Thinking, planning and writing synoptic essays

Exam question

One of the specimen essays is:

'Lenin described the Russian Empire as "a prison of the peoples". To what extent could that verdict be applied to Russia throughout the period from 1855 to 1964?

Let's look at the language of the question

This really focuses on material in **Chapter 1**. This question raises some issues about thinking, planning and writing synoptic essays and is a good starting point. Some key elements in the question are:

- the date – **1855 to 1964**. You should try and cover the whole period and not just part of it;

- **'To what extent'**. The question does not ask you to show the ways in which Russia was a prison house through the period, but to evaluate a judgement; and

- the third is the central concept which needs some explanation before you begin. Regardless of who said it, what does '**a prison of the peoples**' mean?

So getting started means doing some thinking. *First* what are the implications of the quotation and *second*, what is the appropriate factual material that you are going to use? Given that the examiners do not want to see a description and that the essay in the examination should not take more than an hour to write, you are going to have to be selective. This will be helped by the framing of a **thesis**.

> **Thesis**
> A thesis is the forming or proposition of an idea that has to be maintained or proved.

How is the examiner thinking?

The mark scheme gives you a clue about how the examiner is thinking.

'Candidates should focus on the similarities and differences between the treatment of Russians, the repression of the people and the harsh treatment of opponents before and after 1917.'

However, it is important to realise that mark schemes do not establish exactly what you have to put in the essays, but are a guide to what you might include, for example:

- political repression;

- different attitudes to nationalities, and

- religious repression.

The mark scheme refers to 'a line of argument' and this is important.

So assuming that you have looked at Chapter 1 and have read other material, the first thing to do is to make a brief summary of information. Perhaps you might consider looking at political repression; the nationalities and religion. Or perhaps make some brief notes per ruler to help you establish a sort of working thesis to get your essay started:

Alexander II	
Alexander III	
Nicholas II	
Provisional Government	
Lenin	
Stalin	
Khrushchev	

One way forward when you have isolated some key material is to consider the *highest and lowest points* of Russia being a prison. But first you need that crucial definition.

What did Lenin mean?

In a brainstorm, either in class, or with a friend, or on your own – in a dialogue with yourself – consider the implications of 'prison of the peoples'

1. **What characterises a prison?** Lack of freedom, punishment, restriction, a high level of control by the state. It also contains an idea, perhaps of redemption or betterment through punishment. However Lenin may not have had that in mind when considering Tsarist prisons. What about *'of the peoples'* – this might mean either the nationalities or the 'people' in terms of the mass of the workers/peasants.

2. **Try for a clear definition** which best suits the purpose here – which is really to discuss freedom and repression before or after 1917.

3. **In these terms, how do the different rulers of Russia rate?** Where is the highest point of *'prison of the peoples'* in political terms? Does any of the Tsarist repression compare with Stalin and the so-called purges?

3. **In terms of nationalities is it the same pattern**? Bearing in mind that Stalin acquired more subject peoples and certainly oppressed them, but did not necessarily Russify them in quite the same way that the Tsars did.

4. **In terms of religion** – does Tsarist anti-Semitism make religious repression more significant than the campaigns against the churches organised in the Soviet era?

It is now time for an introduction to establish a broad line of argument. Keep this as clear and straightforward as possible.

When you've written the introduction, do a check list

1. Whole period **Yes/No**

2. Definition **Yes/No**

3. Addresses 'To what extent' **Yes/No**

As practice, look at these introductions and attempt a check list. Which one supplies the best match to the question, or would you use parts of each?

Whole period	Yes/No/Partly
Definition	Yes/No/Partly
To what extent	Yes/No/Partly

A: *Under Stalin Russia was a terrible prison with millions arrested, imprisoned and killed. The Soviet era saw a huge increase in prisons and Lenin and Stalin repressed the peoples, their class enemies like the Kulaks, their supposed political opponents, the church and they deported whole peoples like the Chechens whom they distrusted after the war. The Tsars too imprisoned millions, Russified other nations and kept a secret police. They allowed very little liberty until 1906 and then only a restricted amount. Only in 1917 did Russia stop being a prison with prisoners released by the Provisional Government.*

B: *The Tsars were very repressive and Alexander III and Nicholas II both believed that autocracy was right and imprisoned opponents. In the reign of Alexander II there was more liberalism and Russia became less of a prison. Alexander believed in a more liberal regime and he introduced trial by jury and made judges independent. He did not make Russia so much of a prison house, but he had no time for any nationalism among Russia's subject people and was harsh in putting down the Revolt of the Poles in 1863.*

C: *Lenin described the Tsars as establishing 'a prison for the peoples' by which he meant that there was severe repression and lack of political liberty; that the state had powers to suppress political activity and the Russian state imposed Russian language and culture on its nationalities, suppressing any independence. The Tsarist state also was violent towards religious minorities like Jews. These elements of 'prison' however became much greater after 1917. The Tsars were not as efficient as the Communists in establishing prison-like control and by the time of Stalin, the network of prisons and camps exceeded anything that the Tsars had introduced. After 1953 the repression reduced; Russia still had some of the characteristics of a prison as it had even under the liberal Tsar Alexander II, but the extent of repression and lack of freedom was not nearly as great as it had been under Stalin. Thus the term 'prison of the peoples' can be applied with some justification to the whole period, but not equally.*

Common mistakes

Some common mistakes that we all make can be:

- forgetting the question;
- offering a sequential description rather than an overview;
- not making an comparisons or taking a genuinely synoptic approach;
- not responding to 'how far?' or 'to what extent?' elements in questions;
- not backing up generalisations and comparisons, and
- telling the story rather than the argument.

Get the result !

Refresh your memory

Revision checklist

When revising, avoid making simple chronological checklists. Make checklists by theme (for example, the nature of opposition) or by essay practice question as below.

- **Alexander II** legal reforms but repression of Poles and greater political repression with emergence of terrorist groups. Russification.
- **Alexander III** reliance on repression. Pan Slavism. Russification. Anti-Semitism. Censorship.
- **Nicholas II** Russification e.g. Finland. Continuing anti-Semitism. Liberal guarantees. October Manifesto. However, no freedom for Revolutionary groups and intensive police activity. Stolypin's necktie – repression after 1905 Black Hundreds.
- **Provisional Governments**. Release of political prisoners and Liberal guarantees of freedom of association, speech. No plans for federal republic. Suppression of Bolsheviks.
- **Lenin** Emergence of Cheka. Punishments for resisting War Communism. Wartime controls. No political liberty. Separatism in Georgia and Ukraine suppressed. Creation of Federal Constitution. Local development of non-Russian area. In theory end to Russification. Unity based on devotion to Communism and class war rather than enforcement of Russian culture. Respect for linguistic diversity and cultures. Democratic centralism. Political arrests.
- **Stalin** Superficial respect for Peoples, but Stalin repressed Georgia. Economic growth encouraged non-Russians into city and industry. Respect for ethnic diversity, but acquisition of non-Russians in Empire after 1939 – Poles, Latvians, Lithuanians, Estonians. Punishment for non-Russian groups seen as disloyal. Huge increase in prison camps, repression; little recourse of those arrested to law despite Constitution of 1936 guaranteeing rights. High point of imprisonments and arrests 1938. Revival of arrests after 1945 and repression extended to new Eastern European Empire. Leningrad affair and Doctor's plot indicate possible new wave of arrests and anti-Semitism. Relaxation of religious persecutions after 1941.
- **Khrushchev** Police chief Beria executed 1953 and role of gulags (prison camps) reduced. 1956 speech condemning previous tyranny. No relaxation of control over subject groups. Still a prison for dissidents and limited political power of nationalities, though respect for their federal rights, for example, Constitution of 1977. Repression of demands for greater independence within Soviet Union, for example, 1953, 1956. Revival of religious persecutions after 1957.

Use the hotlink code 2428P to visit a website which will help you revise and research Nationalities.

Example answers

Caroline's answer

Russia between 1855 and 1964 was a prison house, but the repression of the people by the rulers varied. There were periods when there was very great repression and periods when Russia became less of a prison. However except for a brief period in 1917 Russia was not free, its people were controlled and at times were being punished.

Under Alexander II there was an attempt to make Russia less of a prison for some of its people. Serfdom was abolished and there were liberal reforms which got away from the prison like atmosphere of Nicholas I. Since 1825 Russia had been dominated by the army and the civil service under a Tsar who did not believe in freedom. Alexander II was more liberal and introduced measures which gave more freedom, such as the creation of the Zemstvos Prisoners do not vote, so Russia was not strictly a prison. There was more freedom in education and legal reforms introduced trial by jury, so Alexander II's reign made Russia less of a prison. However, there was no freedom for the nationalities under Russian rule, particularly the Poles who were cruelly put down when they revolted, so in that sense Russian under Alexander was a prison. Also, there was no question of really sharing power. The Tsar remained firmly in control and when there was opposition he withdrew quite a lot of the reforms he had made, more like a prison governor than a modern ruler. Russians had little control over who ruled them and were not free to express their own opinions. There was still arbitrary trial for those caught opposing the regime. The serfs had been given their freedom, but still had to pay redemption payments and live in communes, so they did not get complete freedom.

Under Alexander III Russia became more of a prison. Shocked by the murder of his father, Alexander III was determined to hunt down terrorists and not to allow any individual liberty. The Law of Exceptional Measures of 1881 increased government power and gave military commanders wide powers. The government took more powers over rural justice in 1889 and the Land Captains kept the peasants under control. Higher feeds for education and state control suppressed students. There were firm policies of Russification, for example by forcing the use of the Russian language and undermining the influence of non Russian in areas such as the Baltic States. There were also severe laws against Jews who were restricted to a special area called the Pale and not allowed full legal rights or to marry non-Jews. There were frequent attacks on Jews.

Nicholas II began by carrying on these policies. He was determined to be an autocrat and appointed reactionary ministers like Pobeodonostev. Finland was put under a lot of pressure to Russify; opposition was crushed by an active secret police, the Okhrana; there was strong action taken against strikers for example at the Lena gold fields in 1912. Anti-Semitism continued. When protestors gathered in St. Petersburg in January 1905 they were shot down. The Tsar was not there, but it was typical of the prison house that he created.

Examiner says:

This sets out an overview, but could do with some more definition of the concept of prison. Think back to the planning stage.

Examiner says:

This is a well supported section, but it gives the impression of a general run through of the period. Caroline might take the Tsarist period as a whole; or she might pick up a theme and take it through the period – for example, political repression. As a start, let's take the Tsarist period as a whole and show some continuity and change and some synoptic writing and synthesis.

After 1905 because of the Revolution, the Tsar was forced to make changes and the creation of the Dumas and the changes made to allow the peasants more freedom to have individual holdings and move to the cities more seemed to make Russia less of a prison house. However, the rebels were severely punished. Under Nicholas II's Prime Minister Stolypin the so called Black Hundreds killed thousands of opponents as well as continuing the pogroms against Jews. The Dumas were manipulated so that there was no real freedom and Russification remained at the centre of policies towards the Empire. The secret police were still active in hunting down opponents and crushing industrial unrest.

When the First World War came, Russia became even more of a prison with greater government control — millions were forced to fight, often with poor equipment and the Duma was virtually ignored. The Tsar took personal control f his forces in 1915.

By early 1916 the prison was even failing to provide food and heat and there were huge demonstrations. The prison guards — the troops — failed to crush the riots and the prison governor — the Tsar — abdicated.

For a brief period in 1917 Russia was much less like a prison. Political prisoners were freed. There was a new representative assembly — the Soviets elected by the people as well as Duma that was free to speak and a Provisional Government which introduced liberal measures to bring Russia into line with parliamentary states in Western Europe. The press was free; there was freedom to form parties and to speak freely about politics.

Political exiles such as Lenin were free to return. However, the revolutionaries saw this false bourgeois freedom. They argued that Russia was still a prison for the workers and peasants.

The coming of the Bolshevik regime made Russia once again more of a prison. The secret police, abolished under the Provisional Government, returned once again in the form of the Cheka, the special committee for security. There was no real parliament as Lenin dismissed it in January 1918. Other parties were not allowed. Even within the Bolsheviks there was the 'ban on factions' and in order to fight the Civil War, there was lack of economic freedom as grain was taken. In practice the nationalities were not allowed much freedom. Separatist revolts in the Ukraine and Georgia were suppressed and communist party controls established. The 1921 Constitution in theory made Russia a federal union with power sharing between the Republics and the central government. In practice, there was considerable control from the centre — strong man Stalin as Commissar for Nationalities made sure of that. Even when Lenin compromised on economic control as with NEP he made sure that the Communists had political control and he was more like a Red Tsar. Russia was still a prison.

Examiner says:

This section on the War isn't adding much, but in the introduction there was a reference to the exceptional period of Russian democracy in 1917

Examiner says:

Let's keep this, but add more on continuity and change

Examiner says:

There is some good material here, but an overview of the Communist period might be more helpful. The Tsars have been compared – now the Communists can be treated synoptically and comparisons could be attempted with the previous period.

Caroline touches on a comparison in 'even more' but doesn't develop it.

Stalin made Russia even more of a prison. The Constitution was a farce. Power was concentrated in his hands and those of his henchmen. His enemies were disposed of and the whole f Russia brought under a dictatorship. There were huge networks of prison camps — gulags. The various secret police organisations — the OGPU and the NKVD — had powers of arrest, imprisonment and after a summary trial, execution. There were millions in labour camps especially in the Yezhovschina period in the late 1930s. Millions were killed not for any real opposition but because they were class enemies, for example the kulaks, or just because Stalin mistrusted them. Russia with its great network of police, prisons and camps, and with Stalin in control of every aspect of life, really did become a prison for the peoples. During the war this was even more so and whole peoples, like the Chechens, were deported for having worked with the Germans. The War brought Soviet control over previous parts of its empire, for example the Baltic and once again the Poles came under control. There was no let up in the prison like atmosphere after 1945 and there was even anti-Semitism and threats of a massive party purge with the Leningrad affair and the so called doctor's plot.

Examiner says:

Caroline touches again on Russia remaining a prison

Under Khrushchev Russia remained a prison but Khrushchev allowed some more freedom. After he denounced Stalin in 1956 there was less repression and the gulags were wound down. Russia was freedom from the fear of mass arrests and purges and within the party there was more discussion allowed. However, Russia remained a prison even if the rules were less strict. The Communist party was the only one allowed; economic life was strictly controlled; there was no freedom of speech. When there was protest, for example in East Berlin and Hungary then the army acted to suppress it — the prison guards were still strong. When there were protests within Russia, they too were met with very severe action. Like China today, modernisation and liberalisation was only on the surface.

Examiner says:

There is good material here, but it could be brought together more to demonstrate the key skills.

Thus Russia remained a prison for the people throughout most of the period, but the rules of the prison were relaxed at some times and the degree of harshness and control varied. Under Stalin Russia was at its most prison-like with millions of prisoners and large numbers of executions. It was as though Russia was being punished. At other times, the level of control was much less harsh — for example under Alexander II and Khrushchev. However, even here Russia was not allowed real freedom and was still a prison.

Examiner says:

Let's keep this, but add more on continuity and change

Let's ask some questions about this essay

1. **Is it about what it is supposed to be about? Has Caroline remembered the question or just written generally about Russia in the period?** There are lots of references to Russia as a prison. Certainly at the end there is an argument about the period as a whole. In every section Caroline deals with the idea of how far Russia was a prison.

2. **Is there a sequential description or an overview?** There is an overview at the beginning and at the end and by and large the information in the answer supports that. However, it is very sequential – we are taken through the rulers one by one – some of the factual information is very strong.

3. **Are there comparisons and a genuinely synoptic approach?** This element is a lot less strong than the focus on the key issue and the factual knowledge. Only at the start and end is there comparison and what we get is a series of mini-essays on the rulers between 1855 and 1964 rather than a sustained synoptic approach. The paper is called 'Themes', but the answer seems happier with taking each part of the period separately.

4. **Is there an attempt to offer a view on 'to what extent'?** Yes, this is done as the essay goes on. There is balance in some sections and there is an overall assessment, but opportunities have been lost to look at the period as a whole. We know how far Russia was a prison under Alexander II; we know that under Alexander III and Stalin there was repression, but the chance for comparison has not been taken – all the assessment in the bulk of the essay is in separate 'boxes'.

5. **Generalisations and comparisons.** In a sense, the whole essay does back up the overall generalisation in the opening; and the final paragraph begins to make comparisons. There is plenty of material here to back up possible comparisons, but the opportunity to reflect and compare has not been taken up. A thesis does emerge, but is not developed in the essay.

6. **Does the essay tell a story?** Not in the sense of running through everything in Russian history, thank goodness. What it does is really to tell a selective story about repression carried out by different rulers between 1855 and 1964. This story is told very well and it is a very thorough and well-focused story with some attempt to look at the period as a whole.

Let's look at the mark scheme

There are two marks awarded. One is for choosing knowledge relevantly, the level of that knowledge, the way that the knowledge is organised and communicated. This is Assessment Objective 1a (AO1a).

So there are four questions that we have to ask about this answer

1. Does it have relevant knowledge – is it about 'prison house' or just about aspects of the period – economic issues or the Tsars/Communist leaders generally.

2. Is there a fair amount of knowledge here or is it rather thin?

3. Does the answer use historical terms properly (e.g. autocracy, Duma, Zemstvo)

4. Is it easy to follow and clearly structured – or does it go from one thing to another without much sense of being organised?

5. Is it easy to read (legibility is one element of the mark scheme!) and grammatical?

Well, for this part, Caroline has obviously done well. There are plenty of facts (look at the section on Alexander III; it gets a bit thinner towards the end, but there is no sense that Caroline doesn't have good factual knowledge and all her writing is clear; there is a structure even it is chronological. So on AO1a this is a clear Level 1 – closer to 1A than 1B. Caroline has worked hard to be able to know so much, especially when writing in an exam.

However, the bulk of the marks (40 out of 60) go for AO1(b) which tests understanding, analysis, substantiated judgements and concepts of continuity and change and the relationship between key features in different periods.

Let's look at Level III (24–27 marks) here

Most of the answer is focused on the question set – **yes**

Answers may be a mixture of explanation and analysis but also description and narrative – **yes**

Answers assess relevant factors – **yes**

But provide only a limited synthesis of developments over most of the period – **yes**

To go higher than Level III Caroline would have to show '**Good synthesis and assessment of the developments**' (Level II)

Excellent/Very Good/Good level of understanding of key concepts **(Continuity and Change**) and for Level 1A 'excellent **synoptic assessment**'

Given that Caroline has broken the back of the work involved, how can she improve her well-informed answer by demonstrating 'synthesis and assessment of developments?

The elements lacking in her answer are

- **SYNTHESIS -** that is pulling together aspects from different periods to support a judgement;
- **SYNOPTIC ASSESSMENT -** a strong overview of the whole period;
- and analysis of **CONTINUITY** and **CHANGE** – which elements were similar and which reflected a decisive change?

She has two choices:

1. To maintain a broad chronological approach, but to offer far more commentary and synoptic assessment. This will mean that some of the factual content will have to be sacrificed.

2. To rethink the structure in terms of themes. Caroline has referred to Russification, nationalities, anti-Semitism. Could these references be pulled out and put in one section? She has referred to police and repression: could this be a separate section?

She has two choices:

1. To maintain a broad chronological approach, but to offer far more commentary and synoptic assessment. This will mean that some of the factual content will have to be sacrificed.

2. To rethink the structure in terms of themes. Caroline has referred to Russification, nationalities, anti-Semitism. Could these references be pulled out and put in one section? She has referred to police and repression: could this be a separate section?

Caroline's improved answer

Both Tsars and Communists restricted the political freedom of the people; both relied heavily on force; both offered restricted opportunities to the different nationalities under Russian control. However, two periods stand out as being of special importance. From February to October 1917 there was a brief period of much greater political freedom and Russia under Stalin was more brutal and prison-like than any other part of the period as a whole.

Examiner says:

This offers more of an overview and makes rather more distinction between periods.

In the Tsarist period from 1855 to 1917 there were common features which made Russia a prison house. The first was a reluctance to offer any self-government to the subject periods. Alexander II for all his liberalism was intent on suppressing rebellion in Poland. A similar attitude to the empire was shown by Alexander II and Nicholas II who insisted on more use of Russian language, repressed nationalist movements, for example in Finland and the Baltic and linked with local elites to ensure Russian control was maintained. Alexander III was particularly enthusiastic in promoting Russianness and suppressing nationalism. Both he and Nicholas II were anti-Semitic. Alexander restricted the Jews to the Pale, reversing Alexander II's more liberal policy; Nicholas II condoned the anti-Semitic activities of the Black Hundreds in the wake of the failure of the 1905 Revolution. Throughout the late Tsarist period, the empire was indeed a prison for the subject peoples.

In terms of political control of the Russian people, there was more variation. Alexander II offered some liberal changes including voting for local self government. This was less prison-like and offered some participation in decision-making. Alexander III for all his repression of opposition did not abolish the Zemstva and Nicholas II was forced to offer Russia a national parliament and more liberal reforms after 1905. However for all this, Russia still maintained prison-like qualities. The secret police were active throughout the period and increased their power and impact after 1881. Repression of opponents was common to all Tsars. This was greater under Alexander III and Nicholas II, but even the liberal Alexander II was forced to withdraw jury trial for terrorist offences and curtail freedom in education. Alexander III passed restrictive laws about educational freedom and his Law of Exceptional measures gave the army wide powers. The high point of repression was probably the period after 1906 when gangs of right wing terrorists took a terrible revenge on the Tsar's opponents including nationalist and ethnic groups. Nicholas II was determined to be an autocrat and appointed reactionary ministers like Pobeodonostev. Finland was put under a lot of pressure to Russify; opposition was crushed by an active secret police, the Okhrana; there was strong action taken against strikers for example at the Lena gold fields in 1912. Anti-Semitism continued. When protestors gathered in St. Petersburg in January 1905 they were shot down. The Tsar was not there, but it was typical of the prison house that he created.

Much less than under the Soviet period, nevertheless this confirmed the nature of Tsarist Russia as essentially a prison, even though concessions were made, for example to the peasants in 1861, towards a more modern legal system, elective local government, and the creation of a national parliament. Thus there was change, but underneath was continuity – the Tsars were committed to autocracy and preventing any major self-government by peoples in the Empire.

This period contrasts strongly with both the Tsarist and Communist eras. There were greater liberal freedoms than in either and much more of a hope that a parliamentary democracy and a liberal capitalist economy might develop. However, the social basis for these developments was limited and Revolutionary extremism was too big a challenge. Kerensky was driven to repressing the July Days and banning the Bolsheviks and also into contemplating an alliance with Kornilov, a potential military dictator merely to ensure some sort of stability. Lenin argued that lack of economic reform meant that gestures towards parliamentary democracy were meaningless and that Russia was still an economic prison with workers being exploited and poorer peasants being denied opportunity to own land. However for all this, Russia became closest to escaping the prison-like repression of both Tsarist and Communist eras in this brief period.

During the period from 1917 to 1964 Russia became more tightly controlled and in many ways more of a prison than it had been under the Tsars. This was partly because the modern state was simply more effective in enforcing control than the Tsarist state. The Cheka which Lenin introduced in 1917 was more ruthless than its Tsarist predecessors because the Bolshevik regime was fighting for its very survival in a Civil War. There was no real parliament as Lenin dismissed it in January 1918. Other parties were not allowed. Even within the Bolsheviks there was the 'ban on factions' and in order to fight the Civil War, there was lack of economic freedom as grain was taken. In practice the nationalities were not allowed much freedom. Separatist revolts in the Ukraine and Georgia were suppressed and communist party controls established.

The mass executions have some parallels with the repression after 1905 but in general the Tsars were not as merciless as the Communists. The repression continued even after Lenin gave up economic controls with NEP in 1921 and reached a high point in the late 1930s. The Stalin terror under Nicolai Yezhov and later Beria was something which had no parallel with either the Tsars or Lenin and was on a scale hitherto unknown. Class enemies like the Kulaks were killed or deported in millions; former party leaders were tried and executed. Millions of ordinary citizens went to Gulags on an entirely new scale of repression. There was some continuity in methods with both Lenin and the Tsars, but none on sheer scale and persistence of prison like restrictions and punishment,

Examiner says:

This doesn't include any more information than Caroline put in, but instead of running through each Tsar in turn it looks at the period as a whole and draws some comparisons. Examiners would find synthesis, some synoptic writing and some comparison – change and continuity

Examiner says:

This offers some balance 'how far' and some comparison.

especially as the terror was recommenced after the war and extended to eastern Europe. The Baltic areas were controlled as severely as they had been under the Tsars. The Poles suffered as much as they had done in the 1860s.

Nominally the Communists set up a federal state where the different 'Soviet Republics' had rights and looked after their own affairs. There was in theory far less repression of nationalities than under the Russification of the Tsars; and less religious persecution. In practice Communism replaced Russification as a means of control and there was a high level of persecution for beliefs – the Orthodox Church had allied with the Tsars to persecute its opponents; under the Communists it was persecuted. There were no longer the pogroms of the Tsarist period against Jews, but after 1948 anti-Semitism was again on the increase and Stalin accused Jewish doctors of plotting against him, possibly indicating an anti-Jewish movement in the wake of the formation of Israel seen as a Western ally in the Middle East.

The central role of the secret police, the existence of constitutions, which seemed liberal on paper but afforded the citizen little protection, and the control of nationalities from the centre, were common features not only of the Soviet period, but of the Tsarist period as well. There were variations on the severity of the prison that Russians suffered under. Alexander II and Khrushchev were more liberal. Khrushchev, like Alexander, followed a very repressive ruler and attempted more liberal political and economic policies. However Russia remained a prison even if the rules were less strict. The Communist party was the only one allowed; economic life was strictly controlled; there was no freedom of speech. When there was protest, for example in East Berlin and Hungary then the army acted to suppress it – the prison guards were still strong. When there were protests within Russia, they too were met with very severe action. Like China today, modernisation and liberalisation was only on the surface.

There is a need to bring all this together and a conclusion would help.

Russia remained a prison house for much of the period. Neither the Tsars nor the Communists accepted the need for personal freedom and the personality of the ruler came to dominate Russia. Both regimes maintained a very high degree of repression, though other rulers punished and imprisoned Russians less than Stalin. There was period of remission from the prison of the state in 1917 and sometimes conditions improved, but the chief characteristics of a prison – lack of freedom and an element of punishment- were sadly present for much of the period.

Examiner says:

Caroline's original conclusion did focus on the issues

Exam question

Now consider this answer to the question
Assess the view that Stalin was more successful in dealing with opposition than any other ruler in the period 1855 to 1964

Tim's answer

The Tsars and the Communists did not allow opposition and both had high levels of repression. However, unlike the Communists, the Tsarist regime was overthrown by opposition. The Communists were more successful in dealing with it and Stalin in particular not only took well-established means of repression to deal with opposition, but used propaganda and his adaptation of Marxist ideology.

Neither autocracy nor the Communist ideology offered any place to opposition. There was no concept under the Tsars, at least until 1905 of a loyal opposition. Opposition was merely treason and went against God's chosen ruler. It therefore deserved punishment.

Similarly, under communism opposition was equated with counter-revolution and an attempt to stop progress towards socialism. What was different was the scale of control and repression. Stalin was easily the most effective ruler in dealing with opposition. Under Alexander II, for example, 3000 political opponents were sent into exile. The Tsars did not imprison millions in the way that Stalin did. The network of gulags – concentration camps was far greater than anything seen under the Tsars or indeed under Lenin. Lenin's career shows that the Tsar's reliance on exiling opponents was ineffective – Lenin came back as did many leading Bolsheviks. Stalin was far more ruthless. There was no question of opponents leading normal lives and plotting further opposition. Many opponents, or would-be opponents were killed and others given long sentences in isolated gulags often among common criminals.

Both the Tsars and Stalin used secret police, spies, political trials and imprisonment and execution. Lenin's own brother was killed. However, Stalin went further than just repression because he was able to use propaganda and ideology far more than the Tsars did. The Tsars expected people to accept their rule and not oppose them because of tradition and God's will. The Communists were offering people a new society. Marx had said that once the 'dictatorship of the proletariat; was over, there would be a golden age of socialism. This gave the people hope and Soviet propaganda – posters, films, exhibitions, music stressed this. Stalin took this further than Lenin and set himself up as the great leader who would bring this about. Some of the Tsars offered reforms, like the Emancipation of the Serfs in 1861 or the creation of the Duma in 1905; but they did not really want a new future and put a lot of restrictions on the reforms. However

Examiner says:

The opening paragraph is well-focused and shows the candidate is aware of the whole period.

Examiner says:

Note that the answer does not immediately go to Stalin, but considers the whole period. It introduces themes – repression, propaganda and ideology which together contributed to control of opposition.

Stalin through his industrialisation did seem to point the way to a new society. This made it hard to offer opposition of his methods. Thus Stalin was more effective than the Tsars and even more effective than Lenin because people could see progress such as the Moscow metro or new towns like Magnitogorsk which they could not under Lenin because of the Civil War.

Stalin used propaganda even more effectively than Lenin and certainly more than the Tsars. For example the Stakhanovite movement which glorified the hard work of young workers. This inspired people to improve Russia. Propaganda too stressed the better life that Soviet citizens enjoyed, the medical care, less crowded housing and greater literacy. The Tsars' reforms had not produced this type of benefit and the Tsars had not used propaganda to reduce opposition by showing benefits. By 1940 Russia had more doctors per head than Britain; Moscow and other cities had big new housing projects and more people could read than at any time in Russia's history. It was hard to oppose this vision of a new society.

What was also used by Stalin was a personality cult. This was criticised by Khrushchev in 1956 and Lenin had never encouraged it. It was much more a feature of the Tsars. Alexander II was seen as 'The Tsar Liberator'; even Nicholas II was held in awe and many fought in the war for him. The repressive Alexander III used his image and there many portraits of him for his subjects to worship. Stalin took the Cult of Personality to new heights because the Soviet propaganda machine was much more extensive than anything that the Tsars had. The image of the Leader was everywhere; films were made showing the young Stalin's brave deeds as a young revolutionary. There were books about his greatness. He was considered an expert in science, art and music and after 1941 in wartime leadership. The war only increased his repudiation. Even the Tsars had not had such an image. Lenin was too ill for much of his time in power to encourage it and the cult of Lenin came more after his death.

All regimes except that of the Provisional Government in 1917 had relied on secret police. Alexander II inherited the famous 'Third Section' and Alexander III expanded the spies, surveillance, censorship and control of the police. The Okhrana with its infamous head quarters 16 Fontanka in St. Petersburg was an object of terror, but usually only to opponents. The Cheka that Lenin created was more powerful still but it was Stalin who raised the secret police – the OGPU and the NKVD to new heights of terror and effectiveness in dealing with potential and actual opposition. Terrorists survived the investigations of the Tsarist police; they were able to maintain contact with each other, work from abroad and sustain terrorism, for example the People's Will. Under Stalin the hand of the state reached everywhere. Lenin was left along in London and Zurich; Trotsky was killed by a Stalin agent in Mexico. The state kept a much closer eye on citizens; absenteeism could be punished by a long sentence in a labour camp, or making jokes about Stalin. This level of repression was unknown before 1917. The repression was less than under Lenin. Khrushchev reduced it by executing Beria, the head of the NVD. By the time Khrushchev denounced Stalinist repression, there was little chance of opposition toppling the system thanks to Stalin's massive terror. However even despite renouncing terror, Khrushchev did use it and the secret police were still a powerful element, even if much less so than in Stalin's day.

Therefore repression of opposition has remained a common theme in Russian history but the Tsars were not as effective in dealing with it as Stalin whose regime remains unique in Russian history in this period for the levels of violence, propaganda and ideological control exercised against opposition. The party members who opposed him were also ousted in the 1920s by a high level of political skill which was rarely exercised by the Tsars. Alexander II failed to prevent opposition building and assassinating him. For all Alexander III's efforts, opposition still existed and Nicholas II faced two revolutions and was unseated by popular opposition. Lenin faced vast opposition and even after the Civil war had to make the concession of NEP. Stalin did face part opposition and resistance in the countryside but opposition stood little chance of making him concede. He used the state far more effectively than any other leader in the period and his repression allowed his successors to dominate Russia until 1989.

ACTIVITY

1 In the first sections, comparative text has been highlighted. Go through the rest of the essay and pick out comparisons.

2 Take a highlighter and indicate where knowledge has been used to back up a point.

3 Take notes on the essay – is it easy to put in subheadings and summarise what is being said?

Let's look at the mark scheme

This is a successful A grade answer. In terms of AO1 (knowledge and communication) it is Level 1 – the knowledge is relevant and the answer is well structured and clear.

In AO2 (understanding, continuity and change, synoptic writing) it is Level 1 – comparison between Stalin and other regimes runs throughout the answer. It is focused, analytical and synoptic.

Examiner's tips

1. You have an hour for each of the essays. Take time to plan. Don't, for example, see Stalin the in the question and rush to write down what you know. Think of the key issue and how to cover the whole period.

2. Don't start to write before establishing an overview –Think in terms of a helicopter over a landscape – how are you going to establish the whole landscape and not just one bit?

3. Always compare, contrast, and look at the whole picture. Themes are much better than a description.

4. Try to cover all the period – don't leave Khrushchev out just because he comes last – this is 14 important years

5. Use your conclusion to sum up your argument.

6. When revising think about key facts that might help your argument (for example how many were arrested under Alexander II and how many under Stalin) or some production figures which might help you compare industrialisation under Witte and under Stalin. Cards will help here.

7. Before the exam, please make sure you've considered the main issues. It's not the time to consider whether workers were better off under Tsars or Communists; or whether the Tsars were more repressive than the Communists; or whether 1917 was a turning point *in the exam room*!

8. There isn't a right answer or a right way to organize synoptic essays – examiners need to see evidence of mature consideration of issues and a way of looking at the period as a whole and not just in individual bits.

9. **This is the key advice.** Give yourself time to **think** during the course, in revision, in tests and above all in the examination.

Bibliography

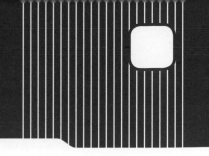

Acton, E. (1990) *Rethinking the Russian Revolution.* Hodder Arnold, London.

Fainsod, M. (1958) *Smolensk under Soviet Rule,* pp. 266–67. Unwin Hyman, Boston.

Gooding, J. (1996) *Russia and its Rulers,* p. 58, Hodder Arnold, London.

Kokovstov, (1935) *Out of my past.* Stanford, USA.

Kurashvili, B. P. (2005) *A History of the Stalin System*: Quoted by: Moshe Lewin, (2005) *The Soviet Century,* Verso, London.

Liebman, M. (1975) *Leninism under Lenin.* Merlin Press reissue 1985.

McCauley, M. (1998) *Companion to Russia Since 1914,* Longman, UK.

Monkhouse, A. (1933) *Moscow 1911–1933.* Gollancz.

Montefiore, S. S. (2007) *Young Stalin,* Weidenfeld & Nicolson (Orion Group) London.

Munting, R. *The Economic Development of the USSR,* p. 86, from Stalin CW 1947, pp. 355–56. Palgrave Macmillan, London.

Munting, (1982) *The Economic Development of the USSR,* Palgrave Macmillan (reprint edition 1984), London.

Letters all quoted in: Pipes, R. (1996) *The Unknown Lenin,* From the Secret Archive: New Haven.

Radzinsky, E. (1996) *Stalin.* Hodder and Stoughton, London.

Volkogonov, D. (1994) (Harold Shukman, trans), *Lenin Life and Legacy.* p. 214. Harper Collins, London.

Volkogonov, D. (1998) (Harold Shukman trans) *The Rise and Fall of the Soviet Empire.* Harper Collins, London.

Glossary

Agrarian – To do with the countryside and farming. Agrarian disturbances are riots or violence by peasants.

Autocrat – Autocrat comes from the Greek – self rule. The Tsars saw themselves as selected by God to rule without being responsible to anyone on Earth; they ruled as absolute monarchs.

Cheka, The – This was the Russian Extraordinary Commission for the Struggle against Counter Revolution and Sabotage – founded late in 1917 by Felix Dzerzhinsky. It was the heir to the Okhrana which had ended when the Tsar fell in March 1917. Russia was without a secret police for only a few months in the entire period 1855–1964

Chinese Great Leap Forward, The – This was a Chinese project of the mid 1950s to establish a new sort of Commune combining agricultural and industrial planning, based on a massive local production of steel in relatively small blast furnaces. It disrupted both agriculture and industry and was a catastrophic failure.

Cold war – Relations between Russia and the West had been strained during the war; the failure of Russia to abide by the West's understanding of the Yalta and Potsdam agreements led to a higher level of tension by 1946. The so-called Cold War escalated in 1947 and persisted through this period.

Collectivisation – This was the process of collecting farms together for communal use. The main campaign was 1928–1933 but the process continued until 1941 and was resumed after the war.

Duma – The Russian word for State (i.e. National) Assembly to Parliament. The first Duma met in 1906 after Nicholas II agreed to a constitution with an elected assembly in October 1905. It met in the Tauride Palace in St. Petersburg. In practice it had little power until its members formed the Provisional Government in 1917. It was suppressed by Lenin. Duma is still the word used to describe the Russian parliament.

Dumas – the name given to the Russian parliaments that met after 1906. The term fell into disuse in Soviet times but was revived after the fall of Communism and the Russian parliament is again called the Duma, though does not meet in the Tauride Palace in St. Petersburg as did the Tsarist Duma, but in the so-called White House in Moscow.

Emancipation – The freeing of the serfs by royal decree in 1861 from being the personal property of their owners. Black slavery in the USA was ended in 1863. There were interesting similarities. Both ex-slaves and ex-serfs found themselves tied by economic necessity to their former lands and both had to wait a long time for full political rights.

Emancipation Act – On 19 February 1861 Alexander II signed the edict in which 'the serfdom of peasants settled on estate owners' landed property is abolished forever'. This affected 23 million serfs but was not fully implemented for two years.

Gosplan – State Economic Planning Organisation, an extension of the overall planning commission set up after the Revolution which made economic decisions and collected data during the Five-Year Plans after 1928.

'Great Spurt', The – was the name given to the considerable growth of industry under Count Witte's guidance. The average growth rate in the 1890s of 8 per cent and the rapid rise in heavy industry, railways and textiles seemed to contemporaries to be more than just normal development and more like exceptional and sudden 'take off' – hence the term 'great Spurt', redolent of the spurt of oil from a well.

Gulag – This was the name given to the prison/labour camps which spread throughout the Communist USSR, particularly under Stalin. Often situated in cold and remote regions, they housed millions of prisoners, especially in the late 1930s. Conditions were inhumane and death rates were high for the ZEKs (prisoners). They were still heavily used after 1945 though fell into disuse after Stalin's death.

Industrial revolution – This is when economic growth becomes so powerful that the nature of the economy is changed permanently and there is a self-sustaining industrial growth leading to mass urbanisation.

Intelligentsia – In the Russian context, this refers to the small number of educated people who devoted themselves to developing their study and understanding of philosophy, political ideas and culture. They were often frustrated by Russia's backwardness and wanted to bring European intellectual life into Russia. Those who were interested in political ideas often became associated with radical politics and fell foul of the authorities. Though there were many Marxist intellectuals, they became victims of Stalin's purges.

Having seen the power of ideas, the Communists were sure to control Russian intellectual life.

KGB – The KGB was the Committee for State Security; the name given to the secret police, spy and security organisation of Russia from 1954–1991

Kolkhoz (kollektivnoe khozyaistvo) – or collective farm. These were distinct from the pure state farms (Sovkhoz) in that peasants pooled their holdings, livestock and tools and worked and lived communally, but were still peasants – they had some land of their own, though the farms were managed by state officials and the state provided machinery through the Machine Tractor Stations.

Kulak – peasants who owned their own farm and as a result were strongly opposed to communist Collectivisation. The term 'kulak' literally meant 'fist' – the idea was to encourage a sturdy Russian peasant middle class to stand between the state and the masses. Under Communism it came to mean 'tightfisted'.

Land and Liberty – a revolutionary group formed in 1877. They relied on terrorism and murder. They evolved into the Peoples's Will group which assassinated Alexander II in 1881.

Mir or Obshchina – The Mir (literally 'world') was the name given to the peasant community. Collective decisions about land use were made by the peasant elders who were also responsible for the community's Redemption payments and obligations to the state.

NEP – The New Economic Policy was introduced by Lenin in March 1921. It replaced requisitioning (seizure) of crops by a tax in kind and allowed private trade by the peasants. It also allowed smaller industrial businesses to be owned and to trade privately. It was seen as a betrayal by hard line Communists; but in reality it was the only way for the regime to survive.

New ideas – They originated from 18th century thinkers, America and the French Revolution. These included the idea that a state should recognise the rights of its citizens to 'life, liberty and the pursuit of happiness'; that a constitutional monarchy should share power; that there should be free trade with an an end to restrictions on trade and manufacture to allow private enterprise to create wealth; that social equality was desirable. These ideas were slower to have an impact on Russia.

October Manifesto, The – This was issued in October 1905 on the advice of Witte to give concessions to the liberals who wanted constitutional change. It offered freedom of person, conscience, speech assembly and union' and a legislative assembly or Duma elected by a broad franchise. The Duma would be consulted by the Tsar and given the right to pass laws. By 1906 the Tsar had regained power and made the position clearer in the Fundamental Law of 23 April 1906 which reasserted his autocratic powers, veto of any laws, appointment of all ministers and to hold all government power.

Obshchina – See *Mir*

Pan-Slav – The prefix pan means 'All'. Pan-slavism was a movement in Russia that thought Russia had a historical mission to bring all people linked racially, religiously and linguistically with Russia together under its protection. Pan-slavism had its modern origins in agitation within the Austrian Empire by the Slav people and there was a pan-Slav congress in Prague in 1848. The defeats of the Crimean War led to more official support for Russification policies.

Peasant land bank – This was a special state funded band which lent peasants money for improvements at reasonable rates. The idea had been tried with some success in Ireland by the British government.

Peasant land seizures – In the Summer of 1917 there had been widespread takeovers of landed estates by the peasants. The government refused to authorise a widespread redistribution of land, so the peasants simply took it. This was accepted by Lenin in his Land Decree in November 1917.

Politburo – The ruling executive body of Communist Russia – the equivalent to the British cabinet.

Political exiles, The – These were the Decembrists, liberal officers and nobles who had tried to prevent Nicholas I from becoming Tsar in a failed revolution in 1825, hoping for a constitution and liberal reforms. Alexander was moved by the plight of these idealistic Russians who had been forced into exile and lost everything in their plans for a more modern Russia.

Purges – The Purges were large-scale arrest and imprisonment, sometimes execution, of a wide range of Soviet citizens thought to be enemies, or potential enemies of the State.

Satellite state – was the term given to countries dominated by Russia in Eastern Europe but who were nominally independent. These were Poland, Rumania, Bulgaria, Hungary, East Germany and Czechoslovakia, collectively known as the Eastern Bloc.

Service State – Peter the Great (1689–1725) had reduced the power of the traditional Russian aristocrats or boyars, instituting a Table of Ranks which made noble status

dependent on the military or administrative service given to the state. The state thus overrode class and tradition.

Social revolutionaries (SR) – They were the heirs of the 19th century radical intellectuals who put their trust in peasant democracy, advocating redistribution of land to the peasants. They formed a party in 1901 under Victor Chernov which was the largest revolutionary group before 1917. They split in1917 and were suppressed by Lenin.

Soviet – These were councils of workers that emerged in the Revolution of 1905. Hastily elected councils of workers and soldiers were formed again in February 1917. They sent representatives to a larger body – the St. Petersburg Soviet – which claimed power over the armed forces. All over Russia these councils were formed and there was an all Russian Congress of Soviets due to meet in October 1917. After the Bolsheviks seized power the Soviet became the unit of local government, though controlled by the Communist party.

Tenure – How land is officially owned. For example if land is Freehold Tenure it means it is owned outright. If it is Leasehold, then the occupier pays for it. Tenure literally means 'holding'.

Thesis – Usually an extended essay, as in a university PhD thesis. Here, forming a 'thesis' is proposing an explanation on a particular subject that relates to the whole period.

Third Section (1826) – was a precursor of the later Okranka and Cheka (secret police). It was a department of the Royal Chancery, run by a close friend of the Tsar, General Benckendorff. It investigated political opposition and rooted out corruption among officials. It relied on spies and denunciations and intervened in a wide range of matters – business disputes, immorality among the higher classes. It processed 31 million documents in 1850 alone.

Trudoviks, The – A group of peasant deputies and intellectuals who numbered 130–140 members in the first and second Dumas and who were more moderate than the SRs and sometimes aligned themselves with the Liberal Cadets. The word comes from the Russian Trudovaya Gruppa (Toilers' or Labouring people's group). Kerensky is their most famous member but Zarduny, a Trudovik, was a minister in 1917 and played a leading part in trying to suppress the Bolsheviks. Lenin suppressed the Trudoviks in 1917–18.

Truman Doctrine, The – On 12 March 1947 President Harry Truman announced that the USA would support free peoples who are resisting attempted subjugation by armed minorities or outside pressures. This was accompanied by aid to Greece, then fighting a civil war against Communism. It was a clear message that the US would 'contain' further communist takeovers.

UKASE – An arbitrary decree. In 1906 the Tsar reserved the rule to rule by UKASE when the Duma was not meeting – something he could decide on by dismissing it.

VZHOD – The title Stalin adopted. It roughly means 'the Boss' or the Chief. Stalin was in theory only the Secretary of the Party; in practice he was the national leader.

White armies – formed from disparate opponents of Communism, the White Armies were geographically separated and their supporters were united only in their opposition to the Reds.

Zemstvos – There was a Zemstvo (plural Zemstvos) for each province and district. They were elected in separate meetings by peasants townsmen and nobles. They could not levy taxes but oversaw local matters: roads, poor relief, prisons, public health and some industrial development. There were urban councils created in a similar way in 1870.

Index

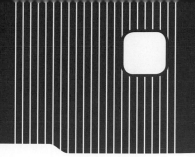

Note: page numbers in *italics* refer to illustrations

A Level Course Structure

AS

978 0 435312 25 1

Democracy and Dictatorship in Germany 1919-1963
Student Book with LiveText CD-ROM and Exam Café

978 0 435312 60 2

Church and State
1529-1589

978 0 435312 61 9

The German Reformation
1517-1555

978 0 435312 62 6

Liberals and Conservatives
1846-1895

978 0 435312 63 3

The Unification of Italy
1815-70

AS Student

978 0 435312 26 8

Democracy and Dictatorship in
Germany 1919-1963
LiveText CD-ROM with Planning
and Delivery Resource

978 0 435312 32 9

Teacher Planning and
Delivery Resource Pack
with editable CD-ROM

AS Teacher

 Written by experienced examiners and subject experts to bring you tailored
support alongside a comprehensive focus on exam preparation.

A2

978 0 435312 42 8

Russia and its Rulers 1855-1964 Student Book
with LiveText CD-ROM and Exam Café

978 0 435312 64 0

The Development of the Nation
State: France 1498-1610

978 0 435312 66 4

Civil Rights in the USA
1865-1980

A2 Student

978 0 435312 43 5

Russia and its Rulers
1855-1964
LiveText CD-ROM with
Planning and Delivery
Resource

978 0 435312 45 9

Teacher Planning and
Delivery Resource Pack
with editable CD-ROM

A2 Teacher

Tailored to the
specification

Our unique Exam Café provides students with a
refreshing way to prepare for their exams.

Your Exam Café and LiveText CD-ROM

 LiveText

In the back of this book you will find a CD version of the Student Book, powered by LiveText complete with LiveText tools.

Within the electronic version of the Student Book, you will also find the interactive Exam Café.

Your Exam Café

Exam café contains advice on study skills, interactive questions to test your knowledge and many more useful features. Load it onto your computer to take a closer look.

Amongst the files on the CD are editable Microsoft Word documents for you to alter and print off if you wish.

Minimum system requirements:

- Windows 2000, XP Pro or Vista
- Internet Explorer 6 (and above) or Firefox 2.0
- Flash Player 8 or higher plug-in
- Pentium III 1GHz Intel® with 512Mb RAM

To run your CD, insert it into the CD drive of your computer. It should start automatically; if not, please go to My Computer (Computer on Vista), click on the CD drive and double-click on 'LiveText.exe'.

If you have difficulties running the CD, or if your copy is not there, please contact the helpdesk number given below.

Software support

For further software support between the hours of 8.30–5.00 (Mon–Fri), please contact:
Tel: 01865 888108
Fax: 01865 314091
Email: software.enquiries@pearson.com